Teaching Theatre Today

Teaching Theatre Today: Pedagogical Views of Theatre in Higher Education

Edited by

Anne L. Fliotsos
and
Gail S. Medford

TEACHING THEATRE TODAY
© Anne L. Fliotsos and Gail S. Medford, 2004

First published 2004 by
Palgrave Macmillan™
175 Fifth Avenue, New York, N.Y. 10010 and
Houndmills, Basingstoke, Hampshire, England RG21 6XS
Companies and representatives throughout the world

Palgrave Macmillan is the global academic imprint of the Palgrave Macmillan division of St. Martin's Press, LLC and of Palgrave Macmillan Ltd. Macmillan® is a registered trademark in the United States, United Kingdom and other countries. Palgrave is a registered trademark in the European Union and other countries.

ISBN 1–4039–6671–0 hardback
ISBN 1–4039–6688–5 paperback

Library of Congress Cataloging-in-Publication Data
    Teaching theatre today : pedagogical views of theatre in higher
education / edited by Anne L. Fliotsos and Gail S. Medford
        p. cm.
    Includes bibliographical references and index.
    ISBN 1–4039–6671–0
        1. Theatre—Study and teaching (Higher)—United States. I. Fliotsos,
Anne L., 1964– II. Medford, Gail S., 1953–

PN2078.U6T33 2004
792'.071'173—dc22   2003070735

A catalogue record for this book is available from the British Library.

Design by Newgen Imaging Systems (P) Ltd., Chennai, India.

First edition: July 2004
10 9 8 7 6 5 4 3 2 1

Chapter 2, Oscar G. Brockett's "On Theatre History: Historical Study in the Theatre Curriculum" is an updated chapter that has previously appeared in Burnet M. Hobgood (ed.), *Master Teachers of Theatre*, Carbondale: Southern Illinois University Press, 1988. Used with permission.
Chapter 3, Patti P. Gillespie's and Kenneth M. Cameron's "The Teaching of Acting in American Colleges and Universities, 1920–1960" is wholly reproduced from *Communication Education* 35 (October 1988): 362–371. Used with permission.
Chapter 8, Beeb Salzer's "Teaching Design in a World Without Design: Part II" is an updated article from *Theatre Design and Technology* 35 (Spring 1999): 32–41. Used with permission.

Dedicated to Patti P. Gillespie, who taught us, inspired us, and was the genesis for this book.

Contents

Preface

Teaching is the greatest act of optimism.
Colleen Wilcox

Theatre in American colleges and universities is ubiquitous. It comprises programs in the thousands. It employs more scholars (and probably more practitioners) than any other kind of theatre. It introduces new generations to the experience of live performance and to an appreciation of theatre's place in the culture. It educates the many to understand better what it means to be human, and it trains a few for careers in the art. All this, yet we have explored little of its theory and history. In fact, it is one of the great ironies of theatre scholarship that what most of us do, few of us study.

Why we should have neglected our own intellectual home as an area of research is puzzling—and also unexplored. Our scholarly neglect does not arise from indifference. On the contrary, most of us in higher education think that what we do is very important. For example, the late George Bryan, a fine teacher and scholar, always dressed to the nines when he met his classes— well-tailored three-piece suit, carefully chosen tie and pocket handkerchief, immaculate shoes and invisible socks. When asked by his more casually dressed colleagues why he bothered, he answered with some version of the following: "Teaching these students is the most important thing I do in my life. I want to show them that I view my classes as a special time for us both. Clothing is one way for me to dignify—to add *gravitas* to—our time together." Although few of us use clothes to signify, most of us signal in other ways our sense of the importance of our teaching: We think about it, talk about it, and strive to improve it. What we don't do much is study it. Why?

A number of only dimly visible forces seem to have pushed us away from such study.

Theatre in American colleges and universities is peripheral rather than central, and, as in Plato's cave, it is thrice removed from the center, triply peripheral: *On campus*, theatre established itself late as a separate field, and it still tends to be overwhelmed by larger departments like English and history when treated as one of the humanities, and by music and visual arts when treated as a fine art. Its designated spaces, if any, often dangle at the edge of no campus, far from the science complexes and business school, sources of money and power in today's university. *In the culture*, the words *American theatre* seem now to denote the for-profit houses and not-for-profit regional theatres found in major metropolitan areas. The early metaphor of tributary theatre, which visualized community theatres joining with campus, regional, and commercial houses to form a mighty Mississippi of American theatre, no longer represents the dominant view. Campus theatre—like community and children's theatre—now lies outside the common understanding conjured by the phrase *American theatre*. Nor is the common understanding entirely wrong. Most graduates of M.F.A. and Ph.D. programs return to the academy rather than entering the commercial or regional theatre. Thus, parallel universe could replace river as the more apt image today. Similarly, *among the arts*, theatre occupies a somewhat hazardous space in the early twenty-first century. Theatre is no longer pedagogue to the *polis* or celebrant for a universal church; it now lacks both the cultural prestige of opera and ballet and the mass, popular audience of television and film. Theatre, an art created for an oral culture, now finds itself adrift in an electronic one.

Research agendas have necessarily been affected. Scholars studying universities have not been likely to choose for study the late-blooming, still-small theatre programs. Scholars interested in American theatre have been unlikely to choose the hermetic world of the academy. Scholars of American culture, seeking representativeness, have been likely to follow the large numbers and study television and film. Practically, to harness a career to studies of practices in peripheral departments within the academy, in marginal strains within American theatre, and in an art now central to neither high nor popular culture may not appear a shrewd path to academic advancement.

Relationships between campus theatres and professional educators have been equally complex—and often troubled. Early in the twentieth century, theatre on American campuses forged links with both teachers of young people and practicing theatre professionals. In scholarly journals and convention programs, university faculty regularly addressed challenges facing elementary and secondary teachers, and when the federal government launched its own theatre program as part of the Works Progress Administration, it was to college and university faculty that it turned for its leaders. Campus theatre was then Janus-headed, facing and thus linking what came before with what came after.

By the 1960s, however, campus theatre had lost part of its head: it had turned away from education. Unlike departments of art and music, which worked hard with professional educators, both on campus and at state departments of education, to maintain strong K-12 programs, campus theatres soon found themselves with no curricula in the early grades and little influence in the high schools.

Several factors conspired to produce this result: Most important of course was that leading campus theatres set as their priority to train students for the profession rather than for education. But there were others. Theatre departments remained small, their faculty overworked by the competing demands of teaching, production, and publication. Most theatre faculty were not qualified as elementary or secondary teachers and so could not be approved to supervise student teachers or teach required courses in pedagogy. The few who were certified were often unenthusiastic, seeing the assignments, usually correctly, as drawing them away from the priorities of the department—and often of the university. None, so far as I know, ever chose to return to the classroom to qualify for such assignments. Nor did they need to. Theatre in many states did not have its own certification, being paired instead with speech and English. Unlike colleagues in music and art who had separate certification, theatre faculty could shunt their educational chores to faculty in other departments, departments that did take the education of pre-college students as a priority. Untethered by departmental courses or colleagues' questions, theatre faculty drifted away from pondering issues of teaching and learning.

The cycle self-perpetuates. With fewer elementary and high school students introduced to theatre, fewer students enter college with interest, let alone skill, in theatre. Lacking experience with theatre education before college, fewer college students of theatre imagine a career in teaching pre-college. In elementary classrooms, fewer teachers incorporate theatre into the classroom; in high schools, graduates in English and speech teach the occasional theatre courses. One result: English and speech graduates teach theatre, theatre department graduates don't teach K-12 at all. And so there is no need for certification programs in theatre or theatre faculty to teach them.

Theatre on American campuses, however, may be atypical. Indeed, the contrast between such theaters in the United States and elsewhere is often stark. The educational setup in England, for example, is almost the reverse of that in the United States. Whereas in the United States, theatre education below the college level is incidental (with little in elementary schools and a course or two in high schools), most American colleges and universities offer a systematic curriculum rich in courses like acting, directing, and design. In England, on the other hand, a powerful theatre-in-education movement has kept theatre at the center of elementary education, whereas the university system, although embracing the scholarship of theatre, has shunted the training of practitioners to specialized academies. The position of campus theatre in many African countries, for another example, is likewise almost the reverse of that in the United States. In Uganda, a nationwide theatre is centered at the Makerere University, from whence it flows to the capital city, Kampala, and to villages throughout the country. The government sponsors traveling theatre companies, facilitated by university faculty and students, to work with villagers in attacking virulent social problems like the spread of AIDS and the abuse of human rights. During my year at the University of Botswana, when students at the university scheduled a performance, the president attended—not the president of the university, the president of the country. What might account for such differing national patterns remains unexplored.

That theatre in American colleges and universities at the beginning of the twenty-first century differs from that of other nations means that its situation was not inevitable. Rather, it grew out of a series of choices made earlier— choices about the nature of American theatre, about the place of theatre in American culture, and about the proper role of theatre education at various levels. At the moment, we understand almost nothing about these choices— why and how they were made, what they effected, whether they were wise.

Happily, there has recently emerged a welcoming new climate within both higher education and theatre education, one that encourages us to think again about what we do and why we do it. Attacks on public education have prompted spirited defenses of it—and calls for alternatives to it. University scholars like E. D. Hirsch and Alan Bloom, by highlighting problems, have provoked public debate. Prodded by the complicity of colleges and universities in the failures of public education, Ernest Boyer has sought to dissolve the tensions between teaching and research by applying the latter to the former: He argues that we should research what we teach, that we should study our educational choices, past and present. At the same time, critical pedagogues like Paolo Friere and Augusto Boal have positioned theatre at the center of their strategies for effecting social change. And empiricism, a research method often inimical to theatre, has been joined (and in some fields replaced) by such theatre-friendly methods as phenomenology, performance, and semiotics as ways of knowing. Theatre education may be moving toward the center.

This collection of essays, taking advantage of today's welcoming climate, is an important first step in our field. It offers us beginning data with which to think about theatre on American campuses, past and present. It exposes some of the critical choices that we have made as a field and allows us to see more clearly, perhaps, their results. It answers some questions and raises many others, and it points new directions for research. If it is true, as the old saying has it, that every time history repeats itself, the price goes up. This collection may serve to dampen the inflation. The volume is sorely needed and long overdue.

Patti P. Gillespie

and developing various courses in speech communication as well as theatre. She has made numerous presentations at professional conferences, such as the National Communication Association, and published in *Negro Educational Review*. She has served her current institution its coordinator of faculty and staff development, and presently functions as its director of institutional assessment.

Michael M. O'Hara is an Associate Professor at Ball State University in Muncie, Indiana where he was named Outstanding Junior Faculty in 2002. He has published in *Shaw, American Drama*, and several book chapters on American theatre of the 1930s. He also published a DVD "iTextbook," *Explore Theatre: A Back Stage Pass*, with Allyn & Bacon, and is working on a book on Bernard Shaw and Federal Theatre.

Michele A. Pagen is an Associate Professor of Theatre at California University of Pennsylvania in California, Pennsylvania. Her work can be found on the Educational Resources Information Center (ERIC). Michele has served as a member of the Teaching and Learning Subcommittee for Faculty Professional Development at California University since her arrival there eight years ago.

Beeb Salzer is Professor of Design in San Diego State University's School of Theatre, TV, and Film. His over 100 articles have been published in *Theatre Design and Technology, Lighting Dimensions, The Chronicle of Higher Education*, and the *New York Times*. Broadway Press published his book *The Skeptical Scenographer*. USITT has awarded him 5 Herbert Greggs Awards for excellence in writing. He continues to design and is a life member of the United Scenic Artists.

Nathan P. Stucky is Chair of the Department of Speech Communication, Southern Illinois University at Carbondale where he teaches courses in performance studies. A former editor of *Theatre Annual: A Journal of Performance Studies*, his published articles appear in *Text and Performance Quarterly, The Journal of Pragmatics, Literature in Performance, The Dokkyo International Review, Communication Education, The Speech Communication Teacher*, and *The Journal of Language and Social Psychology*. With Cynthia Wimmer, he edited *Teaching Performance Studies* (2002). Stucky both writes and directs plays as well.

Jessica Tomell-Presto received her doctorate in the department of Speech Communication at Southern Illinois University at Carbondale. Her dissertation (2003) is entitled, "Performing Irish Identities Through Irish Dance."

Her review of the book *The Body Can Speak* appeared in the May edition of *American Communication Journal*. She is currently an associate editor of *Kaleidoscope: A Graduate Journal of Qualitative Communication Research*.

Michael Wright is the Director of the Interdisciplinary Program in Creative Writing at The University of Tulsa. His books include *Playwriting in Process, Playwriting Master Class, Monologues for Men by Men* (vols. 1 and 2), and *The Student's Guide to Playwriting Opportunities*, 3rd edition. He is founder of the Fictional Characters Writers Collective in Tulsa, National Advisor to Austin Script Works, and U.S. Representative to both World Interplay and the Inter-Scribe Project in Australia.

Introduction

Gail S. Medford and Anne L. Fliotsos

Throughout higher education history, administrators and faculty have argued about the importance of theatre education and its value as an academic discipline within the ivory towers of American colleges and universities. Although American higher education's acceptance of this lively art as a serious discipline has been comparatively slow, its importance to the liberal arts and the support of American theatre nonetheless has become well recognized. Historically, reasons given for including theatre arts in institutions of higher learning were: (1) to teach language and literature; (2) to bind society and culture; (3) to teach Christian virtue; (4) to teach oratory and delivery; (5) to teach self-confidence; and (6) to teach memory. These reasons for academic theatre are fully discussed throughout Phillip A. Coggins, *The Use of Drama* (1956) and addressed in Patti P. Gillespie, "Theatre Education and Hirsh's Contextualism: How Do We Get There and Where Do We Want to Go" (1990). In the second half of the twentieth century, higher education emphasized two additional reasons: to train theatre professionals within academe and to establish a relationship between the college campus and the surrounding community.

While academic administrators, theatre scholars, and artists often discuss these reasons for keeping educational theatre a viable part of the curriculum, very little discussion is given to the art of teaching or the pedagogical aspects of theatre education. Despite the fact that American education (from grade school, to graduate school, to conservatory training) boasts of thousands of theatre programs, the instruction taking place in these programs occurs with little attention to formal pedagogical theory or practice. Perhaps teachers, instructors, and scholars of theatre give little attention to how they teach the art because they themselves did not receive any particular orientation to theatre pedagogy. Nonetheless, theatre educators in all venues continue to offer, with notable success, instruction to majors and non-majors alike in this multifarious and multifaceted discipline. The fact that we find some success in teaching this complex art form should encourage us to give the pedagogy some attention.

What may attribute to successful instructions in theatre and its staying power in higher education can be seen in four premises outlined by Burnet Hobgood in his *Master Teachers of Theatre* (1988). He notes that "theatre teaching... builds on a foundation of emotional and intellectual commitment" and a recognition of the following in theatre education:

1) Theatre is an important, complex art of intrinsic cultural interest that deserves thorough study.
2) The theatre experience is incredibly rich, diverse, and—most difficult of all—ephemeral; yet not only possible but valuable to the future of theatre, and to the young people drawn to it, to devise teaching methods for understanding the art and mastering the crafts of the stage.
3) The theatre requires more than clever minds and willing hands; it demands a full commitment in the use of self (body, mind, and spirit) and an alert awareness of contemporary life (social, ideological, cultural).
4) The art of theatre arises from a distinctive kind of talent, and an essential function of the theatre teacher is the recognition, nurturing, and development of that talent. (Hobgood 1988, 6–9)

These proposed central premises of theatre education only lay the foundation for theatre pedagogy.

Theatre educators entering the twenty-first century are faced additionally with new pedagogical challenges and experiences needed and often required to respond to a variety of late-twentieth century issues in higher education itself. The public's increased call for accountability, the increased number of nontraditional students, the thrust of teaching with state-of-the-art technology, and appeals for better student preparation for successful navigation through a highly globalized and multicultural market are just a few educational concerns driving the twenty-first century pedagogical train, and therefore theatre scholars and teachers.

This book offers both historical and theoretical insights that drove pedagogy in American theatre education in colleges and universities during the twentieth century and into the twenty-first. The works of these contributors are grounded in both the historical reasons for teaching in higher education and premises outlined by Hobgood. The contributors to this volume represent a vast array—from emeritus faculty with years of experience, to tenured professionals in mid-career, to emerging scholars who have begun their research careers though dissertation work in theatre pedagogy. Despite this wide range, all contributors have two things in common: they all teach in U.S. colleges and universities and they all have a burning curiosity to study the "what and how" of theatre pedagogy. From a new generation of professors to the old guard, these essays reflect a continuing interest in researching the history and theory surrounding our pedagogical methods.

The volume begins with a historical and theoretical analysis of theatre curricula. Anne Berkeley, Assistant Professor at the University of North Carolina, Wilmington, examines the theoretical and epistemological shifts underpinning the path of theatre curricula through four generations of change, from 1900 to 1980. She is guided by Oscar Brockett's two timeless questions: "What place, if any, should theatre have in a university?" and "For what are students being educated?" In answering those questions, Berkeley analyzes how priorities and foundations of both our faculty and our educational system have guided the development of the modern university.

Historian Oscar G. Brockett, Distinguished Professor at the University of Texas, Austin, updates his previous essay, "On Theatre History: Historical Study in the Theatre Curriculum" (Hobgood 1988). In his initial essay, Brockett reflected on the changing role of theatre history in the college curriculum. In this updated version, he also examines issues of change at the end of the twentieth century, including the advent of *performance studies* as a field and a new view of learning, through learning communities and service learning.

Scholar Patti P. Gillespie, Professor Emeritus at the University of Maryland, College Park, and co-author Kenneth M. Cameron address the pedagogy of acting during a critical period that laid the foundation for current practices, 1920 to1960. Based in part on a previous study by Clifford Hamar, Gillespie and Cameron examine college catalogues, textbooks, and national convention programs to uncover the nature of acting classes and the ideas that underlay their teaching. In doing so, the authors examine the use of "Stanslavski's system" in American classrooms, as well as the development for alternatives to the system.

Using Gillespie and Cameron's study as a springboard, Anne L. Fliotsos, Assistant Professor at Purdue University, presents research on the pedagogy of directing in U.S. classrooms from 1920 to 1990. By adding interviews to the data from college catalogs, textbooks, and national convention programs, Fliotsos seeks to uncover how professors of directing teach what some artists deem "unteachable." She concludes by structuring a chart of shifting paradigms in directing pedagogy over the course of 70 years.

art as a profession, or simply come to appreciate its beauties and complexities. These men and women, along with the contributors of this book, call upon you, our readers, to share the many and varied successful methods you employ in teaching acting, directing, history, criticism, theory, playwriting, aesthetics, performance studies, design, stagecraft, voice, movement, and all else in this collaborative art we call theatre, that it may continue to play its role in academe and American culture.

Works Cited

Coggins, Philip A. 1956. *The use of drama.* New York: George Braziller.

Gillespie, Patti P. 1990. Theatre education and Hirsh's contextualism: How do we get there and where do we want to go. *Journal of Aesthetic Education.* 24, no. 1 (Spring): 32–37.

Hobgood, Burnet. 1988. *Master teachers of theatre.* Carbondale: Southern Illinois University Press.

CHAPTER 1

Changing Views of Knowledge and the Struggle for Undergraduate Theatre Curriculum, 1900–1980

Anne Berkeley

T heatre curriculum entered higher education at the turn of the twentieth century amid a confluence of economic, political, and educational forces that consolidated the features of the modern research university, fashioned in Germany in the latter half of the nineteenth century. Responding to a necessity to restructure the marriage between capitalism and democracy, the educator Wilhelm von Humboldt developed a plan for a more practical function for higher education that would serve Germany's new status as a unified, sovereign nation-state. After 1865, American scholars traveled to Germany to study Humboldt's plan and returned to the United States to forge a new model of education in colleges and universities—a model that made it possible to envision the study of theatre in the academy. The characteristics of theatre curriculum's subsequent growth and legitimation in undergraduate education paralleled the foundations and priorities that guided the development of the modern university.

My aim here is to trace the conceptual underpinnings of theatre curricula, and to historicize them within generational struggles over the content and worth of liberal education in the modern university.[1] After providing a framework for understanding the changing definitions of liberal education that made possible and shaped theatre's place in the undergraduate curriculum,

I will examine the ideas and arguments put forth by scholars and educators seeking to direct the course of theatre studies between 1900 and 1980, when the rise of electronic technologies, followed by the end the Cold War, signaled the demise of the Humboldtian model. Its end reflects the emergence of a new political and economic order as economic and cultural systems globalize, geographic boundaries erode, and the power and integrity of nation-states weakens. According to Oscar Brockett, the fundamental theoretical questions have always been, "What place, if any, should theatre have in a university?" and "for what are students being educated" (1973, 11)? By tracing the answers to these questions given by theatre educators and scholars, I will explore the connections between the thoughts about educational theatre and the programs that developed, what they wanted the curriculum to become, and what it became.

Definitions of Liberal Education: From Developing the Mind to Managing Society

Throughout its history, the American university has learned to accommodate divergent functions—theological, humanistic, vocational, and scholarly—that have been organized into curricula and legitimized on the basis of changing ideas about the uses of knowledge. Educational historian Herbert Kliebard (1992) has observed that educational sites in the United States constitute contested arenas where specific cultural, ideological, and political interests struggle to control the content and purpose of the curriculum. Subject to a broad range of definitions, Kliebard says, curriculum has been shaped over time by four competing theories of knowledge, those of *mental discipline, social meliorism, social efficiency*, and *child development*. These dispositions progress simultaneously, not chronologically, with one emphasis dominating the curriculum at a certain time, then yielding to another emphasis as social and educational priorities change. The theory of knowledge called *mental discipline* (alternately, "faculty psychology") dominated the thinking of the colonial college, inaugurating a concept of liberal arts education whose presence in the university continues. Derived from the "development of mind" accentuated in the colonial college, *mental discipline* advocates liberal and general (unspecialized) education. Designed to preserve the past and to prepare a leadership of minister–teacher–scholars ("gentlemen"), the early American college promoted classical and theological learning. The curriculum sought to strengthen the faculties of mind that would liberate individuals from cares thought to be incompatible with wisdom, for example, physical appearance, personal gain, and social approval. Set apart from the "servile arts," the liberal arts of classical culture were associated with an "ideal," and as such, centered on disciplined, intrinsically valuable inquiry. Derived from the seven "artes liberales" of medieval universities, the curriculum consisted of those subjects associated with the "higher" things of life: rhetoric, Latin, Greek, Hebrew, and ethics.

Theatre's admission to higher education coincided with the decline of the aristocratic and elitist premises of the classical college during the industrial expanse of the nineteenth century, when the urbanization of society and its steady democratization with the growth of the middle class undercut the dominance of *mental discipline*. Following Humboldt's plan, interest in the social usefulness of the new sciences (chemistry, biology, and medicine) and the introduction of modern tools of scientific research forged new goals for the university. In addition to cultivating the mind, the university was charged with finding solutions to social problems associated with industrialism and with developing strategies and mechanisms for the management of an ever more complex society (Veysey 1965, 113–130). The purpose of liberal education was revised to be "useful," which meant applying scientific knowledge to problems in "real life." In these conditions, scientific research became synonymous with liberal culture.[2] So began a process of democratization and professionalization that constituted radical change and dislocation in the academy.

Utilitarian education gave rise to the twin elements of public service and the culture of expertise. Considered progressive when it developed after the Civil War, utilitarianism through public service emphasized the application of scientific research in the political sphere as a rational substitute for personal influence (Veysey, 116). Curricular models geared to public service express the version of knowledge called *social meliorism,* which stipulates that education should function toward the betterment of society. Initially developing in opposition to utilitarianism, the movement of "pure research" sought to replace "education for citizenship" with "education for knowledge." Proceeding quickly after 1880, this model sought "pure" and "disinterested" knowledge, that is, divested of personal and ideological prejudices and distortions, by way of empirical scientific research. The empirical quest for pure knowledge led to two curricular innovations: the development of knowledge for its own sake and increasing specialization (Veysey, 139). Educational models geared to research express the theory known as *social efficiency* in which curricula functions to solve social problems through the application of empirical research. Contrary to its initial impulse, then, the university reinforced a utilitarian stance by refining its role as a resource for the efficient management of society and its institutions (Veysey, 138–145). Envisioned as the engine of both social progress and social justice and imbued with the power of science, the new utilitarian curriculum was organized according to the priorities of both *social meliorism* and *social efficiency*.

Reacting against the university's growing utilitarianism and the pursuit of knowledge within increasingly narrow disciplinary and subdisciplinary boundaries, humanist education continued as a remnant of colonial classical culture. From the premise that American culture was in decline, the modern humanists promoted the classics, language, literature, and philosophy as a way to raise culture toward an idealized vision of humanity (Graff 1987, 98–118). Drawing inspiration from Matthew Arnold's *Culture and Anarchy* (1869), Irving Babbitt and the humanists (followed after the World War I by T. S. Eliot and then F. R. Leavis) countered aesthetics ("sweetness and light") against their idea of the crass, materialist democratization of industrial society and its manifestation in the bureaucratization of higher education.[3] As it was formulated in the nineteenth century, the primary focus of humanist education was the development of the intellect, and was therefore closely associated with faculty psychology. The basic conception of humanistic education is, first, that it improves the ability to think by cultivating supposedly innate faculties of mind, such as imagination, memory, and reasoning. Second, by association with a set of subjects—literature, the arts, philosophy, history—it was thought to convey the highest forms of expression in Western civilization in general, and the vital core of national cultures in particular. Expected to instill a sense of national identity and pride, humanistic education was used as an instrument in the larger project of strengthening the nation-state. Humanism has been elemental in all models of the liberal arts, for though the subjects that comprise them have varied according to time and place, they have always involved the conscious effort to select those parts of the culture that serve to make one fully human.

So by the turn of the century, the university revolved around two impulses that forged the modern definition of liberal arts education. The first impulse, that of *humanism*, was charged with the safeguarding and dissemination of a national cultural heritage. The second, that of *utilitarianism*, fostered the development of research based, increasingly technological knowledge, with greater social and economic payoffs (Menand 1994, 88–99).[4] Both visions aimed to strengthen the values and integrity of the nation-state. In the transition to the specialized modern research university, marked by the freeing of education from church control, theatre studies formally entered higher education.

Changing Theories of Undergraduate Theatre Curriculum

After two centuries of religious hostility toward theatrical performance, universities officially sanctioned extracurricular dramatic clubs and productions after the Civil War (Hamar 1954, 572–594). By 1910, the mandates of research had become dominant, leading to the expansion and diversification of knowledge, the differentiation of the colonial college's general curriculum into discrete disciplines, and the departmentalization of the entire curriculum (Veysey, 125–134). Such modern categories of "humanities," "sciences," and "liberal arts and sciences" came to designate the varied goals of the undergraduate curriculum. Reconstruction of curricula included the introduction of departments of speech and literature in which dramatic curricula entered (Hamar, 572–594). Theatre studies then developed in four chronological periods that were rendered by, and in turn, reinforced, each pedagogical dispensation Kliebard claims have shaped modern curricula at all educational levels.[5] The first generation began around the turn of the twentieth century when newly constructed departments of speech and English introduced courses in oral interpretation and playwriting. The second generation began in 1925 when George Pierce Baker opened the Department of Drama at Yale University, the event usually credited with legitimizing theatre as an autonomous field of study. The third generation occurred during the so-called boom time for higher education, from the end of World War II through the 1970s, when state and federal legislatures appropriated a large share of mounting national prosperity to the expansion of colleges and universities. During this phase, curricular theatre soared. The fourth generation corresponds with decline of the Humboldtian model as drastic changes in educational funding and student populations that escalated in the 1980s reshaped educational priorities. Still, the curricular paradigm forged during the first three generations remains dominant in theatre studies even as a political and economic order formulates new definitions of liberal arts education.

By consolidating arguments for dramatic curriculum according to both the humanist and utilitarian threads, scholars produced three achievements in the first two generations, from 1900 to 1945: they originated a curriculum out of extracurricular theatre, saw the legitimization of theatre as an academic subject in its own right, and paved the way for the university's eventual role in the rise of the non-profit, professional regional theatre. In accord with humanism and the priorities of *mental discipline*, theorists during the first two decades of the twentieth century aspired to justify drama instruction as an effective method of learning classical literature, and later, modern languages. In English departments, where acting had long been degraded as frivolous, the early drama teachers insisted that to realize a play's full literary value, it needed to be performed. New drama courses that entailed the oral study of plays were "bootlegged" into humanities' curricula with ambiguous titles like "Interpretation of Shakespeare," "Vocal Culture," and "Vocal

expression, arriving thereby at a discovery of his true self and the power of his own thought. The work then is not only practical but educative. (Fiderlick 1936, 452)[20]

The debate's gradual absorption of the values and attitudes of *social efficiency* launched a momentum toward technical training, a dispensation that came to dominate undergraduate theatre in its third and fourth phases. It was not long before the university was envisioned as a theatrical producer:

> As a producing unit, the university theatre will function . . . for the immediate campus, as well as for the public extended throughout the state, as an agency for the dissemination of liberal culture, a means whereby the university may perform in a realistic way its destiny of spreading a living grace to all the people. (McConnell 1941, 7)

The debate's tone became acrimonious when advocates of culture began to worry that theatre studies' unique potential as a humanist pedagogy might slip away. In citing a new educational textbook, John Gassner's *Producing the Play*, George Kernodle noted the field's growing disparity of aims and practices and attacked the field's "disastrous lack of organized thinking":

> There is no organization in the book because there is no organization in our drama teaching. When Gassner wanted to list the forty-five "progressive devices," he arranged them in alphabetical order—from Apron to Montage to Treadmill—because no one has thought long enough to discover any real order in our techniques. Surely it is time for us to take our heads out of the paint buckets long enough to do a little thinking. (1944, 311)

There had, of course, been a record of organized thinking compiled over several decades, a carefully orchestrated campaign to legitimize theatre as a liberal art. A summary of theoretical trends shows that identifying educational values and defining an overarching curricular purpose preoccupied theorists during the first two formative phases of curricular theatre, from 1900 to 1944. The arguments of humanism and public service structured a curriculum in which students interpreted, wrote, and performed plays in an aesthetic and a pedagogy of experimentation and amateurism. In combining technical and intellectual components in the curriculum, according to the priorities of *mental discipline* and *social meliorism*, scholars created a powerful rhetorical and institutional instrument that persuaded administrators of theatre's educational value, potentiating its rise in the academy. But the end of the period saw the working consensus that secured theatre's legitimacy in higher education, signified by the opening of the Yale Drama School in 1925, dissipate in a growing disparity of visions and intentions. The theoretical record of the first half of the century, then, demonstrates the clarification of a coherent, unifying argument and its subsequent unraveling. The loss of consensus seems to have originated with the staging of plays for audiences outside the university. The impetus to enhance local culture bolstered a demand for ever more sophisticated production standards, building an aesthetic and a pedagogy that would replace those of experimentation and avocation, while simultaneously separating the audience from the performer in undergraduate theatre-making. As Dale Riley put it, curricular theatre "tends to raise the standards of acting and production, and the higher standards tend to attract students whose native ability and talent push them still higher, until all other theatrical production . . . tends to drop out of the picture" (Riley 1936, 4). That many had begun over the last decade to characterize the curriculum, in Kernodle's words, as having "gotten away with us" suggests that theatre educators may have unwittingly lost control of their agenda.[21]

To be sure, the modern "multiversity," ambivalent about its role in American life, conveyed ambiguous academic goals, simultaneously general and specialized, which the theatre community incorporated and reproduced. And in spite of the harsh rhetoric, theatre studies' widespread popularity with students led to remarkable curricular growth, for though it took 200 years to secure the right to perform plays at American colleges, it took only 80 for theatre curriculum to grow from a few isolated courses at the turn of the century to well over 14,000 in the 1970s. The steepest rise occurred during the third phase, a product of higher education's unprecedented expansion between 1945 and 1979. Following World War II, the G. I. Bill greatly increased student enrollments, and the National Defense Education Act of 1958 and the Higher Education Facilities Act of 1963 appropriated vast financial resources into program development. The introduction and rise of television, combined with the effects of the depression, had ravaged commercial theatre, and many theatre artists subsequently moved to the non-commercial theatre.[22] Concomitantly, the university theatre developed rapidly. From 1945 through the 1950s theatre courses doubled with most colleges and universities offering theatre instruction, and a quarter of these offering the Bachelor of Arts (B.A.) by 1960. By the end of the 1960s, undergraduate theatre teachers and majors had tripled and courses grew by 71 percent in an increasingly specialized curriculum.[23]

The third generation saw the legitimization of theatre as an autonomous discipline, the professionalization of educational theatre, and its alliance with the professional theatre. Two theoretical developments of the period signaled a major departure from the past two decades. First, theorists broke with tradition by gearing curriculum to the production standards of professional and semi-professional theatre, consolidating a decidedly vocational aim to the curriculum. Second, they derived from then progressive educational philosophies a basis for new teaching strategies and rationales. Both trends revealed the influence of cultural movements of the 1960s from which they drew inspiration.

Although the heated debate between craft and culture intensified in the decades following World War II, Harley Granville-Barker reiterated in 1945 the prevailing commitment to scholarship and intellectual development in theatre teaching:

> We want citizens cultivated to be suitably articulate, keenly critical, and fully appreciative.... I am concerned with the art's general educational uses, which do not demand of the students self-surrender and devotion, but allow for the detached attitude of the scholar adding one more item to the sum of his knowledge. (31)

But production-related courses increased as more theatre departments staged public performances. In turn, the need for trained teachers boosted courses in acting, directing, design, and technology (Macgowan 1947, 51–55).[24] Some rejected "cultural enrichment" altogether and, like Loren Winship, extolled the merits of teaching craft: "[I]n our pragmatic civilization, with its overemphasis on things physical, [our] objective must be bolstered by those of a more practical nature" (Winship 1950, 135). With Edwin Pettet, the advocates of culture attacked the new pragmatism as philistine and dishonest:

> I have never seen a high school play in which the scenery and lighting were not superior to the understanding, the vision, and the intellectual depth before me on the stage.... With a concentration upon the superficial and insignificant, we hope to have found the shortcut to producing students who will be successes. What in fact we have evolved is a slick machine for producing mediocrity. (1950, 8)[25]

In spite of these objections, B. Iden Payne claimed in 1954 that the increasingly specialized theatre curriculum showed a choice had been made to combine general, humanist education with technical training (225). The continuing introduction of aims and rationales heretofore considered beyond the scope of liberal arts had, wittingly or not, reshaped the agenda.

The most important factor in this curricular restructuring was the university's growing involvement in the arts. Theatre educators who encouraged this association sought to link undergraduate teaching to the non-profit regional theatre, concurring with Kenneth Graham that

> [i]f theatre is going to meet the demand of the cultural explosion, rather than be blown up by it, the responsibility will fall in large measure on the educators, in productive alliance with the professional practitioners, to inspire and train the young of our country. (1966, 321)[26]

In order to meet the demand, Graham suggested that (1) schools should work together with professional theatres, and (2) professional theatre should provide models of excellence in performance for colleges and universities, models that would give purpose to students and teachers.[27] By taking these steps, theatre studies would join a coalition of interests in higher education, national arts organizations, and government committed to decentralizing American arts and establishing universities as regional arts centers (Kaelin 1962). The outstretched collegiate theatre project soon found itself at the heart of the professional regional theatre, lessening a historic dichotomy. In 1968, Robert Gard claimed that the professionalization of academic theatre constituted the largest single event in postwar educational theatre, and one of the largest in American theatre:

> The present day trend toward professionalism is being realized in three major ways: (1) many college amateur theatres are evolving toward professional status; (2) some college theatre departments are adding guest stars to their ranks; (3) some theatre departments are fostering the establishment of full-fledged professional companies. (79)

The emergence of a professionalized curriculum was literally cemented by a prolific building program beginning in the 1950s and continuing for two decades in which hundreds of performing arts facilities were constructed at universities and colleges across the nation (Morrison 1973). Highly trained scenic designers, directors, and technicians were hired to teach, and students trained to perform in large venues for paying audiences. The Master of Fine Arts (M.F.A.) and the Bachelor of Fine Arts (B.F.A.) programs multiplied in the new organization of what Burnet Hobgood called the theatre program as a "producing unit" (1990, 14). In 1962, W. McNeil Lowry, the president of

Yale and a prominent commentator on the arts, concluded that, in a major shift, the university had assumed responsibility for training the nation's future artists. Believing this situation to be incongruous with current objectives of liberal education, he urged the formulation of new administrative and curricular strategies to avoid a loss of quality in both educational and professional theatre. But if a contradiction was being instituted between the aims of collegiate educational theatre and its practices, it eluded theatre educators. Evidently, most reacted complacently to Lowry's warnings—and to a generation of critics—for in spite of the steady rise of specialized, practical curricula, most theatre programs clearly stated their chief intent to be the provision of general, liberal arts education (Gard 1968, 78).[28]

So by the mid-1960s, graduate and undergraduate theatre curriculums were functioning as instruments of *social efficiency*, fully engaged with the culture of expertise and specialized knowledge. Once an avocational expression of liberal, humanist inquiry, theatre study had assumed a vocational function.

In the second development of this curricular phase, scholars elaborated the humanist thread with a host of pedagogical innovations from contemporaneous research in cognitive psychology, learning theory, and philosophy. New images like "the whole man," "the education of feeling," and "artistic intelligence" motivated interest in the role of subjectivity in educational experience.[29] Citing Susanne Langer's philosophy of art as "symbolic reasoning," Jack Morrison offered a rationale for arts education as an alternative to the written word for the transmission of culture (1957, 276). Quoting Langer's definition of "personal education," James Clancy pointed to the arts' appeal to subjective intelligence: "What discursive symbolism—language in its literal use—does for our awareness of things about us and our relationship to them, the arts do for our awareness of subjective reality, feeling and emotion; they give inward experiences form, and thus make them conceivable" (1964, 26).[30] John Dewey's pragmatism—"learning by doing," "teaching students rather than subject-matter," "education not as preparation for life, but as life"—motivated a concept of theatre studies that would accommodate both craft and culture in a curriculum whose primary issue would not be "one of subject matter, content or of methodology," as Robert Wills put it, but of "meeting our students individually..." (1969, 194).

The movement prompted the field to embrace innovations of Off-Off Broadway theatre, in its genesis at the time: "[T]oo many of us have failed to keep pace with the changing nature of theatre. No longer can serious theater people ignore Antonin Artaud, Joseph Chaiken, Julian Beck, Jerzy Grotowski" (Wills, 194). Educators endorsed experiential pedagogies—theatre as "educational tool," as "means to an end," and as "process over product"—to fulfill this vision.[31] The proliferation of student-run, "black-box" theatres on college campuses demonstrated the impact of progressive educational and theoretical movements of the day, while the introduction of techniques like role-playing, psychodrama, and sociodrama in the classroom signaled the exploration of theatre curricula as a subjectivist mediation of the environment.[32] In 1968, Brockett offered a spirited summary of these developments:

If we begin with the assumption that education should enlarge experience, sharpen perception, and increase knowledge, it follows that the theatre may be used as an educational tool. In fact, the potentialities of the theatre are so vast that they are not yet fully understood or envisioned. (300)[33]

These pedagogies conform to the fourth theory of knowledge Kliebard identifies, that of *child development*. A product of research into child psychology and therefore imbued with the power of science, *child development* is committed to the psychological and educational needs of the individual. Fundamentally psychological and phenomenological, these theatre teaching strategies attempted to counter education's emphasis on rationalism and objectivity by stressing the role of lived experience in cognitive development. They were also part of a broad attack in the humanities against the preeminence of Arnoldian humanism. In the face of rapid social change, transmission of past knowledge was devalued in favor of preparing students to make meaningful choices in what Jon Roush called the "organized impermanence of contemporary experience":

The typical humanities course or curriculum is a guided tour through a museum. . . . In a world committed to change, what kind of sense does it make to talk about enduring values? If we take seriously the problem of preparing a student for the future, then we must take seriously the responsibility to help him become artful as well as knowledgeable. (1978, 33)

Students of the day needed a new kind of expertise, proclaimed Margaret Mahoney (1973, 120); they needed to know "(1) What information exists? (2) How do I get it when I need it? (3) How can I best use it?"

But with the articulation of lofty new goals, frustration with lax, careless, and poorly taught curricula—indeed with the utter failure of theatre studies to achieve any of its goals—escalated. Hubert Heffner spoke for many in repudiating theatre programs' failure to educate students academically:

> A student appears as a beginning graduate student with a beautiful transcript of undergraduate courses in theatre and drama, but upon taking diagnostic examinations, he reveals that he really knows almost nothing about theatre or drama. . . . He states that he spent his last year or two in college working on productions. . . . (1953, 345)

Conversely, Francis Hodge hammered the field for failing to provide theatre students with adequate skills:

> [O]ne of the principle reasons why the educational theatre has not yet realized its potential contribution is that many of those who now teach . . . design curriculum so inadequate and so superficial that students find it impossible to acquire a comprehensive knowledge of the art and craft of theatre. (1954, 114)

Larry Clark assailed the entire enterprise for its enduring failure to succeed in any aspect of its broad agenda:

> [The field has failed] to prepare trained artists, raise, appreciably, standards of dramatic art, exploit the concept of laboratory—either for production research, or into new techniques or for "defining the human community," coordinate curriculum within programs, and establish continuity with elementary and secondary schools. (1971, 28)

Alan Brody cited reasons for the "failure of the performing arts in academia over the last twenty years": first, there had never been a real understanding or belief in the importance of theatre to the entire university; second, the curriculum was flaccid and "topsy," designed out of necessity to fill the new performing arts buildings (1967, 187–192).[34]

This theoretical impasse raises several questions. To begin with, why did these same charges persist, unabated, since 1930? What caused the shift from the lively theoretical optimism of early years, through the skirmishes of middle years, to the rancorous deadlock of later years? The inability of theatre studies to provide effectively either technical or liberal education vexed several generations of educators. A possible explanation for this conundrum is that educators have been engaged with the wrong questions. Should we be in the business of teaching craft or culture? Is theatre studies a scholarly discipline, a creative discipline, or both? Before examining these questions, I will summarize theoretical trends in the third phase of curricular development. A review of seminal theoretical developments in this phase demarcates clear changes but no resolution of regularly cited problems. As it had since its inception, scholars drafted theatre curricula according to the two axes of liberal arts education in the modern university. During the first few years after World War II, most observers reasserted educational theatre's role in transmitting the humanist ideal. In the 1950s, the aim of training teachers and other practitioners for a growing non-profit theatre increased courses specializing in the crafts of production, establishing a rift between those who favored a general liberal arts focus and those who wished to centralize specialized theatre training. Others sought to combine both goals. With the postwar prosperity, together with a progressive drive in the 1960s, theatre educators sharply diverged from their predecessors by explicitly designing curricula for the burgeoning professional regional theatre. It was during the third phase, then, that theatre studies effectively acquiesced to the ascendancy of *social efficiency* and the culture of expertise, completing a transformation from humanism to utilitarianism—from literary interpretation to technical training, from an amateur to a professional aesthetic, from the classroom as a production lab to the university as a "producing unit."

Beyond Craft or Culture: Reframing the Debate

In sum, the humanist axis, manifested in an aesthetically oriented curriculum that stressed experimentation and amateur theatricals, achieved primacy during the first half of the twentieth century. The utilitarian axis produced a market-oriented curriculum after World War II characterized by professionalism and vocationalism, supplanting the priorities of liberal culture with those of professionalism. But the professionalized curriculum was fundamentally incongruous, for an essentially vocational curriculum was still widely and clearly justified as a form of liberal education. This paradox is a byproduct of cultural, political, and economic forces in university culture whose interests have forged undergraduate curricula on the basis of contradictory aims. While the liberal disciplines intend to broaden intellectual horizons, vocational studies are aimed at more narrow technical proficiencies, job training, and the application of knowledge. Consequently, vocational studies can be regarded as the antithesis of liberal inquiry. In this discordant academic culture, theatre programs rose with speed and abundance. But they rose, too, on the basis of an array of dichotomies—high/low culture, rational/emotional, intellectual/practical, critical/creative—that were never reconciled. This paradox, doubtless the cause of the curriculum's oft-cited disjointedness, evidently frustrated attempts to construct a theoretically coherent framework from which theatre studies could continue to grow and prosper, and led, instead, to the bitter and protracted battle for the heart of the theatre curriculum.

The legacy of this narrative is that theatre studies' impressive rise in American higher education is a patina, for its position in the academy is fundamentally as vulnerable at the start of the twenty-first century as it ever was. The university that accommodates both professional training and liberal study only grudgingly accepts theatre departments, as they do not contribute in an obvious way to either of its major tenets. Thus, theatre programs have little disciplinary and institutional power as departments are dropped from university curricula, and those that remain struggle with diminishing funds, smaller student enrollments, dwindling audiences, and proliferating power struggles among demoralized faculty (Neely 1993, 57–58). The situation is made worse by the diminished status or elimination of the arts at all levels of education in response to the coupling of fiscal crises and the "back-to-basics" movement begun in the mid-1970s.

Where does that lead the field? At a basic level, theatre educators would do well to put to rest once and for all the craft or culture dispute's hammerlock on questions and movements that promise change and progress. Lamentably, the consequences of the building program in the 1960s and 1970s significantly diminish prospects for achieving this goal because decisions about curricular matters—what to teach and by whom—are dictated by administrative fiat. Capacious theatres constitute precious space that must be utilized on campuses strapped for cash. As a result, radical or even creative alternatives to the theatre program's centralizing endeavor—that of producing a "mainstage season"—are deemed impractical and so are dropped or undervalued.

Like all generalizations, this assessment is itself an oversimplification. Nothing in the ever-changing landscape of undergraduate education is inevitable, and certainly intrepid theatre educators, students, and scholars will always move theatre study quietly, and with exigency, toward new horizons. But the craft-or-culture stalemate provides a case study of what can go wrong in the course of an academic subject's formation and development. Kliebard's framework shows that disciplinary histories reflect, above all, struggles for legitimacy, contextualized in a larger process of defining the content and worth of university education. Although theatre's rise in higher education corresponds with changing ideas about the uses of education, and reflects the efforts of scholars to support the university's evolving aims, the record shows a field relentlessly buffeted about by the same source from which it sought countenance. For example, in spite of all efforts within the field to control the course of events, the professionalization and vocationalism of the curriculum actually unfolded inexorably, paralleling the university's responsiveness to the growing demands of the corporate sector. As Lowry observed in 1978:

> In their institutional form, [performing arts] were considered vital to the social, moral, and educational resources of an American community, and therefore *good for business*, especially in new centers of population. The so-called cultural explosion of the fifties and sixties was in great part institutional [italics mine]. (5)

Had theorists better understood the larger forces seeking to control the undergraduate curriculum, they might not have relinquished theatre studies' historic commitments and guiding principles to the juggernaut of *social efficiency*. Had they grasped the incongruous assumptions guiding the modern university's formation, they would have probably avoided those paradoxical questions from which they shaped their discipline—questions that blindly led them to reproduce the academy's own curricular inconsistencies, ambivalences, and paradoxes, ultimately insuring theatre's second-rate status, and making the student the object on which the bureaucratic machinery of the university operates.

The theoretical record shows that the academy will legitimize theatre study in a manner and to a degree that appeals to the university's governing interests and priorities. Neither monolithic nor neutral, however, the university is malleable, with both internal and external influences struggling to determine its principles, functions, and tasks. This perspective suggests that theatre studies' capacity to achieve a high degree of legitimacy is equal to the institutional and rhetorical force of its contribution in formulating new definitions of liberal education. The rescue of theatre studies from its state of decline depends on the willingness of scholars to understand the deep underlying criteria for defining the undergraduate curriculum, and then to actively connect theatre studies to this process. Unless the discipline vigorously participates in university culture, it should expect little control over its own affairs. The tail will continue to wag an ever more recalcitrant dog.

In addition to asking questions about what and how to teach theatre, then, scholars need also to understand how the university itself is transformed by the conditions within which it functions. The values that gave rise to the inclusion of theatre curricula at the turn of the twentieth century have

Crafton, "The Theatre Public: A Question for the College," *English Journal* 10 (November 1921), 511–519; Ray L. Holcombe, "A Plan for a School of Play Directing," *Quarterly Journal of Speech* 8, no. 21 (April 1922), 179–180; and Kahn, 25–28.

13. See also Crafton, 513; Holcombe, 179–180; Hunter 1924, 274–276; Kahn, 32; Koch, "Theatre Today," 64; and Edward C. Mabie, "Opportunities for Service in Departments of Speech," *Quarterly Journal of Speech* 6 (February 1920), 1–7.

14. For further discussion see George P. Baker, "The 47 Workshop," *Quarterly Journal of Speech Education* 5, no. 3 (May 1919), 185–95; Frederick H. Koch, "The Amateur Theatre in the University," *Quarterly Journal of The University of North Dakota* 6 (July 1916), 63–64; and Robson, 411–413.

15. See Baker 1922, 734–744; Henry Curtis, "The Drama in Education," *School and Society* 29 (June 22, 1929), 793–797; and Phillip M. Hicks, "Drama and the Liberal Arts II," *Quarterly Journal of Speech* 13, no. 4 (November 1927), 387–392.

16. For arguments in favor of production-based courses, see also Arthur C. Cloetingh, "An Open Letter to Mr. Coburn," *Bulletin of the National Theatre Conference* 4 (October 1942), 21–24; Robert Gates Dawes, "Undergraduate Curriculum in Dramatic Art," *Players* 7 (March 1941); Alvin Kronacher, "There and Here," *Bulletin of the National Theatre Conference* 3 (December 1941), 6–9; McConnell 1941; F. Cowles Strickland, "Should Universities Sponsor Professional Schools for the Theatre?" *Players* (October 1942), 11–20; and Evaline Uhl Wright, "The Purpose of College or University Training in Theatre Arts," *Quarterly Journal of Speech* 28 (1942), 164–166.

17. See also Crafton; Fleischman 1928; Holcombe, 179–180; Johnson 1919, 162–168; Koch, "The Amateur Theatre," 298–308; Kenneth Macgowan, "A Dozen Rubicons," *Theatre Arts Monthly* 13, no. 7 (July 1929), 480–490; Dixon M. Morton "The Theatre Goes to Yale," *Theatre Arts Monthly* 10, no. 4 (April 1926), 254–261; Donald Clive Stuart, "Drama and the Colleges," *The Drama* (April 1928), 213–224; and "Tributary Theatre," *Theatre Arts Monthly* 11, no. 1 (January 1927).

18. See also W. F. Cunningham, "The College Art Theatre," *The Commonweal* 20 (May 4, 1934), 13–14; H. A. Ehrensperger, "End of a Decade of University Dramatics," *The Drama* 20 (March 1930), 177–179; and Harvey Scott Hincks, "The Place of Dramatics in a Teacher's College," *English Journal* 22 (April 1933), 302–310.

19. Isaacs coined the term "Tributary Theatre" to refer to the growing numbers of "Little Theatres" across the nation. Comprised of non-professional, community theatres, the movement was given this name to contrast them with the "mainstream" theatres of New York and other large cities.

20. See also Edith J. R. Isaacs, "Where Do We Go From Here?" *Theatre Arts Monthly* 23, no. 7 (July 1939), 477–485; and Elmer Kenyon, "Pioneering in Theatre Arts," *Association of American Colleges Bulletin* 22 (November 1936), 434–437.

21. See also Edwin Duerr, "Justification for Theatre," *Players* 17 (March 1941); Monroe Lippman, "An Introductory College Course in Dramatics," *Quarterly Journal of Speech* 24, no. 2 (1938), 192–195; Arthur S. Postle, "Objectives of Teaching Drama," *Quarterly Journal of Speech* 16, no. 1 (February, 1930), 69–74; "Texas Looks Ahead," *Theatre Arts Monthly* 20, no. 7 (July 1936), 549; Walter Trumbauer, "The Forum," *Quarterly Journal of Speech* 24, no. 3 (October 1938), 489–504; and Winn F. Zeller, "Democracy and the College Theatre," *School and Society* 48 (August 1938), 276–278.

22. Throughout the 1920s, for example, there were 5,000 touring companies and 400 stock companies; 80 Broadway theatres opened 200 new plays. By 1957, 50 touring companies and no stock companies remained; 30 remaining Broadway theatres opened only 45 new plays. See Kenneth Macgowan, "The Educational Theatre for Tomorrow," *Educational Theatre Journal* 8, no. 1 (March 1956), 87.

23. For a summary of theatre studies' growth in the academy, see Burnet M. Hobgood, "Theatre in U.S. Higher Education: Emerging Patterns and Problems," *Educational Theatre Journal* 16, no. 2 (May 1964). For detailed information, see American Theatre Association, *Directory of American College Theatre*, 3rd ed. (Washington, DC: American Educational Theatre Association, 1967); Richard G. Ayers, ed., *Directory of American College Theatre*, 2nd ed. (Washington, DC: American Educational Theatre Association, 1967); and Burnet M. Hobgood, ed., *Directory of American College Theatre*, 1st ed. (Washington, DC: American Educational Theatre Association, 1960).

24. See also Crafton.

25. See also Barrett H. Clark, "Professionalism in the American Theatre in the U.S.," *Educational Theatre Journal* 3, no. 2 (October 1951), 99–104; and Payne 1954.

26. See also Macgowan, "The Educational Theatre for Tomorrow," 85–95; William P. Phillips, "University Drama Education: A Modest Proposal," *Educational Theatre Journal* 15, no. 3 (October 1963), 219–223; and Winship 1950.

27. See also Alan S. Downer, "The Teaching of Theatre: A Challenge to Education," *Educational Theatre Journal* 19, no. 2A (1966), 249–252; Robert L. Hobbs, "Is the Liberal Arts Theatre Obsolete?" *Speech Teacher* 13, no. 2 (November 1964), 304–9; Theodore Hoffman, "Dispatch from Academia: HARK! A TREND!" *Tulane Drama Review* 8 (Fall 1963), 5–10; Phillips, 219–223; and Frank M. Whiting, "W. McNeil Lowry's 'The University and the Creative Arts: A Reply,'" *Educational Theatre Journal* 15, no. 2 (May 1963), 158–162.

28. For rationales of theatre in liberal arts curricula, see Hubert C. Heffner, "Theatre and Drama in Liberal Education," *Educational Theatre Journal* 16, no. 1 (March 1964), 16–24; Hobbs; Kaelin 1962; Jack Morrison, "AETA in Education," *Educational Theatre Journal* 13, no. 1 (March 1961), 18–21; and Whiting.

Lowry's call, together with the professionalization of the curriculum, led to the founding in 1971 of the League of Professional Theatre Training Programs, a selective, self-monitoring group composed of thirteen institutions representing the highest quality of training in the field. By the mid-seventies, two more university-sponsored entities were devised to supervise the professionalization of theatre in higher education. The University/Resident Theatre Association (URTA), encouraged the creation of professional quality theatres on campus using students in training, and the use of guest artist contracts. The League of Resident Theatres (LORT) represented professional theatres operating at academic institutions. See Jack Morrison, *The Maturing of the Arts on the American Campus: A Commentary* (Lanham, MD: University Press of America, 1985), 14.

29. See George R. Kernodle, "A Symposium on Aims and Objectives in Educational Theatre," ed. Francis Hodge, *Educational Theatre Journal* 6, no. 2 (May 1954), 107; and Morrison, "Working Myth."

30. Susanne K. Langer, *Problems in Art*; quoted in Clancy 1964.

31. For a summary and discussion of these developments, see Mahoney 1973.

32. Frank Staroba, "Toward Professionalism: Recent Trends in Educational Theatre," *Metropolitan Washington Communication Association Encoder* 1, no. 2 (April 1974), 12–13. See also Paul A. Distler, "Directions for American Theatre," *Theatre News* 11 (September–October 1978), 13–16; Mahoney 1973; Thomas Quinn and Cheryl Hanks, eds., "The Arts at Home in College," chap. in *Coming to Our Senses: The Significance of the Arts for American Education* (New York: McGraw-Hill, 1971); and Roush 1978.

33. See also Clancy, 25–28; Downer; Richard Schechner, "The Bennington Blueprint," *Tulane Drama Review* 10, no. 1 (Fall 1965), 13–22; Delmar E. Solem, "A Course in Symbolic Reasoning: Coordinating the Arts," *The Southern Speech Journal* 27, no. 3 (Spring 1962), 195–201; Harold Taylor, "Education by Theatre," *Educational Theatre Journal* 15, no. 2 (May 1963), 299–310; and Wills 1969.

34. See also Gard 1968, 84–85.

Works Cited

Arnold, Matthew. 1971. *Culture and anarchy: An essay in political and social criticism.* Indianapolis: Bobbs-Merrill. Original edition, London: Smith and Elder, 1869.

Baker, George Pierce. 1922. Our drama today. *Harvard Alumni Bulletin* 24 (May): 734–744.

Brockett, Oscar G. 1973. The historical viewpoint. In Keith Engar (ed.), *Humanities and the theatre*, 5–12. Washington, DC.: American Theatre Association.

———. 1968. Theatre in the educational process. *Educational Theatre Journal* 20, no. 2 (August): 299–302.

Brody, Alan. 1967. The undergraduate theatre department: An opinion and a blueprint. *Education Record* 48, no. 2 (Spring): 187–192.

Ceough, Richard. 1941. The dramatic arts curriculum. *Quarterly Journal of Speech* 27 (December): 573–583.

Clancy, James H. 1964. The performing arts: The necessity for a new tradition. *Educational Theatre Journal* 16, no. 1 (March): 25–28.

Clark, Larry D. 1971. Theatre as a liberal art: A plea. *Communication Studies* 22, no. 1 (Spring): 27–31.

Fiderlick, James J. 1936. The department of drama at Drake University. *Association of American Colleges Bulletin* 22 (November): 451–453.

Fleischman, Earl Emery. 1928. The place of the laboratory theatre in the liberal arts. *Quarterly Journal of Speech* 14, no. 3 (June): 313–333.

Gard, Robert E. 1968. In education: Educational theatre. In Robert E. Gard, Marston Balch, and Pauline Temkin (eds), *Theatre in America: Appraisal and challenge for the national theatre conference.* Madison, WI: Denbar Educational Research Services.

Goodreds, Vincent Spencer. 1935. Dramatics in education? *Players* 12 (November): 6.

Graham, Kenneth L. 1966. Relationships between educational theatre and professional theatre. *Educational Theatre Journal* 18, no. 3A (November): 311–322.

Graff, Gerald. 1987. *Professing literature: An institutional history.* Chicago: University of Chicago Press.

Granville-Barker, Harley. 1945. *The uses of drama.* Princeton: Princeton University Press.

Hamar, Clifford Eugene. 1954. College and university theatre instruction in the early twentieth century. In Karl Wallace (ed.), *History of speech education in America*, New York: Apple-Century-Crofts, 572–594.

Heffner, Hubert C. 1953. Common ground for speech and theatre. *Educational Theatre Journal* 5, no. 3 (October): 341–348.

Hobgood, Burnet M. 1990. A short history of educational theatre. *Teaching Theatre* 2, no. 1 (Fall): 14.

Hodge, Francis. 1954. A symposium on aims and objectives in education theatre. *Educational Theatre Journal* 6, no. 2 (May): 106–119.

Hunter, R. C. 1924. Educational dramatics: Reply to John Dolman. *Quarterly Journal of Speech Education* 22 (June): 274–276.

Isaacs, Edith J. R. 1932. *The American theatre in society and educational life.* New York: National Theatre Conference.

Johnson, Gertrude E. 1919. Dramatic production and the educational curriculum. *Quarterly Journal of Speech Education* 5, no. 2 (March): 158–170.

Kaelin, E. F. 1962. The meaning of Wingspread: Conference overview. *Arts in Society* 2, no. 2 (Fall): 187–193.

Kernodle, George R. 1944. The crossroads in drama training. *Quarterly Journal of Speech* 30: 309–315.

Kliebard, Herbert M. 1992. *Forging the American curriculum: Essays in curriculum history and theory.* New York: Routledge.

Lowry, W. McNeil. 1978. The past twenty years. *The performing arts in American society.* Englewood Cliffs, NJ: Prentice-Hall.

———. 1962. The university and the creative arts. *Educational Theatre Journal* 14, no. 2 (May): 99–112.

Macgowan, Kenneth. 1947. New arts go to college. *Theatre Arts Monthly* 31, no. 7 (July): 51–55.

Mahoney, Margaret. 1973. The opportunities and constraints for the university and the arts. *Arts in Society* 10, no. 1 (October): 118–124.

McConnell, Frederic. 1941. University and theatre. *Bulletin of the National Theatre Conference 3* (October): 3–10.

Menand, Louis. 1994. What are universities for? In David H. Richter (ed.), *Falling into theory: Conflicting views on reading literature*, Boston: St. Martin's Press, 88–99.

Morrison, Jack. 1973. *Rise of the arts on the American campus*. New York: McGraw-Hill.

——. 1957. Educational theatre, a working myth: Or, salt for the tail of the magic bird. *Educational Theatre Journal* 9, no. 4 (December): 273–279.

Neely, Kent. 1993. Economic challenges for the fourth generation university theatre. *Theatre Topics* 3, no. 1 (September): 57–68.

Payne, B. Iden. 1954. The liberal arts vs. the drama major. *Educational Theatre Journal* 6, no. 4 (December): 223–226.

Pettet, Edwin Burr. 1950. Dramatics in the liberal arts college. *Communications Studies* 2 (November): 6–12.

Riley, A. Dale. 1936. The place of the theatre in the university curriculum. *Players* 12 (January): 4.

Roush, Jon. 1978. The humanities museum. In Margaret Mahoney (ed.), *The arts on campus: The necessity for change*, Greenwich, CT: New York Graphic Society, 29–38.

Spiller, Robert E. 1927. Drama and the liberal arts, III. *Quarterly Journal of Speech Education* 13, no. 4 (November): 392–399.

Veysey, Laurence R. 1965. *The emergence of the American university*. Chicago: University of Chicago Press.

Wills, Robert J. 1969. On taking our students seriously: A response to Samuel Seldon. *Educational Theatre Journal* 21, no. 2 (May): 188–195.

Winship, Loren. 1950. Drama and speech: For friendly separation. *Educational Theatre Journal* 2, no. 2 (May): 134–138.

Wray, John Young. 1941. A curriculum plan for a major in play direction. *Quarterly Journal of Speech Education* 27, no. 3 (October): 412.

CHAPTER 2

On Theatre History: Historical Study in the Theatre Curriculum

Oscar G. Brockett

Almost every American college or university that offers one or more degrees in theatre requires some study of theatre history as part of those degree programs. The number of courses devoted to theatre history varies from school to school, ranging from a one-quarter or one-semester survey in undergraduate programs to specialized seminars in doctoral programs. Taken all together, the number of theatre history courses offered in this country is large, although typically the number taught in any one school is small. The emphasis placed on theatre history probably reached a peak in the 1970s, after which a shift in graduate education away from the doctorate with the acceptance of the Master of Fine Arts degree as an appropriate terminal degree led many institutions to abandon their doctoral programs (in which history was a major component) while establishing M.F.A programs, preoccupied with contemporary practice with greatly reduced concern for historical context. (In the United States, there are now about 40 Ph.D. programs in Theatre as compared with hundreds of M.F.A programs.) There is now more information available about theatre history than at any time in the past, but interest in theatre history as such has declined.

I

Since the 1970s, a number of views about teaching theatre history have coexisted. One, the more traditional view, sees theatre history as a body of information (extending chronologically from the ancient world to the present) with which all theatre students should become familiar (at least in broad outline). It treats theatre history as being concerned primarily with knowledge arranged in a linear pattern but with cross-references between countries and time periods.

A second approach tends to downplay chronological study in favor of restricted topics (such as "Female Theatre Managers in 19th Century America" or "The British Music Hall," or "Futurism and Dada in European Theatre During the 20th Century." The possibilities are endless. The rationale for an emphasis on topics is based on the belief that topics encourage study in depth and the development of analytical skills. Some teachers argue that knowledge of chronological development is unnecessary for topical study. This may be true for a specific topic but it can also leave vast holes in the student's knowledge of the theatre's past (and present). It is my opinion that both approaches should be used, one to provide a broad foundation and perspective on the theatre, and the other to delve into specific concerns. Something of importance is missing if either of these is ignored. All too often, however, these two approaches are treated as oppositional rather than as complementary. A variation on topical study is historical study of a specific aspect of theatre: history of acting, of directing, of scenic design, and the like. Such courses are somewhat rare, in part because theatre faculties, usually small, find the need for other courses more pressing.

A third approach is the dramaturgical (which can be thought of as a variation on the topical). Its value lies in making study and research applicable to particular productions. The dramaturg has been an accepted part of German theatre since the eighteenth century and is common in most of Europe today. It is only since the 1970s that the dramaturg has come to be accepted in the United States, although unfortunately there is still no clear agreement about the dramaturg's role. (See Jonas et al. 1997.) It may include some or all of these functions: reading and evaluating scripts; participating in the development and revision of scripts; recommending plays for production; making or acquiring adaptations; assessing the effectiveness and accuracy of translations; collaboration in the formulation of a production concept; undertaking or supervising production research (including historical and critical); providing information for news releases and publicity; assembling material for the printed program given to audiences; writing essays about or related to specific productions; and serving as an in-house critic. When properly used, the dramaturg is an integral part of the production team. Theatre history is only one of his/her many concerns, some of which are more closely related to criticism than to history. The dramaturg's role requires breaching the boundaries between a number of functions and areas of knowledge.

Some theatre departments now offer specific training, courses, and degree programs for dramaturgs. It is one of the ways in which what has usually been thought of as the "academic" aspects of theatre have been made an integral part of the production process, thus breaching what is often a gulf between scholarly learning and performance. Because of this, aspects of theatre history (along with criticism) now often play a larger role in theatrical production than they did before the 1970s.

A fourth approach involves the development of Performance Studies, a field difficult to define because it is so diverse in its concerns. While much of performance studies is concerned with conscious, artistic performance (as in theatre), it may also focus on human behavior in a rather broad sense, having little to do with theatre as such. Almost all human behavior may be considered performative. Some performance studies scholars have little interest in self-conscious, rehearsed, "artistic" performance, but instead concentrate on behavior in which the participants are not aware that they are performing. Richard Schechner, one of the leaders in the field of performance studies, has written that any "twice-behaved behavior" is performance (Schechner 1988, 281). This suggests that almost any human behavior can be studied as "performance"— athletic games, bus riding, business meetings, political gatherings, and so on. Some of these anthropological and cultural interests may have little in common with what we normally think of as theatre, and those who undertake this kind of study often are uninterested in the artistic training of would-be actors or other traditional performers. Thus some courses in performance studies may have no clear link with theatre or theatre history, though many borrow or adapt theatrical concepts in doing their analyses. On the other hand, many of those in performance studies are concerned with performance as traditionally defined—encompassing acting, dancing, directing, and all things involved in artistic public presentations. In performance studies, there is usually considerable emphasis on the cultural context within which performance is created, presented, and studied. Thus, performance studies is often much involved in inquiries that cut across disciplines and departmental lines. Performance studies make for very porous boundaries. Therefore, they may include aspects of theatre history but may do so in a very selective manner or may ignore theatre history altogether. They tend to consider theatre merely a subcategory of performance studies. Thus, the place of theatre history in performance studies may be extremely varied.

These four conceptions of theatre history are not necessarily antithetical. One usually dominates depending on the course and the teacher, but all are often intermingled. There may be still other ways in which the teaching of theatre history is focused, but these encompass the most common patterns.

II

In most theatre departments the primary concerns of students are acting, directing, design, or some other aspect of production. History, students are often told, provides perspective on the present, as well as information about the past, that will be useful and usable in practice. Within the university, theatre history is also often used in making the argument for theatre's academic respectability in those institutions that still have doubts about the wisdom of including theatre in their curricula. In very few theatre departments have students ever been able to give primary attention to (i.e., major in) theatre history. Those departments that have offered majors in theatre history have typically done so only at the graduate level and then primarily in doctoral programs.

Almost all students who enter undergraduate theatre programs do so because of interest in production, most frequently acting. Students interested primarily in theatre history or dramatic literature have usually gone into literature departments, although it is rare for any beginning college student to have formed an interest in theatre history, usually having no incentive to do so. Most undergraduate college students take no courses in this subject beyond what is required, and in fact most theatre departments teach no courses in theatre history beyond those that are required.

At the graduate level, the student's interest in theatre may be more intense, although interest in theatre history often is not. Some programs require work in theatre history for all students at the graduate level, but not all do. It is usually only at the doctoral level that theatre history may become a prominent focus. Most doctorates in theatre now demand a concentration in one, or a combination, of the following: theatre history, dramatic texts, theory, criticism, performance studies, and dramaturgy. The M.F.A is usually considered the appropriate terminal degree for those concerned primarily with "studio" courses (acting, directing, design, technology, etc.). The Ph.D. degree has come to be considered the appropriate terminal degree for those in the scholarly or academic aspects of theatre, although the separation of production and scholarship is less evident than it was a decade ago. Typically, doctoral students come to a concentration in theatre history so late in their academic training that they are faced with trying to cram into two or three years of study what in most fields would have been progressively more detailed work over a period of approximately seven years (in a combination of undergraduate and graduate work). Thus, at every level of academic study, it is difficult for students to gain comprehensive knowledge of theatre history. This difficulty is explained further by several factors. First, theatre history is a broad and capacious subject. As an institution, theatre can be traced back to the beginning of recorded history, and has been present in some form in most societies since that time. Thus, the scope of theatre history is so great that it is virtually impossible to know its entire range adequately. Yet, those who are to teach theatre history may be expected to help students gain an overview of the subject from the beginning to the present (not only in the Western tradition but increasingly in Asian, African, and other traditions). It is probably for this reason that many teachers do not wish to take on the chronological sweep of theatre history and prefer instead an approach through topics, preferring in-depth study of a limited number of topics to the broad sweep of chronology.

The scope of beginning courses in theatre history can be very intimidating to students, since the amount of information with which they are faced is so great that they may feel overwhelmed. In addition, beginning courses usually proceed at such a headlong pace that students seldom get into topics at a depth sufficient to arouse genuine interest. As taught in theatre departments, history is seldom divided into areas of specialization. Most often it is divided in terms of European, American, and non-Western (usually restricted to Asian). A comparison with art history makes the situation clearer. Any art department that offers a doctorate probably has an art history faculty of fifteen or more persons, each with a limited specialty (such as Classical, Medieval, Northern Italian Renaissance, etc.). Similarly in literature departments specialization is typical and often is focused on a single author. Much may be said against such specialization, since it may lead to too narrow focuses that lose sight of the whole. On the other hand, the forced "generalization" that is typical in theatre history study often means that one knows a little about a lot but with no notable depth of knowledge about any one period or topic. Furthermore, it is difficult for the teacher to keep abreast of developments and new scholarship in every period of theatre history, but if one ceases to learn, one soon grows stale as a teacher. Forced generalization does not mean that one cannot develop an area of special interest and research, but it is difficult to do so because one's specialty has only occasional relevance to the broad range of topics one must cover. Even large theatre departments that offer doctorates almost never have more than three or four faculty members who devote their full time to theatre history and related subjects.

A second complicating factor, also related to scope, is the need to approach theatre history as an integral part of the cultural history of the society in which it exists. To study theatre history in isolation is to risk ignoring why it was as it was in that place at that time, and the insights it offers into

curiosity (or developing an inquiring mind). One cannot create an inquiring mind but one can encourage it, and without such a mind most learning becomes mere rote. Without inquiring minds, students are apt to cease learning when they complete their formal education, whereas for persons with inquiring minds the completion of formal education is merely that time when they assume primary responsibility for their ongoing education.

An inquiring mind is not the only necessity for achieving an education. There are at least two others: (1) a reasonable level of intelligence and (2) discipline. I must assume that anyone who has gained admission to a university has the intellectual capacity to learn at a relatively advanced level.

Even if students have a reasonable level of intelligence and are highly motivated, they still need discipline, for without persistence and some systematic approach, motivation becomes mere ambition rather than a road to accomplishment. As teachers, our goal of having students develop discipline often conflicts with our goal of encouraging intellectual curiosity. We tend to do too much toward organizing students' use of their time. All too often, we tell them what to do from day to day and even how to do it; while this may make life easier for us and them and facilitate grading, it also encourages students to expect others to impose discipline upon them rather than developing their own. Unfortunately, after they leave school, this situation often continues, with the result that they permit others to dominate their time and dictate their procedures. Students should have the freedom to choose certain directions (even within a course) and the opportunity to develop the discipline needed to achieve the goals they have chosen. The test of good teaching lies in part, in how successfully freedom and discipline are balanced. As Alfred North Whitehead has put it, "Freedom and discipline are the two essentials of education" (1929, 47).

Teachers should remind themselves occasionally that neither they nor the university is essential to education. Persons with intelligence, curiosity, and discipline can educate themselves—will, in fact, educate themselves. What the teacher and the university can do is save students time by providing direction and system to what might otherwise be wasteful in time and effort and dependent primarily on trial and error. Universities supposedly offer an atmosphere conducive to learning in being communities brought together for the primary goal of encouraging learning.

The concept of learning communities has in recent years attracted the attention of many faculty members in a variety of disciplines, although much disagreement remains about many aspects of this approach. Opponents view the concept of learning communities as a means to completely subvert the traditional educational system, while supporters see it as a way to make school more meaningful by linking seemingly disparate subject areas. Most supporters advocate an approach to curriculum design that coordinates or links (usually two or more) courses into a single program of instruction. Models range from clusters of loosely linked courses to single programs in which several courses have been so intertwined that course divisions are no longer apparent. This supposedly leads students from different major fields to see commonalities by requiring them to think across subject areas. Critical thinking is said to be strengthened as students are exposed to multiple, sometimes conflicting, perspectives on the same issues. One primary aim is to help students understand that learning cuts across separate courses and bridges the gaps among disciplines. Thus a particular course is not viewed in isolation but is coordinated with one or more in the same or other disciplines. This approach to education requires careful planning as well as close cooperation among faculty members. The links may also extend to having the students in a learning community assigned to the same floor in a residence hall, so they may interact beyond the classroom. (For a discussion of learning communities, see F. Gabelnick, J. MacGregor, R. S. Matthews, and B. L. Smith, *Learning Communities* 1990 and Jodi Levine, *Learning Communities* 1999.)

The concept behind learning communities does not necessarily have to involve multiple courses. Learning communities can be created within a theatre history course, especially where enrollment is large. The class may be divided into groups, each responsible for exploring and presenting to the class information about particular issues, events, or problems in performance. They may also branch out into explorations of interdisciplinary topics. This organization gives the students a large measure of responsibility for the course and thereby may increase the motivation to learn. It should also be noted that within a theatre department each production can be treated as a learning community as it draws together faculty, students, and staff from various specialties and encourages the sharing of information and skills from a variety of viewpoints, among them the historical.

A related approach is service learning, which involves providing students with community-based learning opportunities as a way to supplement, extend, and reflect on their academic studies in particular courses. This usually involves practical assignments that take students into schools, juvenile justice facilities, community centers, and similar situations to share the skills and to use the knowledge they are acquiring in the college classroom. The opportunities for application of theatre history in service learning seems more limited than they are in performance, but if theatre history students are part of a larger team that provides community service they may provide some specialized help growing out of theatre history.

Although various approaches to learning communities or service learning can become challenging and productive by focusing on interdisciplinary commonalities and distinctions, much can also be accomplished by concentrating on questions closer at hand. Students may become major contributors to theatre history courses by focusing on the nature of theatre history itself. The greatest error, in my opinion, is to teach theatre history as though it were primarily a factual study. Certainly, history is based on facts (insofar as they may be determined), but it is the interpretation of facts and the search for their significance that constitute the more important and interesting parts. Those teachers who insist that their students commit to memory long lists of dates and names, rather than arousing an abiding interest in theatre history, are apt to create lasting resentment. Facts in themselves are important only as the raw material for answering important questions. A fact is inert; it is given significance by interpretation, and it is the interpretation that can arouse interest. Facts (when they turn out actually to be facts) remain fixed, but our interpretations of their significance usually do not. Almost every generation discovers a new interpretation of events by looking at long available facts from a different perspective. Thus, history is not fixed but dynamic, and it is only when we treat it as fixed that it becomes something to be committed to memory rather than being viewed as a set of flexible relationships.

Some students resent being told that there may be several possible interpretations of the same body of evidence. They want definite answers and are apt to feel there is little point in studying something so indefinite. One cannot force such students to alter their opinions on this point, but one can try to enlighten them about the nature of "historical truth." Ancient Greek theatre offers many opportunities to do this, for the information that has come down to us about aspects of this theatre is so limited that it is easy to demonstrate the necessity of exploring alternative interpretations and seeking the one that seems to account best for the evidence at hand, even as one must acknowledge that other interpretations are possible. It is an easy step from here to show that in any actual historical situation (i.e., in life) the factors at work are so numerous that any interpretation depends upon an assessment of which elements are most crucial and which are relatively unimportant. It can also be shown that by shifting emphasis from one piece of evidence to another, differing interpretations may emerge. It is, of course, essential to stress that the choice of significant evidence is not wholly arbitrary but depends upon perceived logical connections. Nevertheless, such logic is not wholly objective, for what we see as important will depend very much upon whether we look at events within a religious/ritualistic context, a sociopolitical context, an economic context, an aesthetic context, or some other context, for such perspectives determine which set of relationships we are predisposed to accept and which we are predisposed to ignore. Above all, we must remember that in history we deal with probabilities and possibilities more often than with certainties.

A class project or in-class discussion of varying possible interpretations of a body of evidence can help students see that they too may use their analytical and interpretational skills and that it is possible for them to arrive at interpretations on their own—some of which may be no more questionable than those put forth by published historians.

Students also need to be made aware of the role that aesthetic or stylistic preference plays in historians' interpretations of historical evidence. In other words, what historians personally believe to be theatrically effective or aesthetically pleasing often influences their interpretations of how things were done in theatres of the past. Some of the most obvious examples of this are found in treatments of Greek theatre written by scholars of the early twentieth century. Their aesthetic sensibilities apparently were shaped by realism, which led them (perhaps unconsciously) to assume that all good theatre must be conformable to what would be believable in real life. Consequently, despite ancient accounts to the contrary, many early twentieth century historians rejected the notion that the number of actors permitted in performances of Greek tragedy was three, and some did so partially on the ground that this would not have been acceptable to the audience because it would lack credibility. For similar reasons, some also argued for the use of representational scenery in Greek theatre. These examples provide a clear indication of the relationship between aesthetic standards and historical interpretation. When advanced students (usually in graduate courses) are assigned to read scholarly works of theatre history, they should be asked to examine the basic premises (and prejudices) of authors, for these strongly influence how historians select and interpret the evidence they work with.

Another important factor in the student's perception of theatre history is the instructor's presentation of self in relation to the subject. When teachers cannot answer questions posed by students, they should not be ashamed to admit it, but should be willing to help students find the answers and, in doing so, help them recognize that theatre history is not a fixed subject in which the answers to all questions have already been found. For many interesting questions, we have no satisfactory answers now, although diligent research may provide them sometime in the future. The desire of students to know the answer to certain questions can also give the teacher an opening to help them understand historical method.

If theatre history is not primarily a factual study and if not everything can be covered in the typical course, what can be taught effectively in the time that is available? It seems to me that primary emphasis should be placed on a very few concerns, the major ones being the principal characteristics of the theatre in particular periods and the principal changes from one era to another. Ultimately, we should be helping students develop some sense of how the theatre functioned in a particular period/place, what kind of productions it offered its public, the apparent reasons why the theatre was as it was at that moment in time/place, and the role of theatre in its society. At least occasionally, students should be asked to consider how the theatre of a given period/place differed from our own, for studying the past helps us understand the present more fully, just as studying another language or culture should make us more aware of the characteristics of our own.

Obviously, one aid to achieving these goals is to make an era's theatre as concrete and graphic as possible. Although we can never satisfactorily recapture the past, we can encourage imaginative leaps that lessen the distance. One of the most effective approaches is through scripts, in large part because play scripts are usually the most concrete and unchanged artifacts that we have from the past. Students ought to be familiar with several plays from each period in order to gain some feeling for that period's dramatic sensibility, its view of human behavior and motivation, and its artistic style. Although scripts can be interpreted in many ways, attempts to envision how a particular play was staged in its own time can become the focus of important learning. It is very difficult for a present day audience to envision the actor–audience relationship in the Theatre of Dionysus (which held approximately 17,000 spectators). Staging a scene from a Greek play in one end of a football stadium or in a sports arena very quickly impresses on students the importance of spatial relationships and how those in Greece differ from those of our contemporary theatres that are usually designed for a few hundred spectators.

Attempts to visualize performance conditions demand that students bring together information about a wide range of topics: not only the physical space but the spatial relationship of performers and audience, prevailing acting conventions, casting and rehearsal practices, design and visual appeals, managerial practices, financing, performance conditions, legal and social conventions that influence performances, and so on. Such an approach brings into focus around a single script much of the information we have about the theatre of a particular time and place. It requires us to look carefully at the visual and written evidence that has survived. Obviously, there is a limit to how much such work can be done by each student for each historical period. This is one area in which dividing the students into teams, each concerned with a different period during the course can be helpful, each team being responsible for making a presentation to the class about a particular play and its production. (All students read the basic assignments relating to each period. Thus, all the students in the class have a background for understanding and judging the presentations.) The value of this approach is that it helps the students see that though people in the past may have approached play production differently than we do, they still had to deal with the same basic problems; furthermore, they are forced to translate what might otherwise be abstract into concrete terms. It permits students to see process and product in organic relation. There are disadvantages: it is time-consuming; not all members of a group may contribute fully; the grading of individual students may become more difficult; and the imaginative re-creations may become so imaginative that they lose contact with the evidence. But a teacher can probably find out who has done what and can challenge the informational bases of conclusions. In my opinion, the advantages so outweigh the drawbacks that even if the approach is used only for one play, it is well worth the time and effort.

While seeking to visualize productions in the past, it is useful at some point to encourage discussions of how historical information might be helpful in staging the same plays today. Usually a department's theatre season includes one or more "classics" that can be placed on the reading list for a theatre history course, and these plays can provide opportunities for various explorations. Not only might the students seek to determine how the play would have most likely been staged originally, but also the director, designers, dramaturg (and perhaps others) of the current production might be invited to discuss with the class what historical information, if any, they have found useful in planning the production, or how they have sought to make a play from the past meaningful to present day spectators. This offers another opportunity to form another learning community by creating links with other courses within the department, such as those in various aspects of dramaturgy, design, directing, acting, and so on. In many production courses, students are told that they should do research, often involving the historical background, but often they are given no help in determining what they should be looking for or what they should do with what they find. Seldom are they taken through the process in a systematic way. Sometimes they are told that they will learn what they need to know in theatre history courses, but precisely how connections are made between historical information and present-day productions is passed over quickly. Theatre history courses cannot answer this question unilaterally, but teachers can raise appropriate questions and seek to coordinate work with other courses and help to create a desire to see them answered. It is also important for students to understand that though historical information may at times be used effectively, it must usually be adapted or chosen selectively.

There are other less time-consuming approaches to understanding performance conditions of the past. They can be the focus of in-class discussions rather than being made team assignments. In addition, most instructors use slides and technological aids of various kinds to help students envision the theatre of each period. CD-ROMs and videotapes are now available or can be created to show what students have in the past had to try to imagine. For example, many diagrams of complex stage machinery from the sixteenth and seventeenth centuries can be transformed into moving images that permit one to see the machinery in action. For example, a cloud machine can lower, then open to show several gods seated on thrones; the cloud may then divide into several sections and move forward or backward on the stage, allowing one to experience the wonder that the original must have aroused in audiences of its day. Such dynamic and graphic illustrations convey an understanding of the machinery in a way impossible from reading the surviving descriptions. Such aids are becoming increasingly common and more available and more people (including members of theatre faculties) are learning how to create them. Excerpts from contemporary firsthand accounts of the theatre also help to give a sense of immediacy and a flavor of the period. (Many of these excerpts are now readily available in anthologies.) Audiovisual materials showing nontheatrical subjects can be used to establish the dominant visual style of a period. Music may also help students gain a sense of a period's artistic taste and style. In addition, the teacher can add a great deal to student understanding through materials that relate to the social, religious, political, and philosophical context out of which the theatre of the period came. If the theatre "holds the mirror up to nature," then the theatre is a reflection of what its society and age believed about the nature of human beings, their motivations, the causal forces at work in human affairs, and the values that society espoused. The theatre is one record of what human beings have thought about themselves, and our study of theatre history ought to make those views reasonably clear to students. What this adds up to in part is that class time should not be devoted primarily to rehashing what is contained in the textbook or other assignments but should be an extension that clarifies and expands on assignments.

The teacher of theatre history must also be aware of the wide variety of interests among his/her students, ranging through those concerned primarily with acting, to others interested in design and technical production, and still others interested in directing, management, playwriting, criticism, and so on. These interests are usually related to each student's own area of concentration. Teachers can help students appreciate the roots of their own special interests by encouraging (or requiring) them to pursue individualized research assignments. For example, what can an acting student find out about the training, working, and performance conditions of actors in an earlier time? One can never be sure what will pique a student's interest; if the interest is genuine, it should be encouraged (no matter how bizarre it may be in some cases), for we ought to be sympathetic to individualizing interests that help us avoid turning our students into carbon copies of each other. Most courses profit by giving students the freedom to choose some topics for exploration on their own. Such explorations also provide opportunities for students to develop the research skills and discipline they will need for further investigation and learning.

In emphasizing overview and trends, am I suggesting that students need learn nothing about the contributions of individuals or have no awareness of dates or major companies or important theatres? No, but I do suggest that this knowledge is apt to come about relatively easily within the context that I have suggested. If one assigns plays by important playwrights, probably the students will easily be able to identify those writers. Dates and persons are not worth committing to memory unless something so significant is connected with them that this information should be carried in our heads rather than being looked up in sources readily available for consultation. It is what happened at that time that makes a date important, and it is what persons did that makes them worth remembering. Factual information is essential, but I deplore the all-too-prevalent practice of expecting students to memorize facts for the sake of passing exams.

Much of what I have said is most pertinent to the early stages of learning. Further study requires that the field be divided into smaller segments so that the theatre at a limited time or place, or some specific topic can be explored more fully. It is difficult to be interested deeply in a topic about which we have very little information. Advanced study ought to provide in-depth familiarity.

The most advanced students usually are able to take seminars in which a very restricted topic is studied in detail, primarily by requiring students to do research on varying aspects of the topic and sharing the results with each other; not only the teacher but also the students usually comment on and critique the work presented there. And finally, an advanced student seeking a degree in theatre history usually must choose a specialized topic to explore in-depth in a thesis or dissertation, through which he or she seeks to add to our knowledge about theatre history and to demonstrate his or her mastery of the techniques of inquiry, ability to deal convincingly with evidence, and communicate results in a coherent manner. In their turn, most students who progress this far themselves ultimately become teachers of theatre history.

IV

Thus far, I have said little about certain necessary aspects of teaching: course planning, examinations, and grading. Course planning seems to me primarily a matter of logic. If one knows the scope of the course and number of class meetings, one can divide the time to ensure that some attention is paid to each segment that is to be covered. Planning quickly takes definition once one asks what can be done in the time allotted to the course. At that point, one usually begins a process of elimination, for seldom is there time to do all the things one would like or to spend as much time on each segment as one would like. It is helpful (even sobering) to place a calendar showing each class period alongside a list of the things that should be covered in the course. It may be discouraging to find that one can devote no more than two weeks to Shakespeare and the Elizabethan theatre, but this becomes an incentive to decide what one can do through outside assignments, or what one can do through in-class presentations and discussions or learn from watching videotapes. During this process, one's ambitions for a course are quickly reduced to considerations of what is feasible.

If one assumes that for each hour of in-class time, students should do two hours of outside preparation, one also gets a measure of what expectations one may have of the students: how much time will be needed to complete assignments; how many plays can be assigned for reading; what kind of research paper or other projects can be done? This kind of analysis brings into focus the factors that must be considered in planning.

Usually the scope of the course and its place in the overall curriculum have already been defined by the department. But within these definitions, there is usually considerable flexibility about specific goals and the methods that can be used to achieve them. Before deciding what assignments to make and how the time is to be used, teachers need to clarify their own goals and what they need to do to achieve them.

It is seldom possible or desirable to divide the time evenly among all topics. Because of their overall significance, some periods or topics seem to demand more extended treatment than others (e.g., Greek and Elizabethan). It may well be worth spending what on the surface seems an excessive amount of in-class time on a project designed to clarify an approach that will facilitate what will come thereafter. How time is allotted is essentially a matter of aligning goals and available time.

Some teachers seem to know in advance what they will be doing during each class meeting for an entire semester. I need more flexibility. Sometimes topics of major importance require more time with one particular class than with another; sometimes things that one thought would be difficult turn out to be less so; sometimes plans turn out to be wrong for the particular group of students, and another way to accomplish the same goals must be sought. To me, it seems best to make plans for an entire semester's work but not to consider those plans inviolate; the purpose of planning is to achieve goals; if the plan clearly is failing to do that, it is better to seek another plan than to continue doggedly onward to failure.

As another aspect of planning, the instructor should be specific with students at the beginning of the course about the amount and type of work that will be required to complete it satisfactorily—what the overall reading assignments will be; the kinds and number of projects; the number of written exams and preferably the dates on which they will be given (which should not rule out pop quizzes if the instructor thinks them necessary, and so long as students are told at the beginning that quizzes may be given); and whatever else is needed to clarify the teacher's expectations. Unexpected assignments or last minute assignments should be avoided.

Various means are needed to help students fix impressions of the material covered. Among those most frequently used are in-class questioning and discussions; reviews, including time spent to emphasize those things that are most important; quizzes and examinations.

Examinations can be made a learning experience (as opposed to mere regurgitation of memorized fact) by asking questions that require students thoughtfully to put together information in ways not done in class. Such questions may involve comparing aspects of theatre in one or more periods or tracing changes and developments over a period of time or contrasting the work of two playwrights. If students are asked to identify persons or events, they should also be asked to tell why these persons or events are significant in theatre history. Students usually find it helpful, as aids in studying for exams, to be given a set of sample questions or some type of review guide. I recommend limiting questions to those things that are significant enough that students should not forget them. Exams that encourage students to memorize a lot of facts usually contribute only to wasted effort because the facts are forgotten soon after the exam is over.

Grading is the most troublesome part of teaching because the factors that need to be taken into consideration are so diverse. How does one compare brilliant but lazy students (who do well but by no means live up to their potential) with diligent and conscientious but intellectually limited students (who always do their best)? My instinct is to grade the first down and the second up, but that is not a wholly satisfactory solution. One needs a more or less fixed common denominator, but one also needs some means of grading in terms of potential and progress. It is a disservice to brilliant students to let them slide just because their work is as good as that of others when one knows that they are capable of much more, and it is an equal disservice to conscientious students to set goals so far in advance of what they can reasonably hope to achieve that they become discouraged and cease to try. An ideal grading system rewards students for their accomplishments, reminds them of what they still have to do, and encourages them to believe that they can achieve their potential if they will strive to do so.

Teachers tend to develop reputations for being easy or difficult graders. Someone has remarked that grading is an indication of teachers' aspirations for their students. That may be true, but in my opinion good teachers need both high aspirations and high tolerance so as to achieve a balance between over-rewarding students on the one hand and discouraging them on the other hand. Far too much emphasis is placed on grades, but that seems unlikely to change. Meantime, we use grades to suggest the degree of coherence between the course's goals and the students' achievement of those goals, as a symbolic measure of their success—and of ours.

V

It is virtually impossible to specify what makes a teacher good. Some of the qualities that seem to me essential to effective teaching are reasonable knowledge of the subject, obvious liking for the subject, knowledge of other matters so that the subject is placed in a context, and concern for students and sensitivity to their needs and quandaries. That the teacher is at ease with the subject matter and committed to its importance is very important. It is hard for students to take seriously someone who is bluffing his or her way through classes, who knows only what is already provided by a textbook, and who is obviously no more interested in the subject than they are. On the other hand, they may reassess their own attitudes if they encounter someone who is clearly committed to the subject they have no experience with or previous interest in. And if the teacher is willing to take time to deal with their concerns and treat their doubts and questions seriously, students are much more apt to respect the teacher and to believe that he or she may have something to teach them. I think that too many teachers do not realize that students almost automatically recognize the difference between what a teacher tells them they should believe or do and what the teacher really believes and does. Students may parrot back the attitudes they have been told they should have, but they recognize the difference between sincerity and rationalization.

We often hear of students whose lives were transformed by one teacher, sometimes a teacher that no one else seemed to find remarkable. We are lucky if we have such an experience. It is one that should make us wary of trying to lay out too fully how to go about teaching. Teaching skills can be honed and developed, but there are also some that seem to transcend anything resembling a formula. Effective approaches to teaching are always in flux and, while basic principles may endure, how to apply them may need to be reconsidered frequently in light of changing cultural perceptions. Certainly this is true in considering how to teach theatre history.

Works Cited

Gabelnick, F., MacGregor, J., Matthews, R. S., and Smith, B. L. 1990. *Learning communities: Creating connections among students, faculty, and disciplines.* San Francisco: Jossey-Bass.

Levine, Jodi, H. 1999. (ed.), *Learning communities: New structures, new partnerships for learning.* Columbia, SC: University of South Carolina.

Jonas, Susan, Proehl, Geoffrey, S., and Lupu, Michael. 1997. (eds.), *Dramaturgy in American theater: A source book.* Fort Worth: Harcourt Brace College Publishers.

Schechner, Richard. 1988. *Performance Theory.* Rev. and expanded edition. New York: Routledge.

Whitehead, Alfred North. 1929. *The aim of education and other essays.* New York: Macmillan.

CHAPTER 3

The Teaching of Acting in American Colleges and Universities, 1920–1960

Patti P. Gillespie and Kenneth M. Cameron

Today, acting is one of the most popular of our course offerings in theatre. Such was not always the case, however.

A mostly apprentice system before the mid-nineteenth century, actor training moved increasingly into formal schools after about 1880 (Hodge 1954). It came into the college curriculum sporadically from the late-nineteenth century on, and by 1920 (though often called by a different name) it was a part of several colleges' offerings (Hamar 1951). Its theoretical base was largely the "new elocution" (expression), with a continuing strand of American Delsartism (Hamar 1951; Hochmuth and Murphy 1954; Robb 1954; Gray 1954; Shaver 1954). By 1960, not only were courses in acting common, but also the theories of Stanislavski were visibly at their base. However, no serious study of acting curricula from 1920 to 1960 (that is, since the end date of the major previous study [Hamar 1951] and the unequivocal dominance of a new theory) has been undertaken. This lapse is especially significant because the period 1920–1960 saw the foundation of today's practices.

Thus, we used three kinds of evidence—college catalogs (replicating part of Hamar's study, but for the later period), textbooks, and national convention programs—to seek answers to the question, "What was the nature of the teaching of acting in American colleges and universities from 1920–1960, and what ideas underlay that teaching?"

College Catalogs

Of Hamar's original population of 180 institutions, we solicited information from only those 88 that were offering instruction in acting or related skills by 1920 (Hamar 1951, 271). Of these 88, we examined the relevant catalogs of the 58 who could supply them. (The sample seemed sufficient because no systematic bias emerged from the failure of the other 30.)

Our study of catalog materials needed a definition of "acting" more precise than Hamar's, however, for we wanted to differentiate the teaching of acting from closely related subjects like oral interpretation, voice, and movement, on the one hand, and from the preparation of plays, either for class or pubic performance, on the other. It seemed significant that (as Hamar's study showed), the use of the word *acting* in course descriptions and course titles was somewhat late in coming (Hamar 1951, 265). We therefore accepted as acting courses only those that used *acting* or one of its variants in either their descriptions or their titles; as well, we defined three levels of the *acceptance* of acting within a curriculum: (1) when the word *acting* first appeared in a course description and acting was identifiable only as a component of a more general course; (2) when the course title included the word *acting*, either alone (e.g., "beginning acting") or with another word ("acting and rehearsal"); (3) when more than one acting course was offered.

The results are summarized in Table 3.1, which shows that acting generally found its way into the curriculum as a part of another course; that the most rapid growth in the number of new courses took place in the 1930s and 1940s; and that, by the 1950s, *new* acting courses were the exception, but, if introduced, were whole courses rather than components of other courses.

Table 3.1   New Courses in Acting, 1920–1960

Decade	Component of Course	Single Course	Multiple Courses
1920–1929	25	17	5
1930–1939	12	23	12
1940–1949	3	21	18
1950–1959	0	7	3

By 1960 only eight of the 58 schools offered *no* instruction in acting. Acting was by 1960, then, an accepted part of the curriculum of most colleges and universities in our study.

Discussion

Through the 1920s, acting was offered mostly as a part of courses with titles like Dramatic Arts, Dramatic Production, Interpretive Reading, and Dramatic Interpretation. Two approaches seemed to dominate: first, emphasis on the play text, with acting as a step toward the text's performance and therefore its better comprehension; and, second, emphasis on training the instrument, often to develop skills as a performer for platform or stage. In the first approach, little instruction beyond active participation seems to have been given. Thus, in 1920–1921 at the University of Iowa, the catalog said, "Dramatic Interpretation: Principles of dramatic interpretation. Members of the class will take part as actors in plays produced by students in course 133–134 [dramatic production]...." As an example of the second approach, the University of Oklahoma's catalog for 1919–1920 described "Public Speaking 19a. Impersonation: This course comprises dialect work and character study. It is meant to fit one for the platform as a character actor, either in plays or single impersonations...." Preference for either approach seemed to be independent of course title, size, location of school, or administrative unit; that is, courses housed in Departments of Public Speaking (about half), English (about a third), or Expression (about a tenth) did not systematically prefer one approach over the other.

Four words and their variants appeared regularly in the course descriptions of the 1920s: *expression, gesture, pantomime,* and *interpretation,* strongly suggesting that the teaching of acting was still heavily suffused with the ideas of the new elocutionists, and perhaps that acting was not yet considered separate from oral reading. "Pantomime" may suggest the continuing influence of Delsartre (whose ideas were in turn incorporated into some of the new elocution [Robb 1954; Shaver 1954]).

Psychology as a part of actor training was specifically mentioned at Earlham College and University of California-Berkeley, indicating only, perhaps, a general interest in this newly popular field. Mention of psychology, however, may have come from a specific interest in the theories of the expressionist Charles Wesley Emerson or in current psychological theories as represented by the teaching and writing of James Albert Winans and Charles Henry Woolbert, both of whom had published basic speaking texts by 1920 (Gray 1954; Renshaw 1954).

In the 1930s, the number of independent (including multiple) courses in acting increased, but the courses continued to emphasize either participation in plays or systematic classroom instruction in which the influence of expression and interpretation dominated (although the term "interpretation" seemed increasingly preferred). At the decade's end, several schools began to offer courses in radio acting and in screen acting. At a handful of schools (Baylor, Dennison, Iowa, Northwestern, Yale), course descriptions seemed to suggest other new departures. Thus, at Dennison, "emphasis on stage principles and traditions, character creation, emotional interpretation and production"; at Baylor, "theory concerning the playing and creating of a character"; and at Iowa, "survey of the development of dramatic art. Principles of character interpretation in acting."

The 1940s showed change, especially after the war. The old language gave way to a new, perhaps signaling that old approaches to the teaching of acting were being replaced. At least four of the catalogs (Adelphi, Stanford, Washington State, Yankton) showed an interest in a slightly technical approach to actor training. A 1945–1946 course a Stanford called "Technique of Acting" included "a detailed study of stage practice, gesture and movement, timing and pointing of lines, sustaining emotional scenes, effective characterization...." At least two catalog descriptions combined words in ways that almost certainly had their basis in Stanislavski. Macalester's catalog of 1942 described "Fundamentals of Acting" as "a course in the analysis of acting tools as they concern the areas of concentration, memory of emotion, dramatic action, characterization...." Baylor's 1947 catalog listed "Acting Principles and Theory of the Moscow Art Theatre"; regrettably, there was no accompanying course description.

Most of the descriptions, however, were less easily categorized, except to say that they sounded very different from most of those before the war. In case after case, references to *characterization* and *emotion* replaced those to *expression* and *interpretation*. Although many catalogues retained references to *gesture* and *pantomime*, many more now talked in terms of *body, acting,* and *movement*. Occasional references to *experience, observation, ensemble,* and *modern approaches* appeared. A spate of references to psychology came between 1945 and 1949, perhaps a continuation of older interest or perhaps an indication that "inner" work was becoming important, as in the Illinois catalog of 1946: students of advance acting were offered "advanced principles of inner and outer acting technique."

By the end of the 1940s, then, there were four discernible approaches to teaching acting in American colleges and universities, two left over from past decades and two then emerging. Continuing were (1) academic credit for participation in productions and (2) the traditions of expression and inter-pretation. New were (3) an approach devoted to the mastery of external tech-niques and (4) an approach that showed acquaintance with Stanislavski's theories of acting.

Some course descriptions of the 1950s suggested a growing knowledge of Stanislavski: "relaxation, concentration, sensory and emotional recall" (Lawrence cc [college catalog 1951); "character analyses and motivation. Accuracy of observation, recall of emotion" (Knox cc 1952); "exercises in concentration, imagination, and observation" (Smith cc 1955); and "sensory responsiveness; creative memory; character observation; motivation" (Northwestern cc 1958). Others remained more eclectic: Bates and Boston joined Illinois in its implied call to consider "various theories of acting," seeking "the balance between technique and emotion." Some old language persisted: in 1954, for example, two of Whitman's three acting courses echoed earlier decades: "Emphasis is on the art of pantomime and deport-ment.... Emphasis on theatre reading...."

Textbooks

It is reasonable to suggest a rough correspondence between ideas in contem-porary books and ideas in the classroom.

Data from the *Cumulative Book Index* (*CBI*) reveal the number of books on acting available in the period. Because *CBI* varied in several ways across the period, we had to adapt our data accordingly: we included only books having a U.S. publisher or distributor after *CBI* began including all English-language books (1928), and we listed books in multiyear blocks because of *CBI*'s variable annualizing. Textbooks were our focus rather than trade books, but the distinction was often unclear, and books not written as texts sometimes had an impact and so deserved attention.

Table 3.2 reveals a reasonably steady rate of publication before World War II (about 25 books per decade), a precipitous drop in the number during the war (only nine from 1943 to 1948), and then a significant increase from the late 1940s to the end of the period (40 books within 14 years).

Discussion

Probably the most influential books of the 1920s dealt with acting as one element among several: thus, *The Art of Acting and Public Reading* (Talcott 1922), *Play Production* (Smith 1926), *The Art of Play Production* (Dolman 1928), and *Acting and Play Production* (Andrews and Wierick 1925). In these books, the arts of expression and acting remained closely linked: for example,

Table 3.2   Books Under "Acting"
in *CBI*

Years	Number of Books
1921–1924	6
1925–1927	15
1928–1932	10
1933–1937	16
1938–1942	13
1943–1948	9
1949–1952	15
1953–1956	12
1957–1960	8

Talcott defined acting as "the art of presenting literature..., the easiest and most natural form of public expression" (quoted in Ackley 1973, 56–57). The influence of Delsarte remained clear in works like Bosworth's *Technique in Dramatic Art* (a book perhaps organized around the expressionist S. S. Curry's triad of the physical, the mental, and the emotional), which included standard gestures of pity, fear, revulsion, refusal, and so on (Hetler 1957, 148). Indeed, Delsarte's views may have received new, apparently scientific support in 1922 from the publication of the James-Lange theory of emotion, a theory (later discredited) that proposed outward manifestations as the evocation and precedent of inner emotions. Andrews and Weirick (1925) seemed to tie the influence of James-Lange to that of Delsarte, and Dolman advised, "The right actions, thoroughly rehearsed to recur automatically, may have some effect in calling up the desired emotions in the actor and emphatically in the audience" (Hetler 1957, 157).

Two other books of the 1920s were significant, although neither was a text and neither directly treated the training of actors. Both Stanislavski's *My Life in Art* (1924) and Sheldon Cheney's *The Art Theatre* ([1917], 1925), gave support to the burgeoning little theatre movement and presented visions of theatre that were to inspire much of the theoretical work of the coming decades. Important to our study is an understanding that the distinct positions of these two works were seen as competitive and that, of the two, Stanislavski was then considered old-fashioned (Hetler 1957).

Most acting texts of the 1930s continued the tradition of expression. Helena Chalmers, a teacher at the American Academy of Dramatic Art, dedicated her text (1930) to Franklin Sargeant (founder of the school and a new elocutionist). Eva Alberti (1932) echoed Steele Mackay's Delsarte when she referred to "the apex of the triangle in the theatre," advocated "life study," and offered models of gesture and pantomime (Hetler 1957, 169). By 1934, Bosworth had been revised, Alberti's second edition had appeared, and Edward and Alice MacKaye had published *Elementary Principles of Acting*, a close restatement of an earlier book by the actor/elocutionist F. F. MacKay (1913), and called by Lee Strasberg a "manual of expression" (Strasberg 1947, 11).

In 1938, Miriam Franklin's *Rehearsal*, grounded in expression and in the James-Lange theory, appeared and found adoption in more than a hundred colleges and universities. Crocker, Fields, and Broomall (1939) continued the tradition of expression in the teaching of acting: acting was a "skill in ex-pressing" (Hetler 1957, 188–192).

Another approach to acting appeared in books before the end of the 1930s, however. In 1933, Boleslavski's trade book, *Acting: The First Six Lessons*, offered, rather impressionistically, part of what would later be seen as the Stanislavski system. (Parts of the book had already been published in *Theatre Arts* magazine.) Rosenstein et al. (1936) seem to have drawn heavily, but without acknowledgement, upon Boleslavski to publish *Modern Acting: A Manual*, which was endorsed by both Glenn Hughes of the University of Washington and Lee Strasberg of the Group Theatre (which had formally adopted Stanislavski's system as its approach to acting in 1931). With chapter titles like "Observation," "Imagination," "Concentration," and "Characterization," Rosenstein et al. adopted a vocabulary different from that of expression and clearly focused much more on the inner work of the actor. Acting was for them the "means of creating the inner life of the character delineated by the playwright," and their book was to stress "the importance of working within out, or from the inner feeling to the outer manifestation" (Hetler 1957, 190–192).

That same year, Stanislavski's *An Actor Prepares* appeared in English translation and sold six thousand copies in its first six months (Hetler 1957, 104). Also in 1936, Nemirovitch-Danchenko's *My Life*, Norris Houghton's *Moscow Rehearsals*, and an entire issue of *Theatre Arts* devoted to the art of acting focused new attention on the recently old-fashioned Stanislavski.

The books of the 1940s were eclectic. Acting as a form of expression found support in the last of many printings of Bosworth (1940). John Dolman's last edition still relied heavily on James-Lange, although the theory was by then considered discredited. Crafton and Royer retained a focus on Stark Young and the art theatre movement (1934). Several essays on Stanislavski and other Russians appeared in Cole's *Acting, A Handbook* (1947) and in, among others, Cole's and Chinoy's anthology, *Actors on Acting* (1949). Selden in his *First Steps in Acting* (1947) continued the argument of his earlier work (*A Players Handbook*, 1934) that communicating with an audience was the actor's primary task and that technique and careful attention to stage business ("pantomime") were the best ways of assuring successful communication.

Two events of the 1940s, however, focused increasingly serious attention on Stanislavski and his sysem of actor training: the publication of Gassner's *Producing the Play* (1941); and the appearance of Stanislavski's second work on acting in English, *Building a Character* (1949).

The importance of Gassner's work rested on the inclusion of two essays on acting and the actor, one by Strasberg and one by Harold Clurman. Both used the now-familiar vocabulary of *An Actor Prepares*: for example, sense memory, affective memory, concentration, and imagination. Both examined the causes, the motivation, of a character's action. Both emphasized the inner work of the actor. These essays were apparently widely disseminated, for after Gassner's revision of 1953, the book had 122 adoptions in major colleges and universities, including some with established graduate programs—that is, some of those that would be providing the teachers of the next decades (Hetler 1957, 211).

Ironically, *Building a Character* perhaps made less impact than the many essays *about* Stanislavski; although both educators and professionals praised the book, its emphasis on physical and vocal training did not have the effect of *An Actor Prepares*. The book's sales figures were markedly lower, and American exponents of Stanislavski continued to emphasize the inner (Hetler 1957, 267).

The 1950s saw an acceleration in the number of books treating Stanislavski and his system (Stanislavski 1950; Magarshak 1951; Chekhov 1953; Redgrave 1953; Gorchakov 1954). Moreover, by 1955 the popularity of books explaining or advocating some versions of the system was well demonstrated by the sales figures: Cole's *Handbook*, 7,744 copies since 1947; Cole and Chinoy's anthology, 8,317 copies since 1949; Boleslavski's *Six Lessons*, 17,867 since 1946; and Stanislavski's *An Actor Prepares*, 24,548 (since 1924), and *Building a Character*, 8,546 (since 1949) (figures from Hetler 1957, 267). Finally, two exceedingly popular new textbooks seemed to emphasize Stanislavski's position within colleges and universities. The dust jacket of Charles McGaw's *Acting is Believing* (1955) called it a "practical, informative, and inspirational presentation of the Stanislavski method" (quoted in Hetler 1957, 254). Addressed directly to the student of acting, the book sold four thousand copies in its first year, with adoptions at 69 major colleges and universities, including leading graduate institutions like Northwestern, Michigan, and University of California-Berkeley (Hetler 1957, 265).

And probably the most popular of the early introductory theatre texts, Frank Whiting's *Introduction to the Theatre* (1954), specifically recommended Stanislavski's approach to acting as especially well suited for colleges and universities (Hetler 1957, 247). Even Strickland's *The Technique of Acting* (1956), which adopted the technical position far more than Stanislavski's, thought it useful to claim that the text was a supplement to Stanislavski: whereas the Russian's system was designed to keep experienced actors fresh, his own, Strickland said, was designed to teach acting to beginners (ix) and to "help the actor give an intelligent and competent performance, even when inspiration is lacking..." (xiii).

Convention Presentations

Convention records for the major national associations (the parent organization, the Speech Communication Association, and its 1937 offshoot, the American Educational Theatre Association) were unavailable for the years before 1930. However, the records of the national office of the Speech Communication Association were complete thereafter except for 1935, 1943–1946, 1948, and 1954.

The varied nature of presentations at these conventions (papers, demonstrations, performances, roundtable discussions) and the unclear boundaries between acting and, let us say, voice or movement, made comparisons difficult. Still, interest in the teaching of acting clearly increased dramatically in convention programing between 1930 and 1960.

Table 3.3 summarizes the attention give to acting at the conventions from 1930 through the 1960s. The averages were calculated by dividing the total number of sessions and presentations (whether workshops, papers, demonstrations) by the number of years for which information was available.

Discussion

The first convention presentation on acting seems to have been Valentine Windt's paper, "Problems in the Teaching of Acting" (1931). Five years later,

Table 3.3   Acting Sessions at National Conventions

Decade	Average Number of Sessions	Average Number of Presentations
1930s	0.3 (3/10)	1.8 (18/10)
1940s	0.5 (2.5/5)	2.8 (14/5)
1950s	1.2 (12/10)	4.8 (48/10)
1960s	2.8 (28/10)	7.1 (71/10)

he participated in a panel entitled "How Much of Acting Can be Taught and How?" His paper was one of eight (10-minute) presentations and the only titled one: "Acting and the 1935 Soviet Theatre Fesival." In the first joint convention, 1937, Windt participated in a roundtable discussion on "The Teaching of Acting," which included Chester Wallace (Carnegie), Helene Blattner (Iowa), and Lee Norvelle (Indiana). At the same convention, Joseph Smith of Wisconsin talked on "Oral Interpretation as an Aid to Preparation for the Stage" and Constance Welch (Yale) on "Training Voice and Speech for Student Actors." At each of the joint conventions for the next two years, at least one program dealt with issues of actor training.

The 1940s saw an abrupt decline in programs on the teaching of acting. In 1940 and 1941, for example, there was no convention presentation devoted exclusively to the teaching of acting, although there were programs on makeup, history, curriculum, and professional schools. In 1947, however, acting returned as a popular convention topic, although with a somewhat different focus: "Applications of Acting Theories to Oral Interpretation," "A Resident Acting Company in University Theatre," "Using Motion Pictures in the Teaching of Acting." In 1949, Lawrence Carra spoke on "Styles of Acting," and a session entitled "Teaching Techniques in Theatre" devoted five of its ten papers to grappling with the problems of teaching acting in universities and colleges.

Stanislavski's name first appeared in a convention program in the joint convention of 1952—in the *Interpretation*, rather than the Theatre Division—in the title of Leslie Irene Coger's important comparison of Stanislavski and Curry. Not until 1956, however, did Stanislavski appear among the *theatre* programs of a convention. That year his theories, at least as practiced by the American Method teachers, apparently came under attack, for Charles McGaw's paper "The Method and the Educational Theatre" was followed immediately by Ralph Freud's "Style vs. 'the Method' in Acting." In 1959, a clearly non-Stanislavskian panel on "Objective Acting: The Epic Insight" balanced a panel that featured Stella Adler on teaching acting and Jack Clay on sense memory. In addition to this seemingly new interest in Stanislavski, several other issues surfaced in conventions during the decade: stage movement (Juana de Laban's name appears often); voice for the actor (Constance Welch of Yale figured prominently); styles in performance; improvisation in rehearsal; acting for the movies; theatre as therapy.

Conclusions and Questions

The 40 years from 1920 to 1960 saw the acceptance of acting as a legitimate course for colleges and saw instruction in acting (as in most other areas of theatre) become more specialized. Before World War II, the conceptual basis for acting in both courses and texts lay mostly in expression. Before the war, also, interest in Stanislavski seemed focused on his much earlier connection with the art theatre movement. After the war, the number of acting courses, acting programs at conventions, and acting texts increased quickly and substantially, with many courses and books soon showing an acquaintance with some of Stanislavski's theories and practices (as they were understood in America), primarily those related to inner work. A wide (perhaps even general) acceptance of some of his theories and practices by the mid-1950s can perhaps be inferred, for in 1956 and again in 1959, two national convention programs addressed problems of and offered alternatives to "Stanislavski's system"; that is, by the mid-1950s, Stanislavski's ideas may have seemed to many the mainstream against which other ideas were to be measured—a view that has proven prophetic.

Vexing questions are raised, however, by the data and the tentative conclusions. Why do those two areas of the study under academic control—catalogs and conventions—show a lag behind books? And, for that matter, behind the professional mainstream? For it can be easily demonstrated that the American version of Stanislavski had taken firm hold in the profession two decades before it reached the catalogs and the conventions.

Why were the professional conventions—seemingly the most fitting place for the discussion of new ideas—the most laggard? Was there—is there—something in the convention process that militates against innovation?

Why did the ideas of Stanislavski, which had been available in print from the early 1930s (Hewitt and d'Angelo 1932; Boleslavski 1933; Rosenstein et al. 1936), not appear significantly in catalogs or conventions until the 1950s—and why, when they did finally arrive, did they arrive with such a rush that within a decade they were the received wisdom of the time—as they still are?

What may be dimly visible in these data, and what deserves further study, is a problem of transmission—one that may not be limited to acting but that is most certainly visible there. It may involve problems of intellectual receptivity as well as of transmission, perhaps of intellectual curiosity and rigor. These problems are worth examination, however, both to see if they still exist and to discover how they affected (and may affect) the teaching of an influential subject.

Note

Printings and revisions later than the period of our study are generally excluded. College catalogs cited in the text offer the name of the college, followed by cc and the year of the catalog only.

Works Cited

Ackley, B. G. 1973. A comparative study of acting and oral interpretation theory and practice as revealed in selected American college texts, 1900–1970. *Dissertation Abstracts International,* 34, 4454A–4455 (University Microfilms No. 73–31, 316).

Alberti, E. 1932 [1933, 1935]. *A handbook of acting, based on the new pantomime.* New York: Samuel French.

Albright, H. D. 1947. *Working up a part: A manual for the beginning actor.* New York: Houghton Mifflin.

Andrews, H. L. and B. Weirick. 1925. *Acting and play production.* New York: Longmans.

Boleslavski, R. 1933 [1934, 1935, 1937, 1939, 1947, 1949]. *Acting: The first six lessons.* New York: Theatre Arts.

Bosworth, H. 1926 [1928, 1931, 1934, 1935, 1936, 1937, 1940]. *Technique in dramatic art.* New York: Macmillan.

Chalmers, H. 1930. *Modern acting.* New York: D. Appleton and Co.

Chekhov, M. 1953. *To the actor: On the technique of acting.* New York: Harper.

Cheyney, S. 1917 [1925; 1936]. *The art of theatre.* New York: A. A. Knopf.

Clurman, H. 1941. The principles of interpretation. In J. Gassner (ed.), *Producing the play.* New York: Dryden Press, 280–302.

Coger, L. I. 1952. A comparison for the oral interpreter of the teaching methods of Curry and Stanislavski. Ph.D. dissertation, Northwestern University.

Cole, T. 1947 [1955, 1957]. *Acting, a handbook of the Stanislavski method.* New York: Lee.

Cole, T. and H. Chinoy. 1949 [1954, 1957]. *Actors on acting.* New York: Crown.

Crafton, A. and J. Royer. 1928 [1930, 1934]. *Acting: A book for the beginner.* New York: Crofts and Co.

Crocker, C., V. A. Fields, and W. Broomall. 1939. *Taking the stage: Self development through dramatic art.* New York: Pitman Publishing Group.

Dolman, J. 1949. *The art of acting.* New York: Harpers.

——. 1928 [1946]. *The art of play production.* New York: Harpers.

Franklin, M. 1938 [1942, 1945, 1946, 1947, 1950]. *Rehearsal: The principles and practice of acting for the stage.* New York: Prentice-Hall.

Gassner, J. 1941 [1946, 1953]. *Producing the play.* New York: The Dryden Press.

Gorchakov, N. M. 1954. *Stanislavski directs.* New York: Funk and Wagnalls.

Gray, G. W. 1954. Some teachers and the transition to twentieth century speech education. In K. R. Wallace (ed.), *History of speech education in America.* New York: Appleton-Century-Crofts, 422–446.

Hamar, C. E. 1951. The rise of drama and theatre in the American college curriculum, 1900–1920. Ph.D. dissertation, Stanford University.

Hetler, L. 1957. The influence of Stanislavski theories of acting on the teaching of acting in the United States. Ph.D. dissertation, University of Denver.

Hewitt, B. and A. d'Angelo. 1932. The Stanislavski system for actors. *Quarterly Journal of Speech* 18: 440–446.

Hochmuth, M. and R. Murphy. 1954. Rhetorical and elocutionary training in nineteenth-century colleges. In K. R. Wallace (ed.), *History of speech education in America*. New York: Appleton-Century-Crofts, 153–177.

Hodge, F. 1954. The private theatre schools of the late nineteenth century. In K. R. Wallace (ed.), *History of speech education in America*. New York: Appleton-Century-Crofts, 552–571.

Houghton, N. 1936 [1938]. *Moscow rehearsals*. New York: Harcourt, Brace and Co.

Lees, C. L. Ca. 1940. *A primer of acting*. New York: Prentice Hall.

McGaw, C. 1955. *Acting is believing*. New York: Rhinehart.

Mackaye E. and A. Mackaye. 1934 [1935, 1937]. *Elementary principles of acting*. New York: Samuel French.

Mackay, F. F. 1919. *The art of acting*. New York: F. F. Mackay.

Magarshak, D. 1951. *Stanislavski, a life*. London: McGibbon and Kee.

Nemirovich-Danchenko, V. I. 1936. *My life in the Russian theatre*. Boston: Little, Brown.

Parrish, W. M. 1932 [1937, 1941, 1946, 1953]. *Reading aloud*. New York: T. Nelson and Sons.

Redgrave, M. 1953. *The actor's ways and means*. New York: Theatre Arts Books.

Renshaw, E. 1954. Five private schools of speech. In K. R. Wallace (ed.), *History of speech education in America*. New York: Appleton-Century-Crofts, 301–325.

Robb, M. M. 1954. Elocutionary movement and its chief gestures. In K. R. Wallace (ed.), *History of speech education in America*. New York: Appleton-Century-Crofts, 177–201.

Rosenstein, S., L. A. Hayden, and W. Sparrow. 1936 [1947]. *Modern acting: A manual*. New York: Samuel French.

Selden, S. 1947. *First steps in acting*. New York: Crofts.

———. 1934. *A player's handbook*. New York: Crofts.

Shaver, C. L. 1954. Steele MacKaye and the Delsartian tradition. In K. R. Wallace (ed.), *History of speech education in America*. New York: Appleton-Century-Crofts, 202–218.

Smith, M. M. 1926 [1927, 1928, 1930, 1934, 1948, under the title *Play production for little theatres, schools, and colleges*]. *The book of play production*. New York: D. Appleton and Co.

Stanislavski, K. S. 1950 [1961]. David Magarshak (ed.). *Stanislavski on the art of the stage*. London: Faber and Faber.

———. 1949. *Building a character*. New York: Theatre Arts Books.

———. 1924 [1927, 1929, 1935, 1938, 1945, 1948, 1952]. *My life in art*. Boston: Little, Brown.

Strasberg, L. 1947. Introduction. In T. Cole (ed.), *Acting: A handbook of the Stanislavski method*. New York: Lee, 10–17.

———. 1941. Acting and the training of the actor. In J. Gassner (ed.), *Producing the play*. New York: Dryden Press, 128–162.

Strickland, F. C. 1956. *The technique of acting*. New York: McGraw-Hill.

Tallcott, R. A. 1922. *The art of acting and public reading*. Indianapolis: Bobbs-Merrill.

Whiting, F. 1954 [1961, 1969]. *Introduction to the theatre*. New York: Harper and Row.

CHAPTER 4

The Pedagogy of Directing, 1920–1990: Seventy Years of Teaching the Unteachable

Anne L. Fliotsos

The stage director is a modern phenomenon—and somewhat of an enigma.

Regardless of the country, at least in the West, the stage director is recognized as the central figure in the theatre. The definition of a director's job is complex; this pivotal figure must learn about all areas of theatre in order to synthesize the elements of the production into an aesthetic whole. Both a craftsman and artist, the director coordinates the artistic and managerial functions of theatrical production.

Although historians have pieced together the history of theatre education, little attention has been given to the education of directors. Clifford Hamar's study addressed the entrance of theatre into the curriculum and included information about classes in play production and direction. Hamar found that the earliest classes in directing (1912–1920) were geared toward teachers who were expected to direct school plays. Only 12 institutions offered such courses, but a total of 28 offered courses in play production, which included technical aspects of staging a play. The development of these courses over the next several decades, however, remains somewhat mysterious. Presumably directing courses, like other theatre courses, gained popularity after World War II and were boosted by the addition of M.F.A. programs during the 1950s and 1960s.

Statistics from the 1960s and 1970s attest to the growing popularity of directing courses in higher education. The first edition of the *Directory of American College Theatre* (*DACT* 1960) reported that there were 916 undergraduate classes in directing offered nationally. The second edition of the *DACT* (1967) reported a slightly lower number, with 902 undergraduate courses. By the third and final *DACT* (1976), however, the number had increased to 1,462 undergraduate courses and 318 graduate courses in directing.

Despite the central role of the director in theatrical production, the role of American colleges and universities in teaching directing, and the popularity of programs in directing, the instruction of directing in the U.S. has been largely ignored by scholars. This historical study aims to fill this gap by providing an analysis of directing pedagogy in American colleges and universities.

This study is based in part on Hamar's previous research. Because Hamar's dissertation provided information only on the earliest years of instruction in directing (to 1920–1921), this study begins in 1920 and ends in 1990. Although Hamar's study was grounded primarily in evidence from college catalogs (the only evidence available at the time), this study includes analysis of three additional types of evidence: textbooks and conference programs on directing (following the methodology established by Patti P. Gillespie and Kenneth M. Cameron) and interviews with instructors of directing. Critical analysis of these data provide information about what kinds of courses were offered, how they were organized (based on the textbooks), how directing was perceived by its practitioners, what paradigms were in effect, and if or when those paradigms shifted. Although the history of directing pedagogy cannot be reconstructed with complete accuracy, the data provides information for a much clearer picture of directing pedagogy than we have heretofore seen.

Textbooks

As a group, textbooks can indicate trends in both the theoretical and practical approaches to directing in a changing classroom. First, and most obviously, they can document an approach to teaching the subject at a particular time. Textbooks often grew directly from the teaching practices of the author, based on the curricula at that author's institution. In addition, the subsequent adoption of the textbooks indicates a willingness to adhere to the author's approach in other classrooms. Finally, a comparison of textbooks over time provides evidence for change, whether it be a change in terminology, audience, organization, emphasis on subject, or theoretical approach. Frequently, the author reflects upon this change himself, as he justifies his work in the introduction. By identifying gaps in the literature, the author tells us how directing had been approached before he wrote the book, what was lacking in the previous approach, and how his book gives either a unique or more complete approach to directing pedagogy. Although not all teachers use textbooks, books remain one of the few concrete pieces of evidence for past teaching.

A study of textbooks on directing analyzed both the increase in publication from the 1920s through the 1980s and the content of textbooks.[1] In keeping with Hamar's observations, textbooks before World War II were few and were targeted toward community theatre directors and teachers who had to direct school plays. The content was quite simplistic and rule-oriented, often following the steps of the production process and leaving little room for flexibility and interpretation. In addition, the term *play production* often substituted for *direction*, signaling the lack of attention to direction as a separate topic (and reflecting the British tradition of interchanging the two terms).

Several of the early textbooks found a substantial market, for seven were published as new editions into the 1960s or 1970s, and one, Alexander Dean's *Fundamentals of Play Directing* (1941), was published as late as 1989. Dean's book, based on his first-year directing class at Yale, apparently had a significant impact on pedagogy. Two subsequent authors cited Dean's technical aspects as an influence on their own textbooks, and in the interviews, several teachers referred to Dean's textbook as a starting point for both their own study and their own instruction. Other early textbooks proving their staying power included Milton Myers Smith's *The Book of Play Production for Little Theatres, Schools, and Colleges* (later entitled *Play Production for Little Theatres, Schools, and Colleges,* published 1926–1967) and *Modern Theatre Practice* (by Hubert C. Heffner et al., published 1935–1973).

During the 1950s and 1960s, the number of books published on directing rose sharply (see figure 4.1), reflecting the need for such works as theatre departments grew in both size and number. More diverse than the predecessors, the textbooks of the 1950s and 1960s included European directing theory, notably through the publication of Toby Cole and Helen Krich Chinoy's *Directing the Play* (later entitled *Directors on Directing*) and Michael Chekhov's *To the Director and Playwright.* Each of these books presented approaches that were considered innovative. For example, Chekhov's book advocated mixing the order of scenes in rehearsal (echoing one of Stanislavski's techniques) in order to gain a fresh perspective; he also asked directors to look for polar beginnings and endings of each segment of the play, then discover the significant moment between the two. These concepts

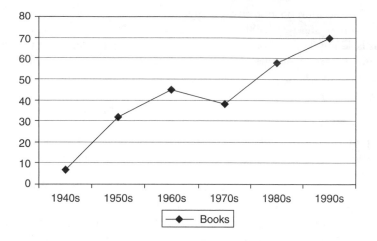

Figure 4.1 Total Number of Books with the Subject Heading *Production and Direction*

would have seemed radical to pre–World War II authors of directing textbooks.

Once people started to question the function and process of the director, a trend toward increasing theory and experimentation emerged, as evidenced in the textbooks of the 1960s, 1970s, and 1980s. For example, James H. Clay's and Daniel Krempel's *The Theatrical Image* (1967) focused on the director's interpretation of the script, relating plays to dreams; they explored experimentation and stylization throughout the book and concluded that there were many valid and invalid methods of interpretation. Increasingly, textbooks also reflected specialized interests, such as J. Robert Wills' book of case studies (1980) or Edward M. Cohen's book on directing new scripts (1988). Overall, the newer textbooks stressed individualism and increasing specialization.

Conference Programs

Conferences on theatre education are an important source of information because they provide a forum for teachers to share classroom techniques or discuss issues that are current and pertinent to their profession. One purpose of educational conferences is for professors to share teaching techniques and discuss both new and popular topics for the classroom.

Analysis of archival copies of conference programs from The Speech Association of America (SAA, which later became the Speech Communication

Association, SCA), The American Educational Theatre Association (AETA, later renamed the American Theatre Association, ATA) and the Association for Theatre in Higher Education (ATHE) provided data on conference sessions addressing directing. Records were available from the 1930s, however, data were limited to the copies on hand at either headquarters for the associations or the archives that held them.

Although not conclusive on its own, the data on conference programs helped to clarify shifts in directing pedagogy. Conference sessions on directing were few in the 1930s, the first decade in which they were offered, in part because directing was still often enfolded into more general sessions on play production. For example, a session entitled "Extra-Curricular Speech Activities for Secondary Schools" in 1934 included the presentation, "Problems of Play Rehearsals." Like the textbooks, conference titles suggested that their audience was mainly school teachers and community directors. Because directing was a new topic, presenters focused on defining directors' roles as well as on their relationships to other production personnel, such as "Author–Director Relationship" or "The Actor and the Director." In addition, some presenters addressed directing pedagogy itself, questioning its goals and outcomes, as with "Academic or Professional Training for the College Director and Actor."

Conference programs revealed the most significant increase in sessions on directing from the 1960s through the 1980s (as shown in table 4.1), most likely because of the growth of the conferences overall.

Despite the revolutionary air of the 1960s, the convention programs of that decade remained oddly conservative, often echoing topics of the 1950s: pedagogy, directing in a variety of spaces, and basic theory. In contrast, textbook

Table 4.1 Number of Sessions on Directing Compared to Total Sessions (Mid-Decade)

Year	Sessions on Directing	Total Sessions	Percent of Total
1935	0	32	—
(1945)[a]	(2)	(78)	(2.6)
1955	1	86	1.2
1966	3	120	2.5
1975	0 SCA/9 ATA	155 SCA/137 ATA	—/6.6
1985	1 SCA/16 ATA	263 SCA/315 ATA	0.4/5.1

[a] SCA Conference Headquarters lost records for 1942–1948 when the headquarters moved, therefore an average from 1941 and 1949 supplied an estimate for the mid-century. Records for 1965 were likewise unavailable, so records for 1966 substitute here.

authors plunged into European theories of directing as early as 1953. It is significant that Patti P. Gillespie and Kenneth M. Cameron made a similar discovery in their study of acting pedagogy. As they concluded, the lag of conferences behind textbooks raises important questions about the transmission of new ideas. Although conferences were ostensibly a place for educators to gather and share information, the most innovative information was in print, not at the conferences. Fortunately, the lag lessened as conferences gained momentum in the later half of the century.

In the 1970s, the sessions on directing again echoed topics of the past, but they treated such topics with increasing specialization. For example, topics on directors' communication included not only their communication with production staff but also counseling skills in directing and semantics of directing. Directors' performance environment, was another old topic to find a new twist; sessions addressed directing in black box, dinner theatre, and Kabuki spaces. Perhaps the newest topic to emerge was that of directors' diversity; session titles reflected a new inclusiveness, addressing contemporary Russian directors, minority directors, and female directors.

The sessions on directing in the 1980s reflected increasing diversity in directing: diverse directors, diverse casts, diverse types of performance (such as deaf theatre), all under diverse circumstances. Several sessions included Brechtian techniques of directing, surprisingly for the first time. Other titles indicated a layering of specialized subjects, such as "Directing the Inexperienced Actor in the Program of Limited Size" or "The Brechtian Approach to Staging and Characterization in Reader's Theatre Productions." In addition, women addressed special issues for female directors in sessions such as "Women Directors in Europe" and "Should We Take the *Woman* Out of *Woman Director*?" Compared to the programs of early decades, the 1980s offered a plethora of specialized issues for the director–educator.

College Catalogs

In this study, college catalogs (also called bulletins) from thirty-one schools in Hamar's study were used to chronicle courses offered in directing for a period of 70 years: 1920–1990.[2] The course titles and their descriptions, when given, provided data which, in turn, furnished insights into the content of directing classes. At the very least, the data provided information about the degree of specialization, from general introductory courses to advanced courses organized around special topics. Furthermore, quantitative data indicated not only the number and range of courses in directing at any given time, but also the rate of increase in directing courses over the 70-year period.

Table 4.2 Specialized Courses in Directing (as Indicated by Course Titles)

	Youth/ School	Specialization of Class				Total
		Styles [a]	History/ Theory	Arena	Other [b]	
1920s	2	—	—	—	—	2
1930s	2	2	—	—	—	4
1940s	8	1	—	—	—	9
1950s	4	2	1	1	—	8
1960s	7	5	2	2	2	18
1970s	5	8	4	2	7	26
1980s	4	11	7	1	10	33
Total	32	29	14	6	19	100

[a] Styles courses include courses in directing for period, modern, or experimental theatre.

[b] Courses in the category "Other" include directing reader's theatre, directing one-acts, directing musicals, directing dinner theatre, directing repertory theatre, script analysis for directors, and communication with designers and actors.

Not surprisingly, the evidence from college catalogs revealed that courses in directing followed a very similar pattern as textbooks and conference programs in terms of content. For example, early directing courses were often enfolded into the classes on play production. As with the textbooks, early courses were structured around the production process, stressing technical skills for amateur directors and school teachers. The need for special courses geared toward teachers of children's theatre peaked in the 1940s, with eight schools offering classes specifically on children's theatre or theatre in the schools. The biggest shift in course content occurred from the 1960s through 1980s, as was the case with textbooks and conference sessions. Courses surfaced on a variety of topics, including theory, history, directing various styles of theatre, communication, script analysis, and directing for certain venues, such as dinner theatre.

The number of semesters of graduate and undergraduate courses increased steadily through the mid-century, with a sharp increase in schools offering more than four semesters of instruction from the 1960s through the 1980s, reflecting the increasing specialization of courses at the time as is seen in table 4.2.

Interviews

Pedagogy is more than a chronicle of curricula or a list of presentations; human interaction, the interaction between teacher and pupil, is key to pedagogical experience. As Max van Manen explained it,

Pedagogy is primarily neither a science nor a technology. Yet it is often treated and researched in a[n] empirically scientific way. ... Only recently has anyone recognized that education needs to turn back to the world of experience. Experience can open up understanding that restores a sense of embodied knowing. (van Manen 1991, 9)

Interviews with directing teachers provided a very different type of data: memories of directing teachers, from their perspectives as both students and teachers. As experienced teachers, they provided intuitive estimations of changes in the field over several decades, something that none of the other sources could provide.

The nine interviewees for this study were chosen from a group of volunteers; there was one exception, Burnet Hobgood, who was recommended as a leader in the field and invited to be interviewed.[3]

One interesting finding regarded the value of course work in directing versus extracurricular work directing productions. Of those who were undergraduates in the 1940s and 1950s, the practical training they received was attributed to extracurricular work, not course work. The exception was interviewees who attended technical schools or conservatory programs, such as Carnegie Mellon, and spoke highly of their course work. In contrast, those students in more traditional college classrooms did not find the course work significant until they reached the graduate level.

Interviewees agreed that their professors employed a fairly standard teaching methodology by combining lectures, demonstrations, and in-class laboratories, which led to final performances. Classes usually followed a "stair step" pattern, leading from one level to the next: Directing I, Directing II, and so forth.

Interviewees often reported that the biggest influence on them was often not the content of their courses but the interaction with their teachers. They described a wide range of professors, from professional mentors to "do-nothings." Even when content was important, it was often linked back to a human factor, such as the study of great directors within the curriculum. Many cited the theory, aesthetics, and practices of past directors, such as Stanislavsky, Craig, and Brecht, as inspirational and highly influential.

The use of textbooks was fairly controversial among interviewees. Significantly, the teachers who were opposed to teaching from textbooks all had M.F.A.s and professional directing experience. Several of them used textbooks for their own benefit, to help them prepare to teach, but they did not require texts for students. Overall, the interviewees agreed that students learned directing by directing, not by reading textbooks on directing.

Given their reluctance to use textbooks, the popularity of textbooks sales is baffling. If so many textbooks were being published, many in multiple editions over several decades, who was buying the books? Community colleges could account for some sales, but it is apparent that many college teachers must have used textbooks to support such a demand for the books. After initially dismissing textbooks, some interviewees later explained that they began their teaching careers using textbooks and abandoned them later. In any case, there seemed to be a stigma attached to textbook use.

Questions about paradigm shifts provided a mixture of answers, and no agreement among the interviewees. For example, David Krasner described a stylistic shift away from Realism in the 1970s and 1980s and an eventual return to realism beginning in the 1990s. Cary Clasz viewed the shift through an economic lens, a shift which ultimately increased bureaucracy in colleges and decreased the amount of time students had to study, due to jobs. Robert Leonard perceived a shift toward an "anything goes" mentality in the classroom, implying that whatever the students produced became an accomplishment of pedagogical worth.

One thing that the interviewees did agree upon was a sense of isolation in the field. Few, if any, had a sense of what colleagues were doing in their classrooms. Several pointed to associations like ATHE or the Kennedy Center American College Theatre Festival (KC/ACTF) as a limited means of communication, but not enough.

A comparison of the interviews indicated that no single variable (period of instruction, geographic location, gender, etc.) had produced a pattern of influence on the group. For example, teachers with degrees 20 years apart were just as likely to embrace or reject new technology. (The teacher's predisposition to risk-taking was probably more influential.) What appeared to be more significant were the individual experiences of the instructors, both inside and outside of the classroom. Not surprisingly, specific instructors, textbooks, teaching experiences, and directing experiences combined in different degrees to produce the teachers that they had become.

A Model of Shifting Paradigms

The combination of data from textbooks, conference programs, college catalogs, and personal interviews supports a new framework for viewing the history of directing pedagogy. This model proposes five major approaches to teaching directing: as Process (both Technical and Artistic), as Problem, as Mastery, as Specialization, and as Idiosyncratic.

Process is, perhaps, the original model for directing classes, dating from the 1920s and retaining popularity well into the 1950s. Considering the goal of early courses to teach community and school teachers in one or two semesters, this approach made practical sense.

The evidence from conferences and textbooks seemed to support Technical Process to very different degrees. Conference titles were usually too vague to determine whether the classes followed a technical pattern, especially in the early years (1930s through 1950s). For example, what kind of preparation was discussed in "Preparation of the Director and Producer" (1936) is impossible to determine. In contrast, the organization and content of early textbooks clearly reflects a Technical Process. Milton Myers Smith's *Play Production for Little Theatres, Schools, and Colleges* (1926), in print for four decades, was one of many early textbooks using it, as revealed by its organization and by the progression of duties a director must fulfill. His four "phases" of rehearsal were (1) Preliminary Study, (2) Working out the Movement, (3) Working for Details, or Characterization, and (4) Working for Finish.

According to both interviewees and course descriptions, Technical Process was not uncommon in entry-level courses into the 1970s and 1980s. For example, Directing I: Principles (1970s) at the University of Michigan was, "A survey of the process . . . from selection to opening." As another example, Scott Strode used *Directing for the Theatre* (Sievers 1961) for years, explaining, "I liked that book because it itself is laid out in an outline form, and so it's very easy and very clear for beginning students to understand the process" (Strode 1997). Likewise, Sidney Friedman described his course, Stage Direction, saying, "The course is organized according to the process of mounting a play. So what's the first thing you do? You figure out what play you're going to do. It's organized according to the sequence of decisions a director usually confronts. The goal is that they direct their first show" (Friedman 1997).

Although Technical Process dominated early catalogs and textbooks, Artistic Process was also evident. In the late 1950s and early 1960s, aesthetic concerns surfaced more and more frequently in course descriptions, with phrases such as "Application of modern aesthetic principles" and "artistic unity, with emphasis on theatre aesthetics." Textbooks also reflected the shift toward aesthetics, often by stressing the director's vision and use of imagery, as with Clay and Krempel's *The Theatrical Image* (1967). In true conservative form, conference programs lagged a decade behind in terms of aesthetics.

The Artistic Process, which continued into the 1980s, was evident in the interviews as well. As one example, Kathryn Ervin remembered a design seminar in which students examined the work of designers in conjunction with directors to understand "how the concept of the play was being articulated."

She added that it was especially exciting at this period in time, when "there were all kinds of visual statements being made to us." Later, she commented on the importance of aesthetics in her own classroom, stressing, "Dean and Carra [*Fundamentals of Play Directing*] is so mechanical" (Ervin 1997).

A second major approach to directing pedagogy is as Problem. This approach dates back to the 1930s and continues steadily into the 1980s. Decade after decade, colleges offered such courses as: Problems and Theories of Play Directing (1930s, Stanford University), Problems in Play Directing in the School Theatre (1950s, University of Illinois), Directing II: Problems (1970s and 1980s, University of Michigan). Why were educators framing the art of direction as a series of problems? Burnet Hobgood explained in his interview:

> The problem approach: the problem of play analysis, the problem of dealing with actors, the problem of dealing with stylization, and so forth.... They came out of my aesthetics study, because I thought there must be some hands-on approach to getting the principles of art and aesthetics, so I invented exercises which would provoke and stimulate students to think about the meaning and beauty of some object.... We have to admit to ourselves that a lot of what we feel about the plays and the materials that we study are not critical formulations, but intuitive responses and how to organize the intuitive response side, that side of your perception. (Hobgood 1997)

In Hobgood's opinion, a problem approach is not a negative approach to directing but an opportunity to evoke individual thinking as applied to the art of directing.

Directing as Problem surfaced in other types of evidence as well. For example, conference programs frequently carried titles of sessions based on problems, ranging from "Directing Problems in the High School" (1949), to "Problems of Arena Staging" (1960), to "Problems of Casting the Original Play for Stage and Television" (1986). Textbook authors were less obvious in applying the Problem Approach; that is, they did not stress the term problem, but they often provided exercises that required problem-solving techniques. J. Robert Wills' book on case studies was an example of an entire book based on problem-solving.

Another popular approach to teaching directing was as Mastery, through study of the great masters of directing. Establishing the onset of this approach is difficult, for it appeared through different media at different times. In terms of textbooks, the clearest date is 1953, with the publication of Cole and Chinoy's *Directing the Play* (thereafter, *Directors on Directing*). However, college catalogs provided a different starting point. Indiana University offered a course as early as the 1940s, which included "the philosophies by Stanislavsky, Craig, Belasco, McClintic, Dean, etc." More commonly, course descriptions did not specify names, but their titles suggested the study of great director-theorists, as with Vassar's Directing Theory and Practice in the 1960s, a more typical starting date for such courses. Courses in the theory and history of directing continued to be offered in the 1970s and increased substantially (to 26 percent of the sample) in the 1980s.

Although conference organizers were late to add sessions on European directors, they managed to squeeze in two sessions in the late 1960s ("Russian Director-Theorists Reappraised" and "Craig's Shakespearian Productions & the Moscow Art Theatre"), only one in the 1970s, and six in the 1980s, as ATHE conferences grew.

The strongest evidence for teaching directing as Mastery came from the interviews with teachers of directing. Many interviewees stressed the benefits of their own study of master directors. Kathryn Ervin recalled her graduate seminars on directing at Wayne State in the 1970s:

> We took seminars on directing theory, where we read *Directors on Directing* and talked about everybody from the Duke of Saxe Meiningen [on]. We had another directing class where we read Clurman, Grotowski, and Meyerhold, maybe. There were three or four of those major directors who had written an approach to directing, and that was a whole semester of study, along with scene work as we were putting things together. (Ervin 1997)

Subsequently, she included the study of these directors in her own course readings and assignments. As another example, Hobgood created a course based on the study of great directors called Directors of the Modern Stage. David Krasner's advanced directing class studied theory through master directors, choosing "at least three historically well-known directors in [...] three periods" (Krasner 1997). In the second semester of the class, he chose one director or subject (such as Brecht or semiotics) for the entire class to study in depth.

A fourth approach to teaching directing is through Specialization. As rudimentary courses began to split into component courses in the 1960s, the trend toward specialization became immediately apparent, peaking in the 1980s. College catalogs logged a variety of individual course topics, including courses on directing children's theatre, school theatre, styles (Shakespearean, absurdist, postmodern, etc.), types (dinner theatre, musical theatre, reader's theatre, repertory theatre), and in various spaces, such as arena.

Conference programs and textbooks confirmed the trend toward specialization by reflecting some of the same topics in courses. In the case of conference programs, there was an additional shift toward diversity, as was apparent in sessions such as "Special Problems of the Minority Director" (1976) and "Directing: Feminist Approaches to Classical Texts" (1986). The shift toward specialization in textbooks had precedents as early as the 1950s, such as Frank McMullan's text on directing multiple styles, but specialization was more apparent in the 1980s with the publication of books such as Lee Mitchell's *Staging Premodern Drama* (1984). Interviewees were less clear about specialized courses, partly because they were never asked specifically about them, but there was an indication that students needed training in a variety of spaces and styles. Robert Leonard reasoned,

> We stage in arena, in thrust, in proscenium—various sizes, and shapes, and styles, and genres. It's like training a conductor; you can't just give a conductor two pianos and two pianists and say, "Learn to conduct an orchestra." (Leonard 1997)

The last approach in this model is the Idiosyncratic, an individual approach that has developed because professors perceived a need that was not being met through traditional teaching methods. Evidence of the Indiosyncratic was most apparent from the interviews with professors. For example, Terry Converse found that most of his own training had been scene study. "Do a scene. Go out and get people and do a scene" (Converse 1997). He found this to be an ineffective way to teach novice directors, citing that they needed guidance with specific skills. This need led him to conceive a series of exercises, which became the backbone of his directing classes. Likewise, Hobgood found a need for students to observe top directors at work and created his Directing Colloquiums, which revolved around observation of directors in rehearsal. Sidney Friedman realized that new directors did not know enough about communicating with actors and created a course on coaching actors based in turn on a course he had taken at Iowa. Each of these teachers saw a need that the traditional curriculum was not fulfilling and acted accordingly.

Such courses were difficult, if not impossible to identify from college catalogs, for course titles and descriptions were too general. Terry Converse's classes were titled Directing I and II, for example. Conference programs were similar in that the titles often did not give enough information about the content of the sessions. For example, "How Not to Teach Directing" could have easily addressed the superiority of the Idiosyncratic over the status quo, or vice versa. However, textbooks were different in that authors could promote their own Idiosyncratic approaches. For example, Terry Converse published his exercises as a textbook in 1995.

With such a variety of approaches to teaching directing, there arose a new question: Was there any approach that was not employed to teach directing? Based on the sample in this study, there was no evidence of what might be called a Collective approach, that approach used by women's collectives and other avant-garde groups from the 1960s through the 1980s. A collective is more than mere collaboration, for collaboration is necessary in any production. Instead, the collective requires both everyone and no one to direct; that is, the group creates together, shaping the work as it develops. No one person has more authority than another, at least in theory. Perhaps academicians neglected this approach because it implied a denial of the need for a director and so threatened the very jobs of directing teachers. Perhaps it was not taught because professors considered it unprofessional (i.e., unmarketable) or simply insignificant. Whatever may be the reasons behind this omission of a Collective approach, the lack does raise some interesting questions about both bias and the importance of marketability within the academic system.

Studies about the past inevitably raise questions about the future. Although this study does not aim to predict future events in the instruction of directing, the patterns of change in the 1970s, 1980s, and 1990s along with the observations from professors in the field may suggest some changes to come in the new millennium.

An overview of the five approaches to directing pedagogy may make the recent shifts more apparent. Regardless of the onset, all of the approaches in figure 4.2 continue through the 1980s and 1990s, suggesting that the more traditional Technical Process and Problem approaches have survived for 70 years and will continue to do so, albeit with more competition. The emergence of the Artistic Process approach in the 1960s suggests a reaction to (or counter balancing of) the Technical. As a teacher from Carnegie Mellon

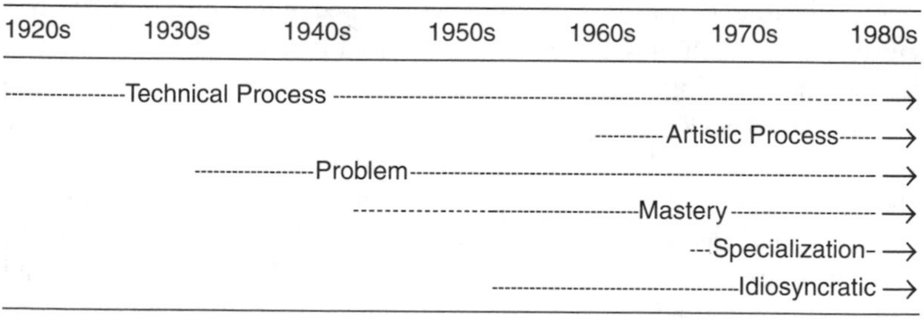

1920s	1930s	1940s	1950s	1960s	1970s	1980s

----------------Technical Process --- →
----------Artistic Process------ →
----------------Problem--- →
-------------------------------------Mastery--------------------- →
---Specialization- →
----------------------------------Idiosyncratic →

Figure 4.2 Approaches to Teaching Directing in the United States, 1920s–1990s

stated, "I teach a class in technique, how to stage, but that sounds aesthetically incorrect these days" (Lehane 1997, 17). Whether in vogue or not, the Technical Process is apparently still relevant to training new directors.

The Specialization and the Idiosyncratic approaches both allow great flexibility for the incorporation of new trends or techniques, which suggests that they will continue with new additions as new needs arise. The increase of specialized textbooks in the 1980s indicates a strong inclination for similar publications in the 1990s (a trend which, in fact, continued). What is not clear is whether the current focus on specialization will continue or whether we will revert attention to The Technical Process as part of a "back to basics" movement. For example, David Krasner foresaw a similar trend when he predicted the renaissance of Realism.

One can hope that the lack of communication among directing teachers that many educators identified will be alleviated through more conference sessions—and perhaps better scheduling—and through journal articles devoted to directing pedagogy. Barring that, the Internet at least makes communication among colleagues fast, inexpensive, and relatively easy.

Although this study has provided some descriptive information about the history of directing pedagogy, much remains to be done. First, we need to know precisely who we are training and what we are training them for. In other words, how do directing students use their education (if they indeed do) upon graduation? As high school and community directors? As professional directors? As professionals in related fields? This information, if it exists at all, is scattered. Second, we need to know more about the training that professional directors have received. Is there, in fact, a high percentage of professional directors with M.F.A.s or Ph.D.s in theatre? If not, what training have they received? Might we alter the curriculum based on the findings of such a study? Robert Hazzard conducted a study of 12 professional directors from 1926 to 1960 and concluded that stress must be placed upon the academic viewpoint of theatre, which does not always prepare the young director for what he will find in the professional theatre. Is that conclusion still valid many decades later?

Third, we need a national survey to establish the state of pedagogy now, an update, in essence, of the *Directory of American College Theatre* of the 1960s and 1970s. These surveys provided a rich source of information from which to base comparisons through the years. We cannot plan effectively for the future if we have not learned from the past.

Notes

1. *Cumulative Book Index* (*CBI*), a catalog of English language books published in the twentieth century, provided the source for the data on textbooks. Examination

of the books confirmed which books were written primarily for instruction (excluding biographies and autobiographies of directors).

2. Hamar discovered 33 schools that offered courses in directing or play production by 1920–1921. Of those schools, only 31 schools were offering courses in directing after 1921. The remaining schools provided a diverse sample, including both colleges and universities, rural and urban settings, and large and small schools; in addition, they represented various geographical regions of the United States.

   Although college catalogs provided an important primary source of evidence for course offerings in directing, Hamar noted several limitations to the evidence, stating, such as the ambiguity of course titles and the inconsistency of schools in offering courses on the books (Hamar 1952, 21). To assure some consistency in the analysis of the data, I placed the following restrictions on the courses to be studied: (1) either the course title or its description had to include the word direct or produce (or one of their variants); (2) in courses with several aims, instruction in directing had to comprise a key element (at least one third of the course, based on the description); (3) course titles or descriptions had to reflect instruction in directing.

3. Of the 21 people who volunteered to be interviewed, I chose nine that approximated the population as a whole, in terms of four major variables: (1) the number of years of teaching experience; (2) the geographic region of their teaching institutions; (3) the geographic region of their degree-granting institutions; and (4) the interviewee's terminal degree. Other considerations were gender, size of the (teaching) institution, and level taught (undergraduate or graduate). I also ensured that women were represented (in this case, three) and that private schools were represented (two). I aimed for some balance of representation from small colleges, mid-sized institutions, and large universities.

Works Cited

Chekhov, Michael. 1963. *To the director and playwright*. New York: Harper & Row. [Later entitled *Michael Chekhov's to the director and playwright* 1977, 1984.]

Clasz, Cary. 1997. Personal interview. Pittsburgh State University, retired. February 17.

Clay, James H. and Daniel Krempel. 1967 [1985]. *The theatrical image*. New York: McGraw-Hill.

Cohen, Edward M. 1988. *Working on a new play*. New York: Prentice-Hall.

Cole, Toby and Helen Krich Chinoy. 1953. (eds.), *Directing the play*. Indianapolis: Bobbs-Merril. [Later entitled *Directors on directing* 1963, 1964, 1970,1972, 1973, 1976, 1986.]

Converse, Terry. 1997. Personal interview. Washington State University. February 22.

———. 1995. *Directing for the stage: A workshop guide of 42 creative training exercises and projects*. Colorado Springs: Meriwether.

Dean, Alexander. 1941 [1962, 1965, 1974, 1980, 1989]. *Fundamentals of play directing*. New York: Farrar & Rinehart.

Directory of American college theatre. 1960, 1967, 1976. Washington, DC: American Educational Theatre Association.

Ervin, Kathryn. 1997. Personal interview. California State University, San Bernardino. February 26.

Fliotsos, Anne L. 1997. Teaching the unteachable: Directing pedagogy in colleges and universities of the United States, 1920–1990. Ph.D. dissertation, University of Maryland, College Park.

Friedman, Sidney. 1997. Personal interview. Boston University School for the Arts. February 21.

Gillespie, Patti P. and Kenneth M. Cameron. 1986. The teaching of acting in American colleges and universities, 1920–1960. *Communication Education* 35 (October): 362–371.

Hamar, Clifford E. 1952. The rise of drama and theatre in the American college curriculum, 1900–1920. Ph.D. dissertation, Stanford University.

Hazzard, Robert T. 1962. The development of selected American stage directors from 1926 to 1960. Ph.D. dissertation, University of Minnesota.

Heffner, Hubert C., Samuel Selden, and Hunton D. Selman. 1935 [1939, 1940, 1941, 1943, 1944, 1946, 1953, 1959, 1961, 1973]. *Modern theatre practice.* New York: F. S. Crofts.

Hobgood, Burnet M. 1997. Personal Interview. University of Illinois, retired. March 1.

Krasner, David. 1997. Personal interview. Southern Illinois University. February 14.

Lehane, Gregory. 1996. The basics: Becoming a director. Interview by Arthur Barlow. *The Journal for Stage Directors and Choreographers* 10, no. 2 (Fall/Winter): 15–20.

Leonard, Robert E. 1997. Personal interview. Pennsylvania State University. February 19.

Mitchell, Lee. 1984. *Staging premodern drama.* Westport, CT: Greenwood Press.

Sievers, W. David. 1961 [1965, 1969, 1970, 1974]. *Directing for the theatre.* Dubuque, IA: W. C. Brown. [Later co-authored with Stanley Kahan and Harry E. Stiver.]

Smith, Milton Myers. 1926. *The book of play production for little theatres, schools, and colleges.* New York: D. Appleton. [Later entitled *Play production for little theatres, schools, and colleges* 1928, 1948, 1962, 1967.]

Strode, Scott. 1997. Personal interview. Manchester College. February 10.

van Manen, Max. 1991. *The tact of teaching: The meaning of pedagogical thoughtfulness.* Albany: State University of New York Press.

Wills, J. Robert. 1980 [1994]. *Directing in the theatre: A casebook.* Metchuen, NY: Scarecrow.

CHAPTER 5

Playwriting: A Pedagogy of Transmutation

Michael Wright

I'm becoming more and more convinced it isn't a question of old and new forms. We have to write not thinking of forms at all, write because it springs freely from our inner being.

Treplev in *The Seagull* by Anton Chekov

The pedagogy of playwriting may be one of the great mysteries of all arts training. In fact, many playwriting teachers and playwright practitioners have posited that playwriting cannot be taught. One can teach the craft, they say, but the art is either present in the writer or it is not. George Pierce Baker, the noted teacher of playwriting, begins his seminal work, *Dramatic Technique*, with this common saying: "The dramatist is born, not made." A few pages later Baker goes on to say, "I wish it distinctly understood that I have not written for the person seeking methods of conducting a course in dramatic technique. I view with some alarm the recent mushroom growth of such courses throughout the country" (Baker 1919, iii–v). William Archer, Baker's contemporary, goes a wry step farther in *Play-Making: A Manual of Craftsmanship*:

There are no rules for writing a play. It is easy, indeed, to lay down negative recommendations—to instruct the beginner how *not* to do it. But most of these "don'ts" are rather obvious; and those which are not obvious are apt to be questionable. It is certain, for instance, that if you want your play to be acted, anywhere else than in China, you must not plan it in sixteen acts of an hour apiece; but where is the tyro who needs a text-book to tell him that? (Archer 1960, 3)

The fact is, of course, that playwriting is taught, though it may be an enterprise that has been, for many decades, a rather singularly American undertaking. John van Druten, in his 1953 book, *Playwright at Work*, mentions the difference in the English point of view:

In a prejudiced way, it would have been assumed that playwriting was not a thing that could be taught; perhaps, even, that it was not a thing that ought to be taught. It was an accidental, and only occasionally profitable, gift that happened to one. (Van Druten 1953, 2)

Van Druten's observation is echoed and broadened in the essay, "The Mission of the Theatre Teacher," in which Burnet M. Hobgood states that

American theatre education is unique among the education systems in the world. In other nations, if training for the theatre is undertaken at all, the instruction of young talents for the stage falls to the theatre profession through programs in operating theatres or in state-subsidized theatres. (Hobgood 1988, 1)

There are now a number of academic training programs in theatre (including playwriting) around the world, so things have changed since Mr. Hobgood's observations in 1988, but the issue of playwriting pedagogy remains fraught with questions. Given that playwriting *is* taught, *how* is it being taught? Who teaches and what techniques do they use? Which is the best approach? There is little published on the subject of playwriting pedagogy, and what is available is inconsistent.

The teaching of playwriting can be best understood in the context of a "transmutable" pedagogy. This is not a new idea, per se, but merely an attempt to establish a newer language and concept base that can link the various perspectives. A critical concept underlying this linkage is a growing recognition in the academy of the critical role of process: the playwright existing in a continual state of evolution and self-discovery, seeking his greatest levels of self-expression. (Note that the context is pedagogy in America. There is even less available information outside the United States, though two recent studies from Australia provide some extremely interesting material.)[1]

The term transmutable has many meanings and correlatives, including the synonym "transformation," a key element of theatre. The verb transmute is defined in *Webster's Ninth New Collegiate Dictionary* as "to change or alter in form, appearance, or nature and especially to a higher form" ("transmute," def. 1). There is also the ancillary alchemical concept of turning base metal to gold. These definitions present wonderful metaphorical images for plays and playwriting students. Finally, the term is used here to suggest the notion of evolving, of being in a continuous progression from one level to the next.

Playwriting, and the teaching of playwriting, are not quite so easy to define, however. Even the basic definition of a play is a difficult prospect. Sam Smiley, in his book *Playwriting: The Structure of Action*, offers this definition:

A drama is a constructed object which exists in a given time span and which can be repeated. Its materials are words and physical activities. Its form is human action, human change. The manner of its presentation requires live performance through acting. (Smiley 1971, 8)

Conversely, Ronald Hayman in *How to Read a Play*, says: "We all think we know what a play is, but no one has ever succeeded in defining it. A novel or a poem is neither more nor less than the words it consists of, but a script is obviously less than a play, while a production is obviously more" (1977, 11). While poets and novelists might take umbrage at Mr. Hayman's thoughts on their art forms, playwrights might find themselves uneasily nodding in agreement with regard to their form.

In addition, there are two prevailing schools of thought which students and professionals alike frequently encounter. These schools present seemingly irreconcilable points of view from equally respected sources. For instance, Buzz McLaughlin, author of a popular book on playwriting, *The Playwright's Process*, writes:

We're just coming out of an era when—and this seems especially true for playwriting—the rigorous teaching of *craft* has not been considered a logical and necessary fi[r]st step. Instead, from the start of a student's training, personal exploration and complete liberation from all time-honored "rules" of dramatic writing have been the norm. To me, therefore, it's not surprising that the majority of new plays being written today never see production. Several decades of an anti-craft mentality have flooded the market with plays that simply do not work on the stage. The fact is that there are a few simple principles of craft which in one way or another need to be respected in all dramatic writing, principles which have been in place and functioning beautifully for twenty-five hundred years. A playwright ignores them at his or her peril. Without exception, every good play I've read or seen—whether written by an established, successful playwright or a student in a beginning course—has somehow incorporated the basic tenets successfully. There is simply no way around them if you hope to write successfully for the stage. (McLaughlin 1997, 12)

Neena Beber provides a different viewpoint in her article in *American Theatre*, "Dramatis Instructus." In the article Beber discusses classroom approaches with six established playwrights who also teach—William Alfred, Maria Irene Fornes, Martin Epstein, Adrienne Kennedy, Len Jenkin, and Mac Wellman. In her introduction Beber notes that

A bundle of rules can be a convenient tool for instructors trying to teach what may be, in the end, unteachable. The best writing teachers, however, seem to appreciate the impossibility of their task and to search out ways to share and inspire rather than dictate. They strive to equip their students with more than a formula. Gone are the rigid prescriptions that can lead to a staid kind of drama; in their place, an innovative cadre of playwright-teachers are presenting new and lively ways of thinking about the writer's craft. (Beber 1990, 22)

These statements represent the two primary views one encounters even in a casual reading of sources. Though not so far apart on the surface, the perspectives are often at complete odds. Is it any wonder, then, that confusion reigns? The teaching of playwriting needs a middle ground: a pedagogy of transmutation.

But what is a pedagogy of transmutation? There are two major aspects of transmutation which will be discussed: the classroom, and the instructor and student.

Transmutation of the Classroom

Playwriting teachers often refer to the classroom as a studio or a workshop. Most instructors approach the classroom not as a lecture hall, but as a forum for discussion, a transformable environment for playwriting exercises, and a reading space for plays written by students. In a survey conducted online for this essay with members of the Playwrights Program of the Association for Theatre in Higher Education (ATHE), the respondents rated lecturing as their least important activity. Some even gave a percentage of zero time spent in the endeavor.

The playwriting classroom itself has no special needs—no barre, mirrors, or formal stage—other than chairs that can be moved into various configurations in order to accomplish sundry transformations. The ATHE survey respondents indicated that their spaces primarily serve two functions during a semester: (1) as a workshop and (2) as a play reading environment. To serve these distinctive activities, flexibility of the classroom space is critical.

The configurations for workshop situations are numerous. Viola Spolin's impact on playwriting pedagogy, through her theories about theatre games and improvisation, is often evident in this context. In some cases, the instructor wants a space with the floor cleared. Maria Irene Fornes, for example, begins sessions with physical warm ups, followed by visualization exercises (Beber 1990, 24). In other instances, the space might need chairs in a circle to facilitate an easier give and take. Spolin-like exercises which involve passing along ideas, images, or other play elements would be assisted by a circular arrangement. Language games, such as "telephone," in which a phrase becomes distorted as it gets repeated by people in a line, sometimes require arrangements where participants cannot see each other easily in order to succeed. There are as many possibilities as there are imaginative teachers of playwriting. The key is that, as Jean-Claude van Itallie writes in *The Playwright's Workbook*, "Playwrights need a supportive physical environment. Preparing the work space will prepare you to write. Whether working alone or with a group, create an appealing writing environment" (1997, 20). "Appealing" certainly includes the transmutability of the space.

Reading student work aloud in the classroom is a critical aspect of learning playwriting. As Sam Shepard remarked in *The Drama Review* issue on playwrights and playwriting, "The spoken word, no matter how you cut it, is different than the written word" (1977, 57). The respondents from the ATHE Playwrights Program indicated that as much as 80 percent of their time is used for reading student work in class. Readings in class can include presenting short assignments, fragments of ongoing work, and full readings of completed scripts.

Readings in the classroom require a change in spatial dynamics. The readers must be seated or stand in an area that is separate from the rest of the class in order to facilitate clarity, character identity, and relationships. This sets up a performance context in which the student/readers become performers and the rest of the class members take on the roles of audience and dramaturgs/respondents. Having the material presented in this fashion moves the script a step closer to its ultimate identity as a play in production. Martin Esslin, in *An Anatomy of Drama*, describes this shift succinctly: "The author and the performers are only one half of the total process: the other half is the audience and its reaction. Without an audience there is no drama. A play which is not performed is merely literature" (1986, 23). Setting up a reading space is an acknowledgment of the desired ultimate result—performance—of the playwright's process. Further, it engenders the eventual reality of collaboration, provides some questions and answers about casting, and draws attention to elements which may not be so obvious on the page, such as language, rhythms, juxtaposition of scenes, structure, and so on.

The transmutation of the classroom is also a critical element to the learning playwright about the nature of theatre itself as an imagining place. Without any production effects, his work comes to life: actors endow the reading space with the power of dramatic possibilities. The classroom chairs become the bar stools, the park bench, the car seat. The reading itself takes on the essential nature of theatre as a witnessed event. As Peter Brook declared in *The Empty Space*, "I can take any empty space and call it a bare stage. A man walks across this empty space whilst someone else is watching him, and this is all that is needed for an act of theatre to be engaged" (1968, 9). When the same chair is transformed in different classroom readings from a judge's bench to an electric chair, the thinking and conceptual processes of the playwright are opened to a new range of possibilities. The transmutable classroom defies and redefines the traditional naturalistic stage environment.

Lastly, the material is often responded to after being read. This creates yet another transmutation: the particular context of the talk-back. The talk-back, or response session, is when the focus leaves the stage and shifts to the audience. The audience in turn is transformed from listeners/watchers to dramaturgs/respondents who will speak to the material they have just experienced. The evolving playwright needs to understand this transformation because it is as fraught with traps as it is with encouragement. The instructor must avoid putting the playwright on the spot. This includes setting the context and rules for responses, and often reconfiguring the classroom. For the talk-back, the "stage" may be replaced by a circle of chairs in order to incorporate the playwright into the group, rather than set him apart.

In all cases, the playwriting instructor needs a room that can serve not only the physical needs of the students, but the mental needs as well. Playwriting is not something learned by sitting and listening to lectures. Nor is it something one learns merely by reading and talking about established writers' plays. The transmutable classroom must be an environment where the student feels as if the play is more a piece of malleable clay than intractable stone, and this feeling arises in part from the classroom space itself being malleable and transformable.

Transmutation of the Instructor and Student

Most playwriting instructors are also playwrights. They understand their own craft, largely from years of having their work produced, plus seeing and reading the work of others, but must undergo challenging transmogrifications in order to teach playwriting. James Palmarini observed this phenomenon in his article "Teaching Theatre," in *Dramatics* magazine:

> ...teaching the craft of playwriting may be as difficult as writing a play. A playwriting teacher must be an instructor setting forth rules (or banishing rules), a role model providing inspiration and guidance, an even-handed critic and editor. She must understand acting, directing, and the conventions, limitations and possibilities of theatre. Plus, there is a nagging question about the teaching of something that is essentially a creative endeavor: Can a teacher who possesses all of the above traits truly help a student writer become a skilled playwright? Nearly four hundred years ago, the great French dramatist Pierre Corneille wrote: "It is certain that there are laws of the drama, since it is an art, but it is not certain what these laws are." (Palmarini 1994, 39)

And, indeed, people remain divided about the validity of laws, or rules, as evidenced in the previous quotations from McLaughlin and Beber. McLaughlin actually puts the word rules in quotation marks, but then uses the synonym tenets without any editorial punctuation; evidence, perhaps, of some sense of conflict. This conflict runs through many commentaries by theorists, and reveals not only a genuine chasm between the pro- and anti-Aristotelians, but within each faction as well, as McLaughlin's wordplay suggests. For example, in *Backwards and Forwards: A Technical Manual for Reading Plays*, David Ball embraces Aristotle's concepts as a foundation, and yet Ball himself says: "It is easy to say, with Aristotle, that a play's main ingredients are plot, character, and thought. But they are results, not first steps. They are what you have to find, *not how you have to find them*" (emphasis Ball's) (1983, 5). The transmutable instructor facilitates the finding process for and with the student, helps define the pathway, and even opens doors to what definition(s) the student will make of such terms as plot, character, and thought.

This split in perceptions about Aristotle has a long history. Dr. Gustav Freytag wrote, in his 1900 work *Freytag's Technique of the Drama: An Exposition of Dramatic Composition and Art*,

> That the technique of the drama is nothing absolute and unchangeable scarcely need be stated. Since Aristotle established a few of the highest

laws of dramatic effect, the culture of the human race has grown more than two thousand years older. (Freytag 1900, 1)

Freytag's position is further modified in 1912 by William Archer. Archer averred, in *Play-Making: A Manual of Craftsmanship*,

There are no absolute rules, in fact, except such as are dictated by the plainest common sense. Aristotle himself did not so much dogmatize as analyze, classify, and generalize from, the practices of the Attic dramatists. He said "you had better" rather than "you must." It was Horace, in an age of deep dramatic decadence, who re-stated the pseudo-Aristotelian formulas of the Alexandrians as though they were unassailable dogmas of art. (Archer 1960, 3)

Are there laws, then, or rules or tenets? Which are the ones to follow? An aside from John van Druten in his book *Playwright at Work* casts a humorous light on the issue:

An interviewer the other day asked me if I always followed the old rule that the first act of a play should be the noun, the second act the verb, and the third act the predicate in the sentence which was the play. I had never heard of the rule, but I immediately began to wonder if it were true, if it ought to be true, if I had obeyed it, if I ought to obey it. (Van Druten 1953, 4)

If a seasoned professional like van Druten found this to be confusing, imagine the student who must suffer under such a dogmatic perspective. It is well worth any student's time and efforts to seek out an instructor who is open to a variety of approaches, who knows when to suggest guidelines and when to let the student follow his own lead. Tennessee Williams offers an intriguing perspective on this, although he does not use himself as an example directly. Williams wrote, in his Foreword to Marian Gallaway's 1950 book, *Constructing A Play*:

A good instructor in dramatic arts knows very well that there may be instances, not frequent but all the more important for being so, when studies and rules of construction and even exercises may be virtually useless. Let us suppose that an undergraduate named Jean Giraudoux had enrolled in a playwriting class, not Miss Gallaway's but that of some instructor less cognizant of exceptional instances and the elasticity demanded of them. This instructor would throw up his hands in holy horror, no doubt, when M. Giraudoux turned in his first assignment, for it would almost certainly violate practically every tenet of recognized craftsmanship except that one very liberal rule of stimulating a sensibility to poetic excitement in that part of the audience capable of responding to such stimuli. However, if the instructor did happen to be the author of this book, who is no ordinary instructor, she would realize that she was up against a case where the rulebook must be set aside in favor of some more mysterious sense of order than that which is susceptible to diagrams and outlines. (Gallaway 1950, viii)

A "mysterious sense of order" raises the issue of how playwriting teachers teach. Are they intuitive or rigidly proscriptive? Do they espouse laws or rules they do not follow themselves? Maria Irene Fornes observed in Neena Beber's article:

Very often teachers don't write the way they teach and don't teach the way they write. And you wonder, "how it is possible?" How can you teach medicine one way and practice it in another? That would be inconceivable, you would say either it's malpractice or it's malteaching. (Beber 1990, 24)

One can only hope these "malteachers" are the exception. The essence of the transmutational approach appears to be where the instructor weaves together his own experiences, conceptual foundations, models, and the self-discovery and expressive techniques found in the work of Viola Spolin, Keith Johnstone, and Augusto Boal (as redefined for playwrights' use in such books as *The Dramatist's Toolkit, Playwriting in Process* and *Playwriting Master Class*).

The available information strongly suggests that the playwriting teacher incessantly invents and reinvents himself, borrowing from previous learning experiences in the academy and the profession, striving always to teach the individual student rather than the subject matter. The late William Alfred, author of *Hogan's Goat*, and highly respected playwriting mentor at Harvard, said in the Beber article that he had "come to believe that the one thing I can give students is a belief in their own gifts" (Beber 1990, 24). Playwright and teacher Susan Miller, author of *My Left Breast*, underscores Alfred's statement: "The real trick is working with each person on the basis of what they've written. A good playwriting teacher doesn't impose what he or she wants a student to write, what they should have written, what someone else

area is that of self-development and transformation. Franklin J. Himes, in *The Janus Paradigm*, describes the findings of educator Burnet Hobgood in regard to the learning process for theatre students:

> Hobgood's research into experiential methods led him to an eventual hypothesis which held that every dramatic arts student experienced four "phases of self-development." Described chronologically, they were (1) the initiatory, which denoted the neophyte's flirtation with the art— involving imitation when first encountering the craft; (2) the formative, where the tendency to imitate continues but the learner also begins a search for "good models with patterns of thought and behavior that transcend the ordinary"; (3) the productive, in which the learner displays a self-trust and authentic interest while "realization occurs that one can think critically without personal prejudice and find the way to original ideas"; and (4) the creative, where the learner "knows his or her limitations but also understands the scope of his or her gifts and has a vision of what can be done with them." (Himes 1998, 9)

Hobgood's description powerfully evokes the transmutative nature of learning to write plays. The concept of the playwriting student seeking his own models beyond what may be provided by the teacher is rich with possibilities, not to mention possible ironies. (Are students who are studying under someone nontraditional secretly gorging on plays by Arthur Wing Pinero?) This suggests that the student transforms himself while learning from the pedagogical approach, pursuing an internal master, in effect, while absorbing the teachings of the external one.

Hobgood's third and fourth points support this image in the sense of transcending one's master or mentor. The notion of thinking "critically without personal prejudice" suggests that the student functions on various levels: assessing his own work, the work of others (both by peers and from the canon), and the value of what the teacher has provided. This includes recognizing the limits of each level as well, in order to move on to other sources of learning and inspiration. It is highly intriguing to note that Neena Beber had studied with five of the six teachers she interviewed for her *American Theatre* piece (1990), and Wendy Hammond mentioned at least three mentors at NYU in her comments in the *Dramatics* article (Palmarini 1994, 39). Part of the transmutation is seeking out a variety of mentors so that the student has a wide range of choices for critical evaluation. Mentors may mean teachers, but may mean models from the canon or other students as well. The key rests in the willingness of the student to go beyond the givens in order to learn that which he most needs. George Pierce Baker extolled this perspective in the Preface to his *Dramatic Technique*:

In all creative courses the problem is not "What can we make these students take from us, the teachers?" but, "Which of these students has any creative power that is individual? Just what is it? How may it be given its quickest and fullest development?" Complete freedom of choice in subject and complete freedom in treatment so that the individuality of the artist may have its best expression are indispensable in the development of great art. (Baker 1919, vi)

With this freedom comes the point of departure from the classroom. It is the point at which the student has accomplished Hobgood's last phase, coming to terms with the scope of one's own gifts. This is when the student has synthesized the first three phases for his own purposes, and reached a point of departure. This phase functions as both an end stage (finishing with being a student) and a beginning (moving into professional life). These phases demand a willingness to continually evolve in order to become prepared for further transformation upon achieving the final plateau of the educational experience.

Baker touched on this when he identified three elements of technique a playwright must possess in order to write truthfully and competently. Baker described these aspects of technique as "universal," "special," and "unique" (1919, 4). ("Universal" is a point which might be debated now, but "special" and "unique" have far greater acceptance and relevance.) According to Baker, universal technique is that which is developed by reading the great dramatists. Special technique comes from developing a clear understanding of what is going on in the playwright's own time, or as Baker put it: "Each period demands in part its own technique" (1919, 3). Unique techniques applies to those elements which are innate to the playwright himself, to his natural abilities and particular world view. The latter two points reinforce the sense of self-invention in the student as he evolves into the playwright he will be.

The dilemma for any artist, of course, is how to trust that his own technique, vision, and expression are valid, especially when they may seem too different from the current mode. The teacher hopes to lead the student to the point where that student's own vision can take over, but it is up to the student to make the leap from there into *terra incognito*. This can be a terrifying situation for a playwright, but if the training has been based in a transmutative pedagogy, the student understands that the first step out into his own vision is just the beginning of a lifetime of transformations. Each new work a playwright undertakes calls upon previously untried elements of his abilities, growth as a human being, experience of the world, willingness to take risks, and many other factors. At the most intuitive level, writing a play is often the pursuit of unresolved personal issues, which are given metaphorical expression. The playwright must transform the inner vision into an externalized expression. Sam Smiley comments on this with images that are particularly apt and vivid:

> An artist, especially a writer, often creates a projection of his good and bad dreams. All men dream, and to some extent all try to make their dreams come true. The artist perfects a medium for the expression of his dreams. These may be short or long, whole or partial, abnormal or universal, but they always possess signification. Stylistically, they may be illusory or non-illusory, objective or subjective. But dreams always reflect the dreamer. As each artist employs his imagination, intelligence, and skill to build an object, he often calls upon his sweet dreams and nasty ones. (Smiley 1971, 5)

Learning to trust one's sweet or nasty dreams as acceptable art is an especially difficult transformation for the playwriting student, but one which must be accomplished in order to move into professional life.

There are many other roles the playwriting student must play in order to access the greatest benefit from any pedagogical approach: learning to function as a respondent, think like a dramaturg, and to look beyond the play toward production, in which case there are design and directorial considerations. The playwright must learn to transform into the thinking modes of all these collaborators, far more than other theatre artists tend to do with regard to playwriting, with the possible exception of dramaturgs. (It is interesting to note that many programs require majors to take courses in acting, directing, and design, but leave playwriting as an elective.)

Thus, the final element of the student's transmutation is that the learning process must go beyond the walls of the physical classroom to have continued value. These experiences include workshops, readings, productions, seeing the work of others, and learning about the nature of collaboration. This applies in two distinct areas: presentations on campus, and in the professional realm.

The majority of the ATHE survey respondents indicated that some form of presentation beyond the classroom takes place. There were four levels to select from on the survey: reading, staged reading, workshop production, and full production. Most of the respondents checked more than one level. Similarly, of the more than 75 colleges and universities represented in

The Student's Guide to Playwriting Opportunities, 2nd Edition, approximately 90 percent provided some form of reading or production on campus (Wright and Carrillo 1998). Many had formal programs under specific titles which occurred on a regular basis each year. The presentation of student work in a public environment is clearly a necessary extension of the classroom. The transformation the student undertakes is complex and dependent to a large extent on the pedagogical foundations which have led him to this experience.

Preparing the student for the public presentation of his work is a major element of the pedagogical approach. There are an endless number of questions students have when their work moves from classroom discussion into rehearsals toward some form of performance. Am I allowed to rewrite? Who has the final say over a line? Can the director do anything she wants with my script? What do I do during rehearsals? Should I attend rehearsals? If I attend, should it be all or some, and if only some, then which? Who do I talk to at rehearsal if I think something isn't quite right, and when do I do that? What should I do during the reading? If there's a talk back after the reading, do I have to be identified?

The experience of rehearsal and presentation can be baffling for the neophyte playwright. In many ways, the playwright's work is over, and he is often reduced to a passive observer unless called upon by the production team. Even in the campus experience he may feel like the proverbial fifth wheel, which is a difficult position to occupy. The playwright knows that his work is only completed when it goes into public presentation, yet it places him in a new context, where his role is sometimes nebulous and self-definition becomes paramount. As Jean-Claude van Itallie expresses it: "The conventional image of the solitary writer is only partly true for a playwright. Choosing to write for the theatre means not only choosing to write alone but also choosing to work with others" (1997, 16). Choosing to work with others means public presentation in one form or another, and the beginning of a kind of pedagogy-by-fire. This is not to cast aspersions on the experience of a reading or production, which are generally positive events for playwrights. However, results often play a more important part than process in these situations, and it is sometimes tricky to evaluate the end product. For example, it may be that the result—the reading—is not quite what the playwright had in mind. The question that must be raised is whether this result distorts the play or simply offers another perspective on it. In this situation, the ability of the playwright to define his role and maintain a clear sense of purpose and perspective while merging with the collaborative team is crucial.

The instructor with professional experience is an invaluable ally at this juncture. He can easily share impressions of prior presentations of his own with the student and take some of the worry out of the process. The instructor can also help give shape to the experience for the playwright by predetermining such elements as the nature of the presentation, the expected outcome of the presentation, and even the style of the talk back.[2] Maintaining perspective through the sequence of rehearsal to performance is ultimately a subjective matter, of course, but the instructor has the capacity to ease the way significantly and continue the learning process. This is especially true if the instructor takes a transmutative approach, and helps the student stay aware of how both he and his work evolve beyond the classroom.[3]

Before concluding, it is important to acknowledge briefly two areas of influence on playwriting which will impact on the pedagogy in the early twenty-first century: (1) influences on playwriting by other media, and (2) the impact of the Internet and long-distance teaching.

Playwriting has been absorbing ideas and values from other media for the past few decades. It is obvious in the work of such writers as Len Jenkin and John Jesurun, among many others, and will be an even greater factor in successive generations of playwrights. David Savran comments on this in his introduction to *The Playwright's Voice*, when he discusses how a

> new generation of writers has appeared that has absorbed the innovations of the experimental theatre of the sixties and seventies: ... [It] moves easily (and without guilt) between realism and various highly theatrical and/or presentational styles. At the same time, this generation, reared on movies and television, has breathed new life into theatre by at once borrowing and keeping its distance from mass culture. (Savran 1999, xxi)

This borrowing from mass culture is rampant in classrooms. Some professors advocate the idea of changing the name of playwriting programs to "performance writing" programs, in order to embrace the media cross-pollination. This is also an acknowledgement of the fact that students not only want to work in film and television, but they recognize that there *is* work in film and television for writers. No one suggests that a playwright will make a living writing plays.

The explosion of computer-based opportunities is having and will continue to have its own impact. Teaching sites online will multiply, as will distance-learning opportunities, and live production via the Internet. Who knows what technology will be capable of by the time you read this essay? Perhaps the ability of virtual reality to create the illusion of being there will allow an audience member to see a play as if he is onstage with it. Imagine being able to walk around on the set of a production of *Hamlet* while it is going on, looking over the shoulder of each character in a scene, or even stepping into the role of a given character. What might a contemporary playwright do with this, then? The mind reels.

* * *

The life of the playwright is complex. On the one hand, he is the creator of his own world. As Jeffrey Sweet describes it in *The Dramatist's Toolkit*: "You set the scene, people it with characters, and establish the logic that dictates their behavior. Your dramatis personae struggle, prevail, or succumb according to your intentions. You call the tune. You set the rules" (Sweet 1993, xi). On the other hand, the playwright creates art which can only find true expression through the abilities and visions of others. The essence of the playwright's life is transmutation and transformation.

It is clear that current pedagogical practices appreciate the myriad roles the playwright must play. That there is no consistent, universal pedagogy of playwriting is to its credit as an art form, which itself continues to morph and evolve. That there is no—as yet—compendium of pedagogical approaches is something that needs to be rectified. Even if such a work is published, however, there is little probability that a single vision would emerge. If it is true that the playwright must reinvent himself over and over, as must the playwriting instructor, the worst thing that could happen would be a cessation of transmutation, and the rise of uniformity.

Notes

1. The two sources are: "The Wright Stuff—an Action Research Project in the Teaching and Learning of Playwriting in the Queensland University of Technology Academy of the Arts" by Don Batchelor and Peter Copeman, published in *Text: The Journal of the Australian Association of Writing Programs* (Vol. 2, No. 1, April 1998), an online refereed journal <http://www.gu.edu.au/school/art/text/april98/copeland.htm>, and a doctoral thesis (dissertation) entitled *Pathways to Playwriting: In the Context of Interplay and Other Selected Playwright Development Initiatives of the Twentieth Century* by Errol Bray (2001) at James Cook University in Townsville, Australia. The Batchelor/Copeman article is a study of how a playwriting course was redesigned (merging two previous courses into one) and the outcomes of the new approach. Although there is little that differs from the basic pedagogical approaches discussed in this essay, the authors/instructors do provide some variations, such as peer mentoring and self-assessment. Bray's thesis gives a broad overview of play/playwright development practices in many parts of the world. Although education/pedagogy are not his

primary focus, the nature of new play development for young playwrights tends to be instructional. The thesis provides a number of insights into methods, as well as the cultural distinctions of various programs. Bray's thesis is published by James Cook University for its own library, and available in microfilm format.

2. For additional insights into talkbacks see "Taking Back the Talkback," by Evan Guilford-Blake in the Spring 2001 *Parabasis* from ASK Theatre Projects, and "Talking Back: A Model for PostPerformance Discussion of New Plays" by David Rush in the March 2000 issue of *Theatre Topics*.

3. Two books that received mention by ATHE survey respondents are helpful works in this area because they identify and underscore the continually transformative nature of the playwright's life. Edward M. Cohen's *Working on A New Play* examines the roles of the various team members in the context of new play development, giving insight into areas that should be taught universally, but are not. The second book is *The Playwright's Survival Guide*, by Gary Garrison. Garrison took a series of articles he wrote for the Dramatists Guild and crafted them into this work, which describes in a very friendly fashion most of the elements a playwright needs in order to build and sustain a career. Garrison's subtitle describes the work perfectly: "Keeping the Drama in Your Work and Out of Your Life." The scope of this essay cannot contain the complicated issues of new play development programs and other professional experiences the playwright might encounter. The hope is that instructors are preparing students for these eventualities beyond the classroom walls.

Works Cited

Archer, William. 1960. *Play-Making: a manual of craftsmanship*. New York: Dover. Original edition, 1912.

Baker, George Pierce Baker. 1919. *Dramatic technique*. New York: Houghton Mifflin Co.

Ball, David. 1983. *Backwards and forwards: a technical manual for reading plays*. Carbondale, IL: Southern Illinois University Press.

Beber, Neena. 1990. Dramatis instructus. *American Theatre* 6, no. 10: 22–26.

Brook, Peter. 1968. *The empty space*. New York: Atheneum.

Esslin, Martin. 1986. *An anatomy of drama*. New York: Hill and Wang.

Freytag, Gustav. 1900. *Freytag's technique of the drama: an exposition of dramatic composition and art*. Translated by Elias J. MacEwan. Chicago: Scott, Foresman and Co.

Hayman, Ronald. 1977. *How to read a play*. New York: Grove Press.

Himes, Franklin J. 1998. *The janus paradigm*. New York: University Press of America.

Hobgood, Burnet M. 1988. (ed.), *Master teachers of theatre*. Carbondale, IL: Southern Illinois University Press.

McLaughlin, Buzz. 1997. *The playwright's process*. New York: Back Stage Books.

Palmarini, James. 1994. Teaching playwriting. *Dramatics* 66, no. 2: 38–43.

Savran, David. 1999. *The playwright's voice*. New York: Theatre Communications Group.

Shepard, Sam. 1997. Visualization, language, and the inner library. *The Drama Review* 21, no. 4: 57.

Smiley, Sam. 1971. *The structure of action.* Englewood Cliffs, NJ: Prentice-Hall.

Sweet, Jeffrey. 1993. *The dramatist's toolkit.* Portsmouth, NH: Heinemann.

van Druten, John. 1953. *Playwright at work.* New York: Harper & Brothers.

van Itallie, Jean-Claude. 1997. *The playwright's workbook.* New York: Applause Books.

Webster's ninth new collegiate dictionary. 1977. Springfield, MA: Merriam-Webster, Inc.

Williams, Tennessee. 1950. Foreword to *Constructing a play*, by Marian Gallaway. New York: Prentice-Hall.

Wright, Michael and Elena Carrillo. 1998. (eds), *The student's guide to playwriting opportunities*, 2nd edition. Dorset, VT: Theatre Directories, Inc.

Annotated Bibliography

(Author's note: this is not intended to be an exhaustive list of playwriting texts or resources; the works included here were contributory to the spirit and ideas of the essay.)

Boal, Augusto. *Games for Actors And Non-Actors.* Translated by Adrian Jackson. New York: Routledge, 1992. Boal uses his theatre games to help create theatre explorations related to aspects of exploitation and oppression in society; the exercises have numerous possibilities for playwrights.

Cohen, Edward M. *Working on A New Play.* New York: Limelight Editions, 1995. This work examines the roles of creative participants in new play development. It does not focus as much on the playwright as it could, but is a very informative read, nonetheless, and shines quite a bit of light on the professional world in an anecdotal manner.

Downs, William Missouri and Lou Anne Wright. *Playwriting: From Formula to Form.* New York: Harcourt Brace, 1997. A work that is praised for its pro and con examination of a formulaic approach to playwriting; a very strong work for beginning playwrights.

Egri, Lajos. *The Art of Dramatic Writing.* New York: Simon and Schuster, 1972. This is the grandfather of playwriting books, with many fine elements to offer the student playwright. Egri advocates an approach that encourages the writer to craft his or her own methodology.

Garrison, Gary. *The Playwright's Survival Guide.* Portsmouth, NH: Heinemann, 1999. A collection of essays written for the Dramatists Guild *Newsletter*, Garrison's book takes a hard but friendly look at life in the business of playwriting. Written in Garrison's inimitable style, this book is a must for students who are about to transition into the profession.

Johnstone, Keith. *Impro.* New York: Routledge, 1989. Johnstone has created a unique look at improvisation, with countless useful games and exercises that will inform and inspire playwrights.

"Playwrights and Playwriting Issue." *The Drama Review* 21, no. 4 (1977): 57. This is a landmark issue of TDR for playwrights, containing in-depth commentaries by Maria Irene Fornes, Adrienne Kennedy, Sam Shepard, and Jean-Claude van Itallie.

Spolin, Viola. *Improvisation for the Theatre*. Evanston, IL: Northwestern University Press, 1970. This is the foundation work for theatre games, story theatre, and improvisational working methods. Every playwright should know this work intimately.

Wright, Michael. *Playwriting in Process*. Portsmouth, NH: Heinemann, 1997. The essential idea of this book is working and thinking theatrically in playwriting, and not from literary or how-to perspectives.

Wright, Michael. *Playwriting Master Class*. Portsmouth, NH: Heinemann, 2000. Seven playwrights respond to a prompt ("there is a key in an envelope in a drawer") by writing a short play and keeping all their drafts, explorations, and notes, which are then edited into chapters. The book is subtitled "The Personality of Process and the Art of Rewriting" and examines a range of approaches.

Wright, Michael and Elena Carrillo. (eds), *The Student's Guide to Playwriting Opportunities*, 2nd edition. Dorset, VT: Theatre Directories, Inc., 1998. A compendium of academic and professional programs for student playwrights, including undergraduate and graduate degree offerings with detailed descriptions of the courses, performance policies, and other elements.

CHAPTER 6

Acting and Movement Training as a Pedagogy of the Body

Nathan Stucky and Jessica Tomell-Presto

American playwright Arthur Miller observed that acting, which he defines as assuming "the character of someone else," is inevitable as soon as we walk out our front doors and into society (2001, 33). Any view of acting holding that each of us acts every day raises questions about the actor's art, the nature of training, and the form any such training ought to take. The ways American institutions have chosen to train actors have varied, but they almost always involve conceiving of the actor as an instrument (in body and voice) that can be adjusted, refined, improved, and tuned. Hundreds of books have been written to aid in the process, and extensive curricula have been arranged to provide the requisite instruction. How is the body conceptualized in actor training? We are concerned especially with how the actor's body, through voice and movement training, is treated.

In this essay we examine two main elements in the academic actor training industry (American university curricula and representative major textbooks) and discuss new issues confronting this training. First, we examine representative curricula in acting, voice, and body, from a range of college and university theatre programs. What do the course offerings and requirements indicate about the way these departments approach the training of the actor? Second, we explore representative acting textbooks to explore further the typical range of instructional materials related to actor training. Finally, we develop two examples (Irish dance and performance ethnography) to explore variations and questions which challenge some of the assumptions in some traditional training.

acidity: "make your own theory, or someone worse will have done it for you.... Few professors are actors, but most of them are directors, and they write the textbooks" (1992, 105).

Although we are concerned here primarily with mid-to-late twentieth and early twenty-first-century practices, it bears pointing out that movement training for the actor has been part of American curricula for well over a hundred years. Indeed, ancient Greek and Roman actors and orators trained their bodies for performance, studying movement as part of developing the roles they played. At the end of the nineteenth century, actor and elocution academies were specifying gymnastics, dance, fencing, posing, and other regimens designed to enhance the actor's stage performance. The long-running debate over a mind/body split has been played out in theatre training as well as physiology, psychology, and philosophy. From the very beginning of theatre training, in one way or another, the mind has been telling the body to go to dance class.

Body and voice training have historically moved from general training, (conditioning, responsiveness, correction of "defects" and perceived inadequacies, and so forth) to particular needs (a Cockney accent, a certain age, particular lines, a fight scene). Training institutions typically construct curricula designed to establish a general skill level under the assumption that once the instrument is trained, particular skills needed for a specific play or production can be learned on the job.

Most academic work, and most texts on acting in U.S. mainstream today, take western realism as the norm. While such presumptions are challenged with increasing frequency, they have become standards against which variations are measured. Such norms shape the whole theatrical enterprise from how theatre is conceptualized, to how actors are trained, to how spectatorship is imagined. Rethinking those norms requires substantial rethinking. As Jill Dolan explains it: "in the illusionist tradition that dominates American theatre practice... [the] spectator has been assumed to be white, middle-class, heterosexual, and male. That theatre creates an ideal spectator carved in the likeness of the dominant culture whose ideology he represents is the motivating assumption behind the discourse of feminist performance criticism" (1991, 1). Of course, the ideal spectator is linked with an ideal theatre, one who relies heavily on "realistic" character development. So it is unsurprising that this, among other norms, can be seen in the approaches to training incipient theatre practitioners. Patrice Pavis discusses these norms in terms of cultural expectations and subsurface determinations: "the actors' bodies, in training or performance, are as though 'penetrated' by the 'body techniques' belonging to their culture, to a performance tradition or an acculturation.

It is (almost) impossible to unravel this complex and compact body, whose origin can no longer be seen" (1992, 9).

Even Augusto Boal asks how believable emotions " 'freely' manifest themselves throughout an actor's body" (1992, 40). An actor must "be able to take on the mechanisms of the character he is going to play" (Boal 1992, 41). For Boal taking on the "mechanisms of the character" comes from intense body training and repetitive scene work. Pavis makes the context of this body training clear when writing: "The culture of the actor, especially the western actor, is not always readable or codified according to a sum of stable and recurring rules and practices. But even western actors are not protected by a dominant style or fashion, or by body techniques or specific codifications, but are impregnated by formulas, habits of work, of their milieu" (1992, 16). The dominant style or fashion becomes ingrained in the expectations of the spectators, who comprise a shifting market for performance; these expectations play out in theatrical practice (including cinema and other forms) and in the formal training mechanisms found in workshops, studios, and universities.

Acting, Voice, and Body in University Theatre Training

University Theatre Departments across the United States offer Bachelor and Masters Degrees in Fine Arts specializing in actor training. The coursework that is required of theatre majors should reflect the knowledge that the university faculty and administration expect an actor to have after completing the curriculum. Implicit in these requirements is also the assumption that the acting styles and techniques taught at the university are necessary for obtaining professional acting work. An examination of university acting programs reflects a privileging of acting, movement, and voice classes for actor training. We studied a range of programs selected to represent geographical distribution as well as liberal arts to pre-professional models (Yale University, Illinois State, Southwest Texas, Florida State, University of Wisconsin at Madison, University of Colorado, Ohio State University, and University of California at San Diego). The list is not exhaustive; surely an even greater sampling would provide additional variety. However, as we discovered, this limited study reveals substantial similarities and intriguing differences across programs.

Many university training programs require an acting class every semester or quarter that a student is in the program. Students are generally required to take a movement or voice class every academic period. These classes are most often offered as separate classes. For some Fine Arts programs, especially Masters Degree programs, a separate movement, voice, and acting class is required every academic period. The movement and voice classes both focus on the body (one emphasizing the body in space, one vocal production); the acting class appears to unite these body/voice skills with critical and analytical skills that utilize the mind. One can see a mind/body dichotomy in the layout of curricula despite likely attempts within the courses themselves to de-emphasize that split.

Yale University's highly regarded acting program describes its first year of study as a "highly disciplined period of training. Through rigorous attention to the text, students learn to identify and personalize a character's driving need (objective) and to engage themselves (voice, body, mind, and spirit) in its active pursuit, informed by character specific listening" (YSD 2001). This description of an acting program explicitly addresses the divisions that acting programs use to educate their actors. The actor's training is typically divided into the training of the voice, body, and mind through coursework in voice, movement, and acting.

Learning discipline and control of the body through repetition and consistent practice seem to be the goal of multiple years of movement and voice classes. The coursework in these classes, therefore, involves an intricate knowledge of the body. Knowledge of the body would allow the actor to manipulate and control his/her movement and voice in order to perform using various acting styles.

Arguably, classes in acting, through scene study, textual analysis, and character analysis, develop the mind. As Yale's statement expresses it, the actor uses his/her mind to pay "rigorous attention to the text." The actor learns "a character's driving need (objective)." These tasks are mental, analytical tasks for the actor to perform in order to know how the character thinks. However, this analysis does not end with learning the character's objective. The actor must then learn to "personalize a character's need" and "engage themselves [...]" in its active pursuit, informed by character specific listening." The actor must "personalize" and "engage." In other words, the goal of the analysis is action or bodily engagement; the actor expresses knowledge of the text and character through voice and movement. Acting classes not only develop the analytical skills necessary to perform, but also put into use the individual skills learned in voice and movement classes. Actor training emphasizes individual, body-centered skills that are learned separately in voice and movement classes. These skills are then combined with the knowledge learned through textual and character analysis in order to embody a realistic character onstage.

The goal of required classes for the theatre major at these universities is an isolation of, and focus on, particular skills to find mastery and then a reuniting of these skills. The goal is a unification or connection of mind and body. In addition to their movement and dance courses, some also offer specialized courses such as the Alexander Technique. The Alexander Technique focuses on finding this connection between mind and body. For the Alexander Technique, the mind/body connection involves understanding the functioning of the muscles of the body. How these muscles interconnect can be discovered through an exploration of posture, movement, and breathing; in learning Alexander Technique, these can be controlled through conscious will.

The acting style that appears to be privileged by the representative universities is a realistic technique. Acting styles that are mentioned within course descriptions and catalogs are frequently those created by Stanislavski or ones specifically entitled, "Acting Realism" (University of Wisconsin 2001). Some programs offer additional classes in dialects in order to train the voice to realistically imitate other regional voice patterns (Southwest Texas 2001 and Florida State University 2001). Classes in stage combat are additional movement classes that a student can elect to take in order to train the body to realistically represent combat situations onstage (DePaul University 2001). Courses in the performance of gender, Latin/Caribbean Theatre (Florida), and African-American dance (University of Colorado at Boulder 2001) indicate a need to realistically and accurately portray, through body movement and voice, marginalized groups that may not be the focus of study in other acting courses. This knowledge would provide a larger range of characters and greater knowledge of characters that the actor could portray.

In the programs we reviewed, courses that do not seem to fall into the classification of "realistic theatre" or "realistic acting" are generally elective courses. These courses are marked as "different" in the course catalog. Restoration Drama, Asian Stage Production and Kabuki Drama are some of the courses offered as alternative classes. The technique necessary to embody these acting styles may not be covered within the required acting, movement, or voice classes. These acting styles may be considered stylistic rather than realistic (as though realism were not itself a style), and are not usually part of the core curriculum. While university catalog course descriptions offer a glimpse into the official purpose of each class, we expect that the actual delivery of instruction by individual teachers varies widely. In some cases, individual acting teachers may significantly modify or extend their courses.

To summarize, the program requirements of most university actor training programs follow a particular pattern. Generally, the student is required to take an acting class and a movement or a voice class every semester or quarter of his/her academic career. The acting course is a standard requirement, but may be described by the individual institution as a course in Acting Styles, Acting Realism, Scene Study, or Introduction to Performance. Courses in movement may also be identified by a number of different names: Dance, Stage Movement, Mask and Movement, or Mime. Finally, a voice class, which may be called Vocal Technique, Voice and Speech, or Voice and Articulation is a common requirement. Additionally, elective courses are offered to augment the acting, voice, and movement training. These courses seem to emphasize a realistic acting technique: Dialect; Stage Combat; Gender, Race, and Performance; Latin and Caribbean Theatre; and African-American Dance. Classes that are also offered as elective courses, but are typically described as using a stylistic rather than a realistic technique are Asian Drama, Kabuki, and Restoration Drama.

Acting Books

Acting books are another source of common methodologies for training the actor. Acting books are used as a resource by the professional actor who reads them to improve his/her technique, by the university student who uses them as textbooks for his/her courses, or by the layperson who desires access to professional technique. A number of recurring themes about actor training are evident in the books that were examined.

The first approach within the representative literature is a recurring metaphor that describes how the actor should view the training of the body; the body is compared to an instrument. Second, like university coursework, acting books tend to make recommendations for training the actor through improving his/her voice and movement. Third, it is necessary to understand one's own body before being able to take on the physical characteristics of another person or character onstage. A final approach is the connection between understanding the physical movement of a character and understanding the character's mental processes; a character can be "found" or understood through physical characterizations.

The first approach is the metaphor used repeatedly by the various authors. Many acting books describe the body as an instrument that must be tuned, trained, and perfected. In *Respect for Acting*, Uta Hagen describes the body as a musical instrument: "Essential to the serious actor is the training and perfecting of the outer instrument—comprising his body, his voice and his speech. This instrument is the violin on which he will play. He should be aware that it can be comparable to a Stradivarius and that he must turn it into and treat it like one" (1973, 14). The implication is that the body can be changed and tuned like the strings on an instrument; it is flexible and pliable, if kept in good condition. Gates and McGaw describe actor training using this metaphor as well: "The answer is that the actor's voice is developed in much the same way that one learns to play a musical instrument" (Gates 2000, 3). McGaw states, "These truths are obvious. The actor's need for a well-trained voice and body is equally obvious. A musician is at a disadvantage if he has to perform on an inferior instrument. An actor is at a similar disadvantage if his muscular and vocal control are not all that they could be" (McGaw 1980, 10). According to these authors, the body is an instrument that can be controlled and re-educated.

For Stanislavski, in *An Actor Prepares*, the body is an instrument, but is characterized more like a machine than the musician's instrument: "In order to express a most delicate and largely subconscious life it is necessary to have control of an unusually responsive, excellently prepared vocal and physical apparatus" (1969, 15). A machine is much more predictable; similar results should occur upon each use. This predictability may be reassuring for an actor who must perform the same role multiple times in a day or week.

Hagen and Stanislavski focus on the body, with its connection to the mind being less explicit. Kristin Linklater, however, uses the metaphor of the instrument with explicit reference to its use with the mind and imagination: "The actor's instrument is composed of the body, the voice, the imagination, the emotions, the brain, and the life experience of the human being that actor is" (Linklater 1976, 201–202). Like Hagen and Stanislavski, the natural division between the body and voice, the parts of the instrument, is still apparent in Linklater's description. However, in using this metaphor, she includes the mind, or imagination and brain, as well as the voice and body, as part of the instrument. This inclusion of the mind and the possible connection between mind and body differs from how the other authors conceptualize the actor's instrument.

Linklater Technique is one exception to the common division between vocal and physical training. Linklater decries this fragmentation in the training of the actor and argues for synthesis:

In the old days a young would-be actor went to ballet classes to learn graceful control of the body, to singing classes to learn to manage the voice, and to an acting studio to study whatever approach to acting a particular teacher had devised. It would take a well-integrated personality to triumph over such fragmentation of function. It is now understood, in theory at least, that taking a human being apart, developing the parts and

technique assumes that emotional life may sometimes be more easily aroused and fixed for performance through work on the physical life of the role, rather than through inner work" (Carnicke 2000, 26). This technique strongly links the mind and the body in acting technique. The body, through voice and movement, triggers emotions in the mind of the actor. A well-studied walk, posture, dialect, or gesture is the link to understanding the psychology and emotional state of the character. "An outward imitation of attitudes suggesting suffering, for example, will help to bring the corresponding inner feelings" (Albright 1959, 26). The leap from experiencing the emotions and understanding the psychology of the character to performing an authentic and believable character is then made.

The performance of a character that is authentic and believable becomes the end goal for the actor when a realistic technique is expected. According to Carnicke's discussion of Stanislavski, "the Moscow Art Theatre established itself as the leader in realism" (2000, 12). Stanislavski's Method is a predominant training method for actors today. Acting books continue to advocate a natural or realistic performance style: "Good reading of dialogue has the quality and effect of real conversation" (Albright 1959, 40). Charles McGaw, in *Acting is Believing*, describes the reason for using a realistic technique: "It is necessary to the actor to believe what he is doing, and his first responsibility to his audience is to induce their belief in his actions" (McGaw 1980, 16). As Jerry Crawford notes, there may be several ways to this end: "No matter what the style required, the initial and central problem of an actor is to use personalization to establish comfort and familiarity with his role or activity. Then he must communicate the intentions of the playwright as revealed by action and characters of the script or the theatrical activity. Language, mood, emotions, thoughts, and physical activity are all parts of personalizing and communication" (Crawford 1980, 118). Crawford's point that "it is a common mistake to call any non-realistic play or theatre experience 'stylized' " (1980, 118) may help the student understand that, although the university curriculum tends to segment the training process, individual acting classes may attempt to bridge the gap; an individual acting teacher might draw upon a similar perspective to point out that "realism" is itself a style.

Movement, Dance, and the Ethnographic Body

To play out some of the ramifications of actor and movement training we turn now to two examples. In the first, an exploration of training in Irish dance, the relationship of the body training to implicit and implied "character" points to assumptions about the relationship between bodily representation and that which is represented. In the second, an instance of performance ethnography is developed to raise questions about the possibilities of realism, especially where verisimilitude in performance intersects with the subject (or text) of performance.

Movement training can take a variety of forms for the acting student. For the university student, course listings from the dance department are possibilities for fulfilling that requirement. For any actor, the desired training to learn to control the body can be found in a variety of dance classes offered within and outside the university. For one of the authors (Jessica Presto), the bodily knowledge and control that would aid in the acting process was found in Irish step-dancing lessons. These particular dance classes seemed especially relevant when trying to understand a character of Irish descent.

Learning cultural norms through dance is also the motivation for and method chosen by many dancers and parents of young dancers. According to a study done in Boston, "the dancing teacher contributes to the socialization process of Irish-American children and to the perpetuation of a dance form indicative of Irish identity" and "the dancing school is the only other institutional means by which an awareness of heritage is instilled in the child" (Sughrue 1985, 11). "[E]thnic heritage features [. . .] and a sense of self-identity are conveyed to the young members of the Irish community through [. . .] the Irish dancing school" (Sughrue 1985, 14). According to *Dance Magazine*, Michael Flatley, a Chicago native, head choreographer for Riverdance and Lord of the Dance, "was sent to Irish dance classes to keep him in touch with his roots" (Parry 1997, 72).

Dance theorists Ann Cooper Albright and Susan Leigh Foster credit John Martin with creating terminology for the bodily knowledge gained through watching a dancer or learning a dance. The muscles of a dancer and even of an audience member respond empathetically while watching another dancer. Martin's term for this response, depending on whether Albright or Foster is writing, is metakinesis or kinesthetic empathy, respectively. Foster, in the endnotes to her introductory article in *Choreographing History*, cites Martin as defining kinesthetic empathy as when "bodies respond proprioceptively to the shaping, rhythmic phrasing and tensile efforts of other bodies" (Foster 1995, 20). Certainly, this kinesthetic empathy is similar to the bodily knowledge and understanding of a character that an actor hopes to achieve in moving, gesturing, and transforming him/herself into another body.

As an adult novice dancer in the United States, my experience of Irish step-dancing comes late in life in comparison to most Irish dancers. Most Irish dancers begin their training while still in grade school. My reflections on Irish dance are consequently made by an older, less experienced dancer, one who has not participated in the dance competitions or feis that are the concern of most young dancers and dance schools. Although the schools claim to teach Irish heritage with or through the dance, what complicates the process is the possibility that the culture of the schools and feis becomes part of the curriculum as well. In fact, my ability to learn Irish dance as an adult was hindered more by most dance schools' dismissal of anyone who is not a potential competitor, in other words, someone fifteen or older, than by my inability to learn or perform any of the steps.

To the novice dancer (Jessica), Irish step-dancing differs from other dance styles in two major respects. First, the posture of the dance is significantly different from other dance styles. Second, the costuming of the dancer has become a significant element of Irish dance. The current costuming of the dancer may be more an element of the culture of the Irish dance schools and competitions than Irish cultural heritage; however, this element has become almost inextricable from the dance. The claim is that the costuming is "Authentic Gaelic" dress. These two aspects of Irish dance, posture and costuming, are only two of the possible ways that Irish dancing differs from other dance styles and embodies a particular cultural identity. The focus in this example will be on these two aspects because they are immediately recognizable as aspects particular to Irish dance.

The posture of Irish dance is easily recognizable because of its stiff upper torso and stiff, still arms. All of the movement in traditional Irish dance happens below the waist. The reasons given for this technique vary. Some dancers claim that this technique was developed in reaction to the Queen's command that Irish dancers perform for her; they were required to dance, but did not want to seem to be enjoying it. Others claim that the dance could be masked from parish priests or British soldiers by restricting movement to below the waist. This folklore often becomes part of the instruction in Irish dance classes. Regardless of the true meaning behind the decision to limit the upper body movement in Irish dance, the explanations hinge around historical events that are key to Irish identity. Additionally, to the novice dancer, the stiff, regimented posture of the Irish dancer, seems to personify the attitude, perseverance, and discipline of the "Irish character."

Susan Leigh Foster in *Corporealities: Dancing Knowledge, Culture and Power* and John O. Perpener in *Researching Dance: Evolving Modes of Inquiry* discuss the influence of ballet on colonized people and the indigenous dances. Both authors are concerned with the ideologies presented through ballet. Ballet and Irish dancing have been linked in technique and style. Although ballet may not have been specifically introduced by English dancers, the style is not that of the indigenous dance of Ireland. Perpener states, "In the example just cited, classical ballet, such investigations could expose the sociopolitical underpinning of an art form that has gained its hierarchical status, in large part, because it is historically rooted in empires that achieved their cultural dominance and built images of superiority upon the subjugation and denigration of non-European people (as well as European people of lower classes)" (1999, 341). The indigenous dance style also seems to be connected, even if it is only in the minds of the dancers, by Ireland's colonization; the reasoning for the arm technique is often explained as a result of England's influence. According to Foster, "Today's ballet, a sanitized geometry, emphasizes physical discipline and dedication.... In these landscapes of virtuosity, both *her* and *his* bodies bear the marks of colonization and colonial contact. They stand against indigenous forms of dancing as bodies estranged" (Foster 1995, 2). However, it would seem that the estranged bodies in Irish dancing are those of the Irish dancer who purposely marks him/herself as different, as estranged, through movement technique, or in this case, lack of movement.

The costuming of Irish dancers appears to be regulated by tradition, however, there is also some debate about this as well. Female dancers appear at family functions, local gatherings, pub performances, and feis in elaborately detailed dresses. These dresses come in a variety of colors and fabrics. Recently, neon greens, yellows, and oranges are colors of choice. These dresses apparently conform to the NAFC's (North American Feis Commission) regulation for "Authentic Gaelic" dress. Some dance historians claim that "Authentic Gaelic" dress would be a brown wool dress or kilt. Male dancers, although in past years were required to wear a kilt in competition, normally appear in black pants. Male dancers would seem to have permission not to wear "Authentic Gaelic" dress. Another reason for avoiding the traditional garb in competition is given by a young Irish dancer in her website: Theresa describes one of the disadvantages of wearing a kilt for boys is that "they are sometimes subject to jokes and mocking" whereas "pants are less likely to be made fun of by peers" (Siamsa 2000). Female dancers are not given the choice between wearing a kilt, dress, or pants. Theresa also claims in her website that the costuming affects the dancer and how the dance is viewed.

Some obvious gendered norms, which are based, depending on the critic, on either tradition or contemporary cultural standards, are taught through Irish dance. These norms, however muddled in terms of being "authentic" or "traditional," reflect the Irish identity taught by the dance schools. The Irish dancer's movement reflects, to some extent, Irish history and the Irish character. Additionally, the tradition that is embodied by the Irish dancer is one with specific norms for feminine and masculine appearance and behavior. Although this example was limited to a short exploration of the posture and costuming of Irish dancers, other norms for behavior are learned through the types of steps that are taught female dancers versus male dancers, the elaborate hair curling rituals that are the norm for young female dancers, and the comportment and etiquette of the dancers, all of which could be explored in further research.

The discipline of Irish step-dancing is a pedagogy of the body in a number of respects. The body is disciplined to move in a style that differs in significant ways from other forms of dance. The body is conditioned to reorient itself in order to perform movements that are not natural to the human body, the recognized posture of the Irish dancer with a stiff upper-torso with hands stiff at the sides along the waist. The costume associated with Irish dancing forces the Irish dancers' body to move in a particular way and to be treated or to react socially in a particular way. The motivation for conditioning the body to move in this particular manner for the dancer is the desire to know and follow a tradition. The motivation for the actor is to be able to duplicate this bodily movement and learn control of the body in order to take on a realistic, historically and culturally accurate, character. The learning of these traditions cause the dancer and the actor to embody, consciously or unconsciously, a culturally distinct and gendered body. Dance scholars have addressed the importance of deciphering how various bodies communicate these cultural and gendered identities as well as the body's and movement's role in history and politics (Roman 2003).

The university curricula and acting texts we examined ask the student to address questions of developing a character. The pedagogy of those lessons is often couched within specific conventions of style or genre. How would a given character speak or move given particular circumstances of period or dramatic moment? For example, one way to take on an Irish character is to perform certain dance movements, and by performing certain movements to take on an Irish character—something that goes beyond the movements and costuming alone. Learning Irish dance carries implications about culture and gender for the performer in the context of audience expectations, real or anticipated. Much as an investigation into learning Irish dance, or any other specific performance skill (e.g. stage combat) reveals underlying assumptions about gender and culture, an investigation into the concept of "character" reveals complexities about the nature of self and other. To bring teaching "character" into sharper focus we turn to performance ethnography where questions of subject and object, what is real and what is true, have been the subject of ongoing discussion.

Performance ethnography provides a unique way of investigating the relationship between the body and the role. Because the role played originates as a live human being (instead of a fictional character in a play), the model (the character within the dramatic text) is constantly shifting, and the performer's relationship to the subject, too, must be taken into account. As Norman Denzin explains, "The field is caught between those who produce ethnographic performances that report on and reproduce reality on stage and those who critique reality and its representations"(Denzin 1997, 114). When the ethnographic subject (a real person) is transformed into a written text (ethnographic description) questions of authorship (is the live human the author or is the author the ethnographer?) and authenticity (who presents the real character?) begin to turn what seemed like a relatively simple acting task into a complex maze of interlocking puzzles. And, since we are all acting everyday when we step out our front door (see Arthur Miller's quote at the beginning of this essay), the very representations we undertake in performance ethnography have their origins in everyday acting as well.

The challenges of reproducing an "ethnographic subject" in performance can perhaps be seen through a performance example. In 1999 one of us (Nathan Stucky) arranged to present a public performance that included representing (or presenting?) his Tai Chi teacher. It seemed there were significant differences between the performer (Nathan) and the subject he wished to portray, his teacher, Master Han. Among the challenges were these: the age difference (about 18 years); the size differences (6'1", and 5'; c. 200 lb, and c. 95 lb.); language differences (native English speaker with no knowledge of Chinese, and native Chinese speaker using English as a second language); cultural experience differences (merely consider the categories Midwestern American, and Chinese/Taiwanese to imagine the gap in general terms); educational differences (American university liberal and fine arts education, and Taiwanese electrical engineering plus Tai Chi training in Taiwan). This list could go on, but identifying differences in age, body size, language, cultural experience, and education, points to significant differences between the performer and the performed. Despite all these differences, in a discussion after Stucky's performance of Master Han, several members of the audience reported that they "really saw" the character of Han even though the performance itself explicitly suggested the impossibility of this actor convincingly playing that role.

One form of performance ethnography, Everyday Life Performance (ELP) (Hopper 1993; Stucky 1993) provides a method to produce high-fidelity replication of ordinary conversational interaction—a kind of hyperrealism. This performance technique involves carefully transcribing recordings using a notational system developed by conversation analyst Gail Jefferson, which identifies such paralinguistic details as simultaneous utterances, overlap, intervals between utterances, rising and falling intonations, laughter, louder and softer utterances, extended syllables and so forth. The ELP rehearsal process, rather like learning to sing along with a musical recording while following a score, leads an actor into a precise mimetic performance of the way people actually talk. Scripts, which develop from conversation analysis materials, contain a higher level of detail than a typical dramatic playscript. They present the actor with specific challenges for replication and they "raise questions about *mimesis* and *verisimilitude*" (Stucky 1993, 168). In the Tai Chi performance of Master Han then, the question of character becomes problematized as ELP acting techniques are employed. As the actor gains technical accuracy the gap between the performed and the performer, between the role and the actor, becomes more difficult to identify. In ELP the audience is simultaneously presented with a "real" character and a real actor. In contrast to American versions of Stanislavski's method acting, with their focus on psychological and internal elements of characterization, ELP requires a careful examination of empirical evidence of an "original" performance of a real-life person. In method acting the actor asks, "What would I do *if* I were this character?" In ELP the actor asks, "Exactly what did the person do?" "The end result of ELP often looks astonishingly realistic (like some method acting), but the underlying logic is more akin to presentational theatre or storytelling than it is to Western realism because the actor is, in effect, performing a carefully rehearsed quotation" (Stucky and Daughton 2003, 482).

If we take the challenge of realistic acting seriously, or in ethnographic performance, what Denzin identified above as "ethnographic performances that report on and reproduce reality on stage," then we can see that verisimilitude, or the appearance of truth, may be elusive. If this extreme example leads one to say, in the context of realism, that such would not be appropriate casting, then the question becomes one of degree. That is, how close to some ideal must the actor be in order to qualify for the role? What assumptions about race and culture arise if, for example, one were to cast a Japanese-American student to play a Chinese character? The examples can get complicated even while familiar: Italian-American actors have been frequently cast to play Native American Indians in Hollywood films; and, even when Native Americans are cast, there may be disproportionate casting from the great plains tribes (e.g. Sioux) rather than other tribes perhaps because they fit a certain "Indian look." Along this line, then, we can arrange a series of related issues confronting the theatre, and especially educational theatre: cross-race casting, cross-ethnic group casting, cross-age casting, cross-gender casting, and so forth. How do we rate the less tangible? For example, what value is placed on a match of personality type between actor and role compared to a match of age or race? Each crossing forces us to ask what is being crossed? What are we privileging in these supposed crossings? While performance ethnography provides some methods for actor training, it also raises questions of representation. We point here to some of the fundamental questions that arise from ingrained realism in actor and movement training today. Performance ethnography allows us to inspect more clearly what is present in acting a more traditional dramatic role, and it helps clarify what it means to embody a text, whether that text is another live human being or a dramatic role. It allows us to reconsider the assumptions we make regarding difference and similarity, and the underlying qualifications appropriate for taking on a character.

Conclusion

One way to put acting a dramatic character into perspective is to consider modes of performance which problematize "acting like another character." The gender assumptions in everyday performance of self, for example, are highlighted in complex ways through transgender performances of varying kinds. Judith Butler's analysis of gendered performances makes us rethink what is often assumed to be effortless or natural. Performance ethnography, because it draws its characters from studies of real life persons, blurs the boundary between text and performance. That is, how can a person be a "text" in the same sense that a character in a drama is a text? Oral history and folklore performance, while sharing the textual complexity of performance ethnography (characters who originate as real life persons), also reorder the performance event. In traditional theatre the writing of the drama usually precedes the performance event. However, in the performance (or re-performance) of oral history, one begins with a live performance that is subsequently turned into a script or text. That script may later become the basis for another performance. Everyday Life Performance finds theatre in mundane conversation and repositions the actor to play with mimetic precision in an outwardly representational but fundamentally presentational mode.

One way to assume another character, for one person to approach the body (voice and movement) of another person, is to ask what is claimed by the embodiment of both the performer and the performed. How does the facial affect of the Irish Dancer relate to the Irish character? Performance ethnography, in the broadest context, asks what it means to perform another—a person from another culture in contrast to a fictional character in the drama. What assumptions and presumptions about culture and personhood are involved? Performance ethnography raises questions about the epistemology and ontology of performance. Performance ethnography grapples with the impossibility of playing another while dramatic acting grapples with the possibility.

Training an actor increasingly is seen as a complex task whether conceived as a liberal arts preparation for living a fuller life or as a path to a specific career. Theatre training programs, built on a tradition of western realism, have begun to widen their course offerings to include a variety of styles as well as courses that recognize the diversity of theatrical performance. At the beginning of the twenty-first century, acting books as well as university training, while still firmly rooted in realism, are challenged with new theatrical forms and expanded notions of what it means to "assume the character of someone else."

Works Cited

Albright, Harry Darkes. 1959. *Working up a part: A manual for the beginning actor.* Boston: Houghton Mifflin.

Boal, Augusto. 1992. *Games for actors and non-actors.* Trans., Adrian Jackson. New York: Routledge.

Carnicke, Sharon Marie. 2000. Stanislavsky's system: Pathways for the actor. In Alison Hodge (ed.), *Twentieth century actor training.* London: Routledge, 11–36.

Crawford, Jerry. 1980. *Acting in person and in style.* Dubuque, Iowa: Wm. C. Brown.

Crow, Aileen. 1980. The Alexander Technique as a basic approach to theatrical training. In Lucille Rubin (ed.), *Movement for the actor.* New York: Drama Book Specialists, 1–12.

Denzin, Norman. 1997. *Interpretive ethnography: Ethnographic practices for the 21st century.* Thousand Oaks, NJ: Sage.

Dolan, Jill. 1991. *The feminist spectator as critic.* Ann Arbor: U. Michigan.

Florida State University school of theatre. Florida State University. March 24, 2001. <http:/www.fsu.edu/~theatre/>.

Foster, Susan Leigh. 1995. An introduction to moving bodies: Choreographing history. In Susan Leigh Foster (ed.), *Choreographing history.* Bloomington: Indiana University, 3–12.

Gates, Linda. 2000. *Voice for performance: Training the actor's voice.* New York: Applause.

Hagen, Uta. 1973. *Respect for acting.* New York: McMillan.

Hopper, Robert. 1993. Conversational Dramatism and everyday life performance. *Text and Performance Quarterly* 13: 181–183.

Huston, Hollis. 1992. *The actor's instrument: Body, theory, stage.* Ann Arbor: U. Michigan.

Linklater, Kristin. 1976. *Freeing the natural voice.* New York: Drama Book Specialists.

McGaw, Charles. 1980. *Acting is believing: A basic method.* New York: Rinehart and Winston.

Miller, Arthur. 2001. American Playhouse: On politics and the art of acting. *Harpers* 302 no. 1813 (June): 33–43.

Ohio State University course offerings. Ohio State University. April 7, 2001. <http://www.the.ohio-state.edu/Courseinfo/CourseDiscriptions.htm>.

Parry, Jann. 1997. The Irish dance phenomenon: Celtic crossover. *Dance Magazine* 71, (October): 70–73.

Pavis, Patrice. 1992. *Theatre at the crossroads of culture.* New York: Routledge.

Perpener, John O. 1999. Cultural diversity and dance history research. In Sondra Horton Fraleigh and Penelope Hanstein (eds), *Researching dance: Evolving modes of inquiry.* 334–351. Pittsburgh: University of Pittsburgh Press.

Pisk, Litz. 1975. *The actor and his body.* New York: Theatre Arts Books.

Relph, Patricia. 1980. The bodily expression of emotional experience. In Lucille Rubin (ed.), *Movement for the actor.* New York: Drama Book Specialists, 29–49.

Roman, David. 2003. Theatre journals: Dance liberation. *Theatre Journal* 55: 395–588.

Siamsa. Personal Webpage. October 15, 2000. <http://www.geocities.com/Broadway/Alley/9643/claddaghmain.html>.

Southwest Texas State University: Department of theatre. Southwest Texas State. May 29, 2001. <http://www.finearts/swt.edu/theatre/index.htm>.

Stanislavski, Constantin. 1969. *An actor prepares.* Translated by Elizabeth Reynolds Hapgood. New York: Theatre Art Books.

Stucky, Nathan. 1993. Toward an aesthetics of natural performance. *Text and Performance Quarterly* 13: 168–180.

Stucky, Nathan P. and Suzanne M. Daughton. 2003. The body present: Reporting everyday life performance. In Phillip Glenn, Curtis LeBaron, and Jennifer Mandelbaum (eds), *Studies in language and social interaction* Mahwah, NJ: Lawrence Earlbaum. 479–491.

Sughrue, Cynthia. 1985. The O'Shea dancing school as a socio-cultural medium in a Boston Irish community. Working Papers. Northeastern University.

Theatre and drama: University of Wisconsin Madison. University of Wisconsin-Madison. March 24, 2001. <http://polyglot.lss.wisc.edu/tnd/theatre/undergrad/unergrad.html>.

Theatre at Illinois State University. Illinois State University. March 24, 2001. <http://orathost.cfa.ilstu.edu/theatre/program/UGframe.html>.

The theatre school: DePaul University. DePaul University. May 29, 2001. <http://theatreschool.depaul.edu/resources/act_mc.htm>.

UCSD graduate acting. University of California at San Diego. April 7, 2001. <http://www-theatre.ucsd.edu/gradtheatre/grad-acting.html>.

University of Colorado at Boulder. April 7, 2001. <http://www.colorado.edu/sacs.catolog00-01/c.html?3-6201>.

faculty either of how much their artistic work depends on the audiences the course supplies or of how difficult mutli-purpose courses are to teach.[2]

In addition to its ambivalent reception within the department, the course reaches students from many disciplines, some distantly related to the arts, and like patrons of productions, they behave as patrons in the theatre classroom. "They'll eat you alive if you don't keep them interested,"[3] one senior faculty member told a beginning lecturer, so with the student expectation that they are in a course that is supposed to be "That's Entertainment," combined with the departmental insistence on keeping both academic standards and enrollments high, the pressure on the Introduction to Theatre faculty is almost implosive.

Has the Introduction to Theatre class always been this demanding? At least since 1973, as evident from Gillespie's analysis, the problems deriving from budgetary issues have existed. Apart from fiscal concerns, have curricular designs in the past better integrated the course with strong academic programs in theatre and drama or has Introduction to Theatre functioned as a distant rich relative supporting the nuclear family of the department?

A review of current literature illustrates that much work has been completed on interactive learning strategies in education (Amirahmadi 1990; Brell 1991; Jackson and Poulter 1995; Davis 1997), and interdisciplinary strategies that use theatrical approaches (Gagon 1998), with few articles that deal specifically with the teaching of Introduction to Theatre; those notable exceptions by Ronald Willis (1991); Kae Koger (1994); David Carlyon (1998), ask questions about target audiences for the course while providing techniques for reaching those specific audiences. None of the articles attempt a historical perspective to the teaching of the course to illustrate how the questions scholars ask at the end of the twentieth century derive from dilemmas that developed at its beginning.

By surveying the history of the teaching of the Introduction to Theatre from its earliest traceable beginnings to the present in the United States, repeated patterns and practices of instruction can be outlined. Because this is an analysis of the pedagogical history of the course and not a quantitative study, the answers to several qualitative questions will be sought: first, what was the course initially mandated to accomplish and how has that mandate changed; second, how have changing students populations altered the goals of the course; and third, how are instructors currently meeting the demands of students who are sophisticated in areas of technology and sometimes naïve about what happened in history before they were born.

The evidence for the study is divided into three parts: first, for the earlier history, a summary of courses and curricular models from the turn of the century to the 1970s illustrates changing trends in course development; second, a survey of textbooks illustrates shifting pedagogical emphases, with a focus on those published since the 1980s; and third, panels from two different conferences in 1999 and 2000 on the teaching of Introduction to Theatre bring current issues to the discussion. I make no pretense that this is a global study, but rather a survey that attempts to summarize pedagogical trends so as to provide course designers with information as to how others have solved the rather perplexing problem of being "all things to all people."[4]

Pedagogical History

Introduction to Theatre inherited pedagogical tendencies that had developed from the late nineteenth century until 1936. During this period theatre as an academic discipline passed through the stages of serving as an extra-curricular activity to a semicurricular one, finally arriving at the curricular phase (Beckerman 1971) in which three emphases emerged: the close examination of the play text derived from the study of literature and literary criticism, the practice of elocution often considered a subdivision of the latter (Smith 1954), and the development of artistic stagecraft (Carrie Wright 1924). Theatre arts as a separate field of study did not emerge in the formal curriculum of American colleges and universities until the 1920s, and it wasn't until 1936 when the American Educational Theatre Association was established that a "thrust for excellence in theatre education began" (Geltner 1980, xiii).

During this period, a discussion began that has ensued throughout the decades regarding the function of the departments of theatre which very much affected the later development of the Introduction to Theatre course. On the one hand, theatre departments trained theatre practitioners, and on the other hand, they served the goals of the liberal arts with the objective of broadening the minds of theatre students so as to make them more "susceptible to the influences of beauty and truth" (Spiller 1927, 398). The debate over the needs of production and training versus those of developing the whole individual became even more focused in the 1940s as educators expanded the liberal arts base of dramatic education to that in which dramatics "should have as one of its major objectives the development of the personality of the individual student" with a secondary goal of the "particular skills and insights that will be of professional value" (Pollack 1941, 2). The move toward a generalist approach to theatre education expanded to what Evaline Uhl Wright described in 1942 as training students to be artists in an educational program with high standards for "actors, designers, playwrights, technicians—the *producers* of theatre—and high standards for the members of the audience—the *consumers* of theatre" (165). It is significant that as early as 1942 the role of the student as consumer had already entered the discussion as to the content of university theatre courses, a factor that as yet plays into the development of Introduction to Theatre courses.

The debate between training and educating was ongoing after World War II when in 1946 Ralph Freud argued that with the advent of motion pictures and radio, the nature of theatre education had radically changed because theatre workers had been diverted from the theatre art. The uniqueness, however, of departments of drama lay in their ability to "enrich the theatre by developing students culturally and personally so that they may be able to give the theatre what it lacks most seriously at this moment—ideas" (Freud 1946). The curriculum proposed by Freud has been lost, but it is said to have influenced the subsequent curriculum developed by Monroe Lippman. In a list of five aims of a liberal education, Lippman includes the need for "a cultural background in and appreciation of Theatre Arts and their contribution to the development of our culture." More significantly, for the first time, a course entitled "Introduction to Theatre" is proposed. Subsequently, the college and university work project committee of the American Educational Theatre Association advocated a course that was "a study of plays, analysis of plays and play structure, consideration of the development of the theatre, in terms of its equipment, literature, aesthetic principles, and styles of production" (Lippman 1946). The following year, 1947, the chairman of the subcommittee on college curriculum, Edward Wright, went even further in promoting the liberal arts basis to the curriculum by recommending the "integration of courses...and an emphasis on the place of the Theatre, not only as an art form, but as a form in the social, religious, and everyday life of the individual as reflected through its history" (Reports of College 1948). In the following year, the subcommittee expanded their vision by concluding with what could be considered a mandate for the teaching of Introduction to Theatre:

> Our final recommendation is that we should not center all our attention on Theatre majors but should gear the basic courses to meet the needs of those students with only a passing interest in Theatre. We can furnish them with the opportunity of molding personality, realizing artistic achievement and perhaps finding a valued avocation in later life. They can and often do bring great gifts to the department and the college theatre program. (Reports of Subcommittee 1949)

For the first time in the teaching of theatre in the United States, curriculum designers included the consideration of non-majors as part and parcel of the design of the introductory course.

By the middle of the century Introduction to Theatre was both a base to professional training and a means of personal enrichment for non-professionals in a liberal arts curriculum. Ironically, as theatre education broadened its goals, other disciplines narrowed theirs with an emerging emphasis on science and technology. By the end of the 1950s an unexpected, mercurial reversal occurred in theatre education: to compete with increased funding to scientific research, liberal arts colleges returned to a focus on professionalism with a diminishing emphasis on liberal arts (McGrath 1959). Again, theatre educators struggled with the dilemma of training and educating simultaneously in a cultural context in which specialization, as influenced from the sciences, was becoming the norm.

In the 1960s when both universities and theatre programs were growing rapidly (Fliotsos 1997), a new set of paradigms for the teaching of theatre were generated. Burnet Hobgood proposed criteria that contained multiple purposes so that each college or university could "formulate its own conception of higher education" (Hobgood 1964, 150). His five paradigms differentiated program characteristics crucial to quality and policy, including: recreational, advocational, liberal-arts humanistic, liberal arts-vocational, and pre-professional. The recognition that no one model applies to all educational situations reflected not only the student empowerment of the revolutionary sixties in which previous standards for education were suspect, but also augured the acceptance of difference as a measure of intellectual validity. The assumption that knowledge could be communicated through courses designed by experts for both majors and non-majors began to shift toward a new paradigm in which groups of diverse backgrounds could express their own ways of knowing, using dramatic literature and theatre practices as their tools. Implicit to this change in educational strategy was the growing awareness of the student as consumer.

It was in response to this major shift in educational expectations that Gillespie proposed the multi-purpose course referred to earlier in this discussion, an experiment, not unique but documented, that reflected the changing trends in the teaching of Introduction to Theatre. This course at the University of Iowa was intended to provide "identifiable, definable, and in some way measurable goals" while simultaneously meeting the objectives of "the department . . . and the needs of the College of Liberal Arts (for a course in the historical-cultural humanities)" (Gillespie 1973, 148). Organized around lectures presented three times a week, discussions conducted by graduate assistants were subdivided into three different topic areas: production, history of ideas, and cultural climate. Extensive slide shows and musical selections developed with specialists in the art and music departments were "identified, previewed, cataloged, and incorporated into the lectures" (Gillespie 1973, 149). Designed to present a wide range of information through tightly structured lectures that crossed disciplines and media, the class targeted students of various academic backgrounds who were free to select one of three discussion topics, and, in fact, were welcomed in as many discussions as they wished to attend. According to Gillespie, the course achieved its aims in minimizing the impersonality of the large lecture by providing the smaller discussion sections while maximizing the breadth of the survey approach.

The significance of this 1973 model is its reflection of the need to open curricula to a wider base of students. While Gillespie's model broadens the traditional tri-fold approach of history, dramatic literature, and theatre practices to an interdisciplinary consideration of cultural context, it is evident from the need for its development that the demands of the market were pressuring the actual design of courses. A shift in student receptivity resulting from a range of social causes—the protest movements of the late sixties, changing expectations of what constitutes knowledge, and increased awareness of idiosyncrasy in learning styles—created the need in the theatre departments to seek ways to keep students attentive and attending.

In 1976, Oscar Brockett addressed the Forty-first Annual Convention of the Southern Speech Association with a concern that marked a kind of milestone in the discussion that had proceeded from the 1930s. He said:

> These days I hear many complaints about schools that are claiming to give professional training, though they are not. Unfortunately, one does not hear many complaints about what is even more prevalent—schools that claim to be giving a liberal education and are not.... Thus, they have done all too little to lead students into the kinds of inquiry that would develop the qualities traditionally associated with a liberal education. Unfortunately, there is often much more truth to the charge that those who major in theatre are neither trained nor educated. (Brockett, The humanities, 1976, 143)

What was changing that caused this apparent crisis in purpose? After 40 years of defining curricula, debating the educational focus of theatre departments, and evolving more complex courses to meet the needs of increasingly vocal and diverse students populations, theatre programs seemed to be as yet unsure about their objectives. Brockett, whose textbook as yet dominates theatre history, represents traditional scholarship, whereas the mid-seventies marked the beginning of what Anne Fliotsos labels "the Idiosyncratic, an individual approach that has developed because professors perceived a need that was not being met through traditional teaching methods" (Fliotsos 1997). The transition from the period of multi-purpose presentations to managing shifting ways of knowing is reflected in the quantity and quality of introductory textbooks that exploded on the market beginning in the 1970s.

That's Entertainment

The textbooks published from 1935 to the 2001 that can be considered introductions to theatre reflect the changing trends in theatre education as they reflect the changing marketplace of the university. Their selection in the earlier period is based on the few that were then available, and in the later periods, on the basis of those texts cited in scholarly articles and by conference panelists. In addition, I surveyed the texts that have been sent to me (many in their third or fourth editions) since the mid-1980s when I began teaching Introduction to Theatre as illustrative of the variety in approach that has now become available.

Hubert Heffner's *Modern Theatre Practice* provides a model of the material considered important for the training of practitioners. In a brief introduction to the one section of twenty-one that deals with play analysis (the other twenty sections focus on elements of production), Heffner admonishes his student directors to respect the drama as the Word:

> The idea that a play is a mere script to stimulate the creative imaginations of theatre artists is an example of misguided egotism born of ignorance. The supreme art that has come out of the theatre is drama, a making with words, the creation of man in action by poets. Theatre reaches its highest artistry in the faithful interpretation of great plays.... Its misinterpretation can but make the judicious grieve. (Heffner et al. 1946, 27–28)

In a position that argues a worshipful respect for the text, Heffner illustrates an intellectual stance in which knowledge is transmitted as a one-way exchange. I use Heffner's book as a beginning, not because students studying the Introduction to Theatre were necessarily exposed to it, but because it marks an intellectual center that radically changes as the century progresses.

The first text entitled *An Introduction to the Theatre* appeared in 1954 by Frank M. Whiting (Whiting 1954). Although the table of contents would suggest a focus on practitioners with parts titled according to the various professions (plays and playwrights, directing and acting, architects, designers and technicians, and professional work in theatre), a closer examination reveals that each section includes a history of the specialization. The text, therefore, is at least 50 percent history with a minimum of photos, but clearly representative of a liberal arts approach to the study of theatre. It assumes an audience that seeks information beyond the scope of theatrical training and represents the interest in liberal education that was dominant at the time the book was published. What is particularly noteworthy is that the material contained within each chapter is quite comprehensive in its treatment of both history and the elements of art, but the style of presentation, with a rare photo among the pages of uninterrupted text, is almost scientific. Nothing about the text is designed to attract the uninitiated to the field.

In 1964 Brockett published *The Introduction to Theatre* (Brockett 1964). Of the over 600 pages of text, 10 percent is dedicated to art, audiences, and the play text, 24 percent to the roles of the artists, and the remaining 66 percent to the development of theatre throughout history. Illustrating a liberal arts base to curriculum through the study of historical context, the text provided a model that authors of introductory texts appear to have either adopted or reacted to for the rest of the century.

A sampling of textbooks on Introduction to Theatre between 1976 and 2001 falls into three groupings: the first group introduces performance and text (audience, artist, critic, play script), with the rest of the material divided in various configurations between history and production; the second group focuses more on dramatic literature integrating history and production with the examination of plays and playwrights; the third grouping focuses almost exclusively on production with a sprinkling of history and dramatic literature throughout. As the various texts have gone into multiple editions, the glossiness of printing quality has increased, as have the number of high quality photographs as well as inserts and boxes throughout that provide summaries of information. Some of the more recent books are accompanied by handbooks of guidelines on how to both read and see a play. While the original division of information along the lines of history, dramatic literature, and production still seem to be in place, the approaches used have radically changed. In addition, a fourth focus has emerged since 1998 that is based mostly on play texts with a slant that appears to have an anthropological basis with an obvious influence from developments in performance studies.

The first group, those organized with a major historical component, include George Kernodle, Portia Kernodle and Edward Pixley, *Invitation to Theatre* (Kernodle et al. 1971), Oscar Brockett, *The Essential Theatre* (Brockett 1976), Kenneth Cameron and Patti Gillespie, *The Enjoyment of Theatre* (Cameron and Gillespie 1980), and Robert Cohen, *Theatre* (Cohen 1981). Each varies depending on its apparently different target audience.

Kernodle, Kernodle, and Pixley have organized their content as "The Audience, The Play in its Time, and The Play in Production." Written for the "theatre novice to appreciate a wide variety of theatre genres while discovering the links that connect theatre of the past to those of our time," the writers have combined literature and history in what amounts to a history of genre in such categories as the "Theatre of Exaltation (Greek tragedy, medieval drama to modern tragedy), and the Theatre of Laughter (farce and high comedy)" (Kernodle et al. 1971, viii–ix). Simplifying the complex, the categories are easy to remember and the writing style is easy to read.

Brockett's text is a condensed version of his earlier introductory text with the added features of summary boxes on plays and artists and inserts of glossy colored photographs. As with the other texts in this grouping, *The Essential Theatre* contains an introduction to art, audience, and play script, with its two major divisions between a straightforward history and the elements of production. In a style characteristic of Brockett, the writing is dense and rich, rendering the book more of an introductory history text than one for novices in theatre.

By contrast, Cameron and Gillespie (1980) have experimented with their approaches throughout the five editions of *The Enjoyment of Theatre*.[5] The first edition opened with a section that has been sustained throughout, "Theatre as Art" (in later editions to "Theatre as Performing Art") comparing theatre in its social milieu with other performance forms. While the remainder of the text is divided among play analysis, history, and production, the earlier version rearranged history, beginning with the contemporary period and working backwards with the practitioners as the last section in the text. In the later editions, this rearrangement has been undone so that the practitioners are presented first and then history proceeds in chronological fashion. What is interesting about this experimentation in format is that the authors were apparently arranging history in a manner that would cause students to engage with it; their concern with student receptivity was paramount, therefore, to their pedagogical choices.

In similar fashion, Robert Cohen has produced two texts: *Theatre* (Cohen 1981), and *Theatre, Brief Version* (Cohen 1981). *Theatre* follows much the model of the other books in this grouping with a large portion of the text devoted to history interspersed with plays and critical comment throughout. The smallest section of *Theatre* focuses on practitioners, but Cohen compensates with his second text by removing history all together. *Theatre, Brief Version* belongs in the third grouping of texts that focus on production and is an obvious effort to appeal to a different kind of reading public.

The text that diverts from the historical approach to the teaching of Introduction to Theatre is Edwin Wilson's *The Theatre Experience* (Wilson

1976). As evident from its many editions, the text has been received well, partially, perhaps, because it offers a structure different from any of the others; it focuses on integrating plays and theatrical production without the chronological presentation of history. Wilson, with Alvin Goldfarb, has also written a history text, *The Living Theater* (Wilson and Goldfarb 1983) as well as an anthology of plays (Wilson and Goldfarb 1998) which may be used to supplement Wilson's introductory text. The most recent edition of *The Theater Experience* contains photos on almost every page and chapter references to web sources. While the content is substantial, the approach is clearly audience-centered, with images that change quickly and boxes of data that are easy to read. The text, therefore, is designed to appeal to the general audience member, the paying public, or the non-major in the university environment.

The third grouping of introductory to theatre texts are designed to engage the novice in the excitement of theatre. Books in this category abound, but some samples include Cohen's *Theatre, Brief Version*, Jeffrey H. Huberman, James Ludwig, and Brant L. Pope, *The Theatrical Imagination* (Huberman et al. 1997), Stephen M. Archer, Cynthia Gendrich, and Woodrow B. Hood, *Theatre: Its Art and Craft* (Archer et al. 1999), and Tom Markus and Linda Sarver, *Another Opening, Another Show* (Markus and Sarver 2001). All of the texts center on production, with variation in the target audiences. Cohen's *Theatre, Brief Version* brings an academic approach to the material, with significant attention to contemporary playwrights and directors as wide-ranging in scope as August Wilson and Ariane Mnouchkine. *The Theatrical Imagination* is appropriately organized according to artistic imagination and choices: the artists, the consumer, the playwright, the directors, the actors, and the designers. Integrating brief references to dramatic literature and history, the text is particularly concerned with the processes of creativity. *Theatre: Its Art and Craft* fulfills what its title promises as each theatre practitioner is considered in turn. The last text, *Another Opening, Another Show* is obviously written either for the young or the inexperienced, but contains some of the clearest explanations available of classical categories such as style and genre. While the book is unpretentious, complex ideas are made accessible to unsophisticated audiences.

The final text stands as a transitional piece away from the groupings divided according to the traditional categories of history, dramatic literature, and production, as it reflects models of learning emerging from performance studies programs. Stephanie Arnold's *The Creative Spirit* (Arnold 1998) "proposes that theatre results from a matrix of diverse social negotiations" that ultimately build community (Kuftinec and Underiner 2000). Beginning with a consideration of the impulse to perform "personal performance, community performance, and professional performance" (Arnold 1998, viii) and following with drama (several full-length multicultural plays), style, and history, Arnold puts the general reader at the center of the discussion by beginning with performances practiced in every day life.

Beginning in 1954 with Whiting and ending in 2001 with Arnold, the textbooks introducing theatre have transformed from a scientific-like presentation of facts to glossy, photo laden invitations to participate. As student populations have become major consumers at universities with tuition fees unimaginable in the 1950s, the materials for these courses reflect a purpose unknown in prior generations: to educate through seduction. The beauty of the textbooks alone attests to the need to attract; with the emphasis in learning shifting from an established body of knowledge, which only the experts know, to each reader, listener and participant in the learning situation as "knower," the mandate of the course is to teach and to please.

All Things to All People

Two conferences serve as signposts for where Introduction to Theatre is going as the twentieth century turns. Not a comprehensive survey of conferences, but rather an examination of two case studies, I assess what questions teachers of Introduction to Theatre are asking and what answers they are finding. Practical solutions to complex pedagogical problems are represented, not as prescription for what should be done in a variety of teaching situations, but as examples of how creative faculty are expanding the boundaries imposed on them so that students may discover that theatre can enliven both their academic learning and their personal development.

At the 1999 National Communication Association (NCA) Convention in Chicago, Gail Medford chaired a panel entitled, "Squaring the Circle in the Introduction to Theatre Course: Sharing Innovative Ideas in Teaching." Likewise, at the 2000 American Society for Theatre Research (ASTR) Conference in New York, Brett Crawford and I co-chaired a seminar, "Teaching Introduction to Theatre: All Things to All People." The two events differed in format in that the NCA program was a panel in which four presenters spoke and a respondent answered. At ASTR, the format was that of a seminar in which 12 presenters discussed papers that had been read by all presenters beforehand and were available as abstracts for the attendees on site.

At NCA, techniques for expanding the breadth of Introduction to Theatre were introduced. Michael O'Hara described how "Technology Enters Introduction to Theatre" through web pages and email exchanges he society" and foster connections between the performance of popular culture and performances in their own lives (Dennett 2000).

Third, concern about the *function* of the course considers its role within the university structure; supporting theatre departments through large enrollments, the course also serves as a training ground for teaching assistants,[6] in some cases as many as ten a semester. A sore point for many of the participants, Ken Cerniglia questioned managerial and status issues in the administration of the course, first, because of blatant attempts to market "the field to a vast and diverse group of non-majors," and second, because the withdrawal of senior professors from the class creates the mentality that the person with least seniority "gets stuck" with teaching 250–300 students rather than the maximum of 35 in other classes (Cerniglia 2000). By contrast, Sonja Kuftinec and Tamara Underiner reclaim community in the 500 student format at the University of Minnesota by incorporating active learning strategies and by significantly increasing the role of the section instructors so as to create pedagogical communities among their teaching assistants (Kuftinec and Underiner 2000).

Fourth, *community* formation undergirds the majority of the presentations in this panel, and its importance is the focus of several. Susan Applebaum positions her students as tellers and receivers of story, believing that "students become engaged in community...only by getting physically, intellectually, and emotionally in theatrical process." Describing contemporary theatre as an "explosion of new practices and mixed forms...why would we make the choice within the academy to remain stranded on the shoals of traditional boundaries through the transmission of knowledge through standard lectures to large classes of disconnected students?" (Applebaum 2000). Student engagement is critical to her methodologies.

Lastly, all members of the panel acknowledged the many advantages to mastering new *technologies* in their teaching. Leslie Pasternack proposed using the Internet "as an *illustration* of theatrical performance rather than the *antithesis* of theatre" by presenting the web site as a playing area for live performances. She further elaborated on the use of list serves, web site links, and multimedia collaboration within fine arts departments as a means of paradoxically connecting students to liveness through the use of virtual realities (Pasternak 2000).

The panel "All Things to All People" concluded with the recognition on the part of most participants that, in fact, it is impossible to be all things to all people. The paradoxical trends, however, represented by the move from text to performance, from live to virtual realities, and from delivered to performed lectures reflects a final explosion of the spark begun with the multi-purpose course in the 1970s. That the courses are filled with numbers

of students in the thousands nationally, and that committed theatre faculty
are exploring the boundaries of culture to engage their students is a promis-
ing commentary on the field and its junior faculty. Recognizing that teaching
Introduction to Theatre is in itself a specialization, a new community of
re-energized faculty emerged at the conclusion of the seminar.

Concluding Observations

In surveying the teaching of Introduction to Theatre in the United States
from 1936 to 2001, several trends emerge: first, the course was a scale for
balancing liberal arts education and professional training at the university
level with the weight shifting from one side to the other in different decades;
second, as audiences to the public theatre waned, the course expanded in
importance so as to attract audiences to university productions and potentially attract majors and future practitioners to the field; third, "multi"
became the key prefix for the design of the courses (multi-purpose, multi-
media, multi-realities) as diverse ways of knowing were recognized; fourth,
with the consumerism of the 1980s, the rising costs of higher education, and
with its legitimacy as an established humanities course in the core curriculum of most major universities, Introduction to Theatre became subject to
the will of the public, a surrogate for contemporary theatre in the educational
situation—an audience pleaser.

In the current cultural context, another development in the Introduction
to Theatre course has emerged. With the increased competitiveness of graduate
programs in theatre and performance studies in the United States, a new wave
of educators has entered the scene who both as junior faculty and doctoral students at major universities[7] are embracing the course as a place to practice
their own theories on the value of interactive classrooms. Through the application of ideas of thinkers such as Victor Turner[8] (1982), Jürgen Habermas[9]
(1984), and Augusto Boal[10] (1979) faculty are theorizing their teaching by
turning their classes into self-conscious communities that contradict both the
consumer mentality and the corporate model overtaking universities. In curricula that broaden the base to what is considered a liberal arts education,
young[11] theatre faculty are developing courses in which "students and their
experience, rather than the contents of a syllabus, are brought to form." They
are seeking to hear student voices, to inspire student projects, and to encourage student performance regardless of the size of their classes or the indifference of the social milieu, drawing on an eclecticism that recognizes the
"inherited practices of known cultures... multi-media and electronic drama-
tizations" (Berkeley 1998, 206), amateur improvisations, and dramas that

solve social problems. Understanding that upcoming student populations have their own way of knowing, innovative faculty bring them into the world of the play by playing in their world *while* teaching them dramatic literature, theatre history, theatrical practices, and the importance of performance in their daily lives. Not all things to all people—but enough to many to regenerate theatre departments and create communities that extend beyond the classroom into the public arenas of professional theatres, educational institutions, and even politics. Would that Plato could see us now.[12]

Notes

1. In the impersonal teaching environment of the large lecture hall, students of the Introduction to Theatre course are sometimes misinformed about the proper decorum required in play attendance and show up at theatres in athletic clothes or baseball caps. Their ignorance provokes disdain from theatre majors, usually operating the front of house. When a fire drill occurred just before an intro exam at the University of Maryland in 1996, a senior faculty member commented to the lecturer, "Well, of course it's one of your students."
2. Not all departments are guilty of this kind of benign neglect. The department of theatre at the University of Vermont, for example, provides full support from both administration and faculty to the Introduction to Theatre course.
3. The faculty member in question was an expert at teaching large lecture classes, and, in fact, was extremely popular with the student body. He was unable or unwilling, however, to transfer his expertise to the lecturer and graduate students assigned to the Introduction to Theatre course.
4. The Title of a panel I co-chaired with Brett Crawford at the American Society of Theatre Research (ASTR) Conference, "Method and Discipline: Current Practices in Theatre Studies," New York, November 9–12, 2000.
5. In 2003 a 6th edition was published, which included an instructional DVD.
6. Ken Cerniglia notes that at the University of Washington, enrollments of 250 students in ten sections are being encouraged to double within a year.
7. Participants on the two panels included representatives from two of the first universities to establish Introduction to Theatre courses in their curriculums, the University of Minnesota and the University of Washington, as well as those from programs of national reputation, Northwestern, the University of Maryland and the University of Texas at Austin.
8. Victor Turner is the source for the concept of communitás as I have used it in much of my teaching of Introduction to Theatre which loosely speaking is the building of community.
9. Jürgen Habermas notes that cultural modernity begins with the collapse of a unified world view.

10. Augusto Boal, argues for theatre for social change that creates actors out of spectators.

11. Young in the sense of up-to-date, experimental, as yet optimistic, rather than in terms of age. They are often what students refer to as "cool" because they understand youth cultures including their music, television shows, movies, and web sites.

12. As we all know, Plato had little regard for actors, believing that "when any of these pantomimic gentlemen, who are so clever that they can imitate anything, comes to us, and makes a proposal to exhibit himself and his poetry, we will fall down and worship him as a sweet and holy and wonderful being; but we must also inform him that in our State, such as he are not permitted to exist...we shall send him away to another city." *The Republic* in Dukore.

Works Cited

Amirahmadi, Hooshang. 1990. Emerging trends and the quest for universalism in planning education and research: Toward an interactive pedagogy. Rutgers University: Working Papers at the Center for Urban Policy.

Applebaum, Susan. 2000. Community, collaboration, and story: One approach. Seminar. All things to all people: Teaching Introduction to Theatre. American Society of Theatre Research Conference.

Archer, Stephen M., Cynthia M., Gendrich, and Woodrow B. Hood. 1999. *Theatre: Its art and craft*. San Diego: Collegiate Press.

Arnold, Stephanie. 1998 [2001]. *The Creative Spirit*. Mountain View, CA: Mayfield.

Barnette, Jane. 2000. Not just what Jane says: The intro class as community. Seminar. All things to all people: Teaching Introduction to Theatre. American Society of Theatre Research Conference.

Beckerman, Bernard. 1971. The university accepts the theatre: 1800–1925. In Henry B. Williams (ed.), *The American theatre: A sum of its parts*. New York: Samuel French.

Berkeley, Anne. 1998. Toward a critical aesthetic praxis: Theorizing undergraduate theatre curriculum for a culturally diverse democracy. Ph.D. dissertation, University of Maryland, College Park.

Boal, Augusto. 1979. *Theatre of the oppressed*. New York: Urizen Press.

Brell, Carl. 1991. Reconciling dichotomies in higher education: Theoretical and practical implications of an interactive educational conception. Thesis, University of Massachusetts, Amherst.

Brockett, Oscar. 1976. The humanities: Theatre history. *The Southern Speech Communication Journal* 41: 143–148.

———. 1976 [1980, 1984, 1988, 1992, 1996, 2000] *The essential theatre*. Fort Worth: Harcourt Brace.

———. 1964 [1969, 1974]. *The theatre: An introduction*. New York: Holt, Rinehart and Winston.

Cameron, Kenneth and Patti Gillespie. 1980 [1989, 1992, 1996, 2000]. *The enjoyment of theatre*. New York: Macmillan and Needham Heights, MA: Allyn and Bacon.

Carlyon, David. 1998. Theater is action: Teaching a task oriented intro class. *Theatre Topics* 8, 1: 1–12.

Cerniglia, Ken. 2000. Taming the beast: Drama 101 at the University of Washington. Seminar. All things to all people: Teaching Introduction to Theatre. American Society of Theatre Research Conference.

Cohen, Robert. 1981 [1988, 1994, 1997]. *Theatre*. Mountain View, CA: Mayfield.

———. 1981 [1988, 1994, 1997, 2000]. *Theatre, brief version*. Mountain View, CA: Mayfield.

Cosdon, Mark. 2000. Teaching Intro: Frustrations of a first-time professor. Seminar. All things to all people: Teaching Introduction to Theatre. American Society of Theatre Research Conference.

Crawford, Brett and Lynne Greeley. 2000. Seminar. All things to all people: Teaching the Introduction to Theatre. American Society of Theatre Research Conference.

Davis, David. 1997. *Interactive research in drama in education*. Straffordshire, England: Trentham Books.

Dennett, Andrea Stulman. 2000. Pedagogy, performance studies and theatre: From wrestling and ritual to popular culture. Seminar. All things to all people: Teaching Introduction to Theatre. American Society of Theatre Research Conference.

Fliotsos, Anne L. 1997. Teaching the unteachable: Directing pedagogy in colleges and universities of the United States, 1920–1990. Ph.D. dissertation, University of Maryland, College Park.

Freud, Ralph. 1946. Unpublished letter or report. New York Public Library.

Gagnon, Pauline. 1998. Acting integrative: Interdisciplinarity and theatre pedagogy. *Theatre Topics* 8, 2: 189–204.

Geltner, Jr., Frank Joseph. 1980. Standards and accreditation for Theatre Arts Programs in American higher education: A history and analysis. Ph.D. dissertation, University of Oregon.

Gillespie, Patti. 1973. Drama and western culture: A strategy for organizing a multi-purpose course. *Speech Teacher* 22: 147–153.

Habermas, Jürgen. 1984. *The theory of communicative action, volume I. Reason and the rationalization of society*. Trans. Thomas McCarthy. Boston: Beacon.

Heffner, Hubert, Samuel Selden, Hunton D. Sellman, and Fairfax W. Walkup. 1935 [1939, 1946, 1959, 1963, 1967, 1973]. *Modern theatre practice*. New York: Appleton-Century-Crofts and Meredith.

Hobgood, Burnet. 1964. Theatre in U.S. higher education: Emerging patterns and problems. *Educational Theatre Journal* 16: 150–158.

Huberman, Jeffrey H., James Ludwig, and Brant L. Pope. 1997. *The theatrical imagination*. Fort Worth: Harcourt Brace.

Ignatieva, Maria. 2000. Aristotle and pretty woman. Seminar. All things to all people: Teaching Introduction to Theatre. American Society of Theatre Research Conference.

Jackson, Tony and Chrissie Poulter. 1995. Learning through theatre: New perspectives on theatre and education. *Theatre Research International* 20, no. 2: 179.

Kernodle, George, Portia Kernodle, and Edward Pixley. 1971 [1978, 1985]. *Invitation to theatre.* San Diego: Harcourt Brace Jovanovich.

Koger, Kae. 1994. Teaching Introduction to Theatre today. *Theatre Topics* 4, no. 1: 59–63.

Kuftinec, Sonja and Tamara Underiner. 2000. Introducing theatre in a different way: A view from the University of Minnesota. Seminar. All things to all people: Teaching Introduction to Theatre. American Society of Theatre Research Conference.

Lippman, Monroe. 1946. Letter to College Curriculum Study Subcommittee. Theatre Collection. New York Public Library.

Large classes: A teaching guide. 1996. Center for Teaching Excellence. Office of Undergraduate Studies. University of Maryland at College Park.

Markus, Tom and Linda Sarver. 2001. *Another opening, another show: A lively introduction to theatre.* Mountain View, CA: Mayfield.

McGrath, Earl J. 1959. *The graduate school and the decline of liberal education.* Teachers College, Columbia University. Institute of Higher Education, Bureau of Publications.

Nathans, Heather. 2000. What's this got to do with theatre: Intro and the public sphere. Seminar. All things to all people: Teaching Introduction to Theatre. American Society of Theatre Research Conference.

O'Hara, Michael. 1999. Technology enters the introduction to theatre. Panel. Squaring the circle in the Introduction to Theatre course: Sharing innovative ideas in teaching. National Communication Association Conference.

Orr, Shelley. 2000. Reading and writing about theatre: Teaching critical thinking tools. Seminar. All things to all people: Teaching Introduction to Theatre. American Society of Theatre Research Conference.

Pasternack, Leslie. 2000. Web spectatorship: Teaching theatre studies online without losing the live. Seminar. All things to all people: Teaching Introduction to Theatre. American Society of Theatre Research Conference.

Plato, *The Republic* in Bernard Dukore. 1974. *Dramatic theory and criticism, Greeks to Grotowski.* New York: Holt, Rinehart and Winston.

Pollack, Thomas C. 1941. The function of instruction in dramatics in a teaching-training program. *Quarterly Journal of Speech* 27: 2–22.

Reports of College and University Work-Project Committee. 1948. AETA Reports.

Report of Subcommittee on College Curriculum Study. 1949. AETA Reports.

Riddell, Richard. 2000. Introducing students to a balance between theater study and practice. Seminar. All things to all people: Teaching Introduction to Theatre. American Society of Theatre Research Conference.

Smith, Donald K. 1954. Origin and development of Departments of Speech. In Karl R. Wallace (ed.), *History of education in America.* New York: Appleton-Century-Crofts, 178–194.

Spiller, Robert E. 1927. Drama and the liberal arts. *Quarterly Journal of Speech Education* 13: 398–412.

Turner, Victor. 1982. *From ritual to theatre.* New York: PAJ Publications.

Moreover, theatre departments have agreed to disagree about various theories of educating designers. Some offer B.F.A degrees with specialization at the undergraduate level while others believe that design education should only be started at the graduate level after a well-rounded liberal arts grounding. Professors disagree about whether or not creativity can be taught. They differ in the aesthetics they teach, from favoring the realistic kitchen sink set to stressing the more abstract designs found in Europe or to more flamboyant operatic design. It is no wonder that the way computer assisted design is taught also covers a spectrum of possibilities from little use of computers to instruction that is completely computer based. Much depends on how a department perceives its mission. Some believe their graduates will only design for theatre, others see students designing either for theatre, television, or film. At the extreme, is extensive computer training which prepares students for film animation and video games, predicting that the future lies outside of theatre.

I typed the first article on a five-year-old Osborne computer, a word processing workhorse which never broke down or gave error messages. The cursor was moved by keys rather than a mouse. There was no color nor were there design programs. Today I am writing on a Mac loaded with painting, 3D modeling, and photo programs, applications hardly dreamed of in 1989. With increasing frequency I find that my three-year-old computer lacks the connections or operating system to add new applications or equipment. Every few years I must consider yet another hardware upgrade. But then, the necessary software upgrades eat up even more memory. I often feel I have fallen behind with no hope of catching up.

Besides not being able to keep up with the equipment and programs, I find that each year, my students are more computer savvy and experienced than I am. Where once I knew a bit more than they did, they now teach me. So I make no claims to being a master teacher of computer use, or of anything else for that matter—my students would laugh at that. What authority I do have is based on longevity, standing on a vantage point which permits me to look back on nearly 40 years of professional and academic work and at the same time consider the future while I am still *compos mentis.*

In the beginning was the brush and pencil. For hundreds of years, from the Renaissance to the 1960s, design ideas were communicated by two-dimensional drawings. For 30 years, from the 1960s to the 1990s, model making became popular. Now we are in the age of the computer, a time when changes seem to happen by the minute. Keeping up and learning new techniques can be a full time job. It was not always so.

The insightful A. S. Byatt sums it up in *Babel Tower*: "Anyone's idea of teaching and learning...comes from his own experience of being taught" (1996, 142). That was true for me when I started to teach. As graduate students my colleagues and I presented a watercolor sketch and ground plan or a number of costume plates for a different play each week. At the end of three years, we had struggled with a variety of design problems in nearly 75 plays, operas, and musicals. Although we did not completely solve many of these problems, we realized later in our professional work that we had a leg up. We knew how to deal with new problems by relating them to similar examples we had studied. Specialization was not emphasized because the union, the United Scenic Artists, was not yet divided into categories; we were examined in set, lighting and costume design as well as scene painting.

As for drafting, make-up, and technical production, we were expected to learn this on our own through experience. With neither Xerox machines nor calculators, we did a lot of tracing and adding up dimensions by simple arithmetic. We rarely made models except for rough ones to check sightlines or study difficult shapes. Lighting templates had not become ubiquitous; we cut our own out of flimsy plastic. I still have my antique yellowed quarter-and-half inch templates.

In those days, professional theatre was not scattered throughout the country. Productions started in New York, so most of us gravitated to the city. It was the time of piano box resistant dimmer boards run by five or six electricians exiled to a basement, where ghost lamps burned to equalize the wattage capacity of each dimmer. Peggy Clark used about two hundred instruments and twelve strip lights to light a major musical, *Wonderful Town* (Rubin and Watson 1954, 18–19). In this less complicated and more leisurely time, there was no need to reinvent a way of teaching design. When I started teaching, the only adjustments I had to make involved teaching undergraduates rather than graduate students.

The arrow of time in design is not strictly one directional. Ironic swings of the pendulum occur. Big musicals today have many times the instruments Peggy Clark used, primarily because computers can keep track of them. But interestingly, computers are also responsible for the advent of moving and color changing lights so the numbers of instruments are starting to drop. Maybe soon there will be even fewer than 200 on a musical. Although we predicted that computers would eliminate jobs, manpower has not been reduced. As productions become more complex, with computers running lifts, turntables, winches, and wagons, with mics and sound systems to control, and with massive scene shifts, each show employs at least as many, and maybe more, stage hands, electricians, wardrobe, and prop people (Pogrebin 1998, 5).

We also do a convoluted dance in education. When universities had computer-controlled dimmers before professional theatres, we debated whether or not to resuscitate piano boxes so that students could gain experience with the equipment they would use after graduation. Today, while universities are at the forefront of computer design, most campuses can not afford the range of the equipment that computers control in professional productions. Educational institutions have always claimed that the productions they mount are laboratories for classroom work, the equivalent of science labs. But technologically, our budgets put students in "science labs" with only salt, pepper, sugar, and a Bunsen burner for experiments.

As a teacher, I view budget constraints as a minor consideration compared to the aesthetic paradigm shifts created by computer design. Tossed about in a roiling sea of rapid change, we have little idea of the end result. However, we do know that major changes come with trade offs. The shift from sketches to models is an example. Looking back, it seems only natural that, as productions moved out and around the proscenium, becoming more three-dimensional, the means of demonstrating a design idea also became three-dimensional. The trade off came, first of all, because building a model took more time than painting a sketch, thus reducing the number of different design assignments each term. Consequently, students confronted far fewer problems during the course of a degree program. Second, students became agile at manipulating the materials to make models but they seemed to lose their facility for painting and drawing. Third, they have increasingly been unable to understand perspective.

Enter the computer and the big question: Will students ever again have to draw and paint or know perspective? My students answer this question in various ways. Some tell me that they want to learn to draft by hand in preparation for those times when computers crash. Others say in using a pencil they have a better feeling for the aesthetics of a drawing, line weights, and placement. One student told me that she feels her spirit moves through her hand to the paper when she is drawing with a pencil.

I am not sanguine about the future of pencils, T-squares, and triangles. Surely there was a time when artists must have claimed that grinding their own pigments was far superior to those new fangled tubes of paint. All of my colleagues, save one, agree that for the novice, the hand is better than the mouse. The one dissenter may well be right.

I conned my university into providing me with a laptop computer, a painting program and a digitizing tablet when they first became available. We wanted to see if students using a computer could learn to draw and paint from nature. They would take this equipment anywhere they could take a sketch book. As with all the best-laid plans, this one showed its drawbacks from the start. In the beautiful light of out of doors, the laptop screen was barely readable; when it was, the colors produced had no relation to what was seen or what the student intended. We considered concocting a black cloth with two eyeholes, but hiding the student inside a dark tent did not seem a comfortable alternative.

Indoors, students were fascinated by the painting program, particularly the variety of media which could be called up by a tap of the stylus. Without buying expensive art materials, students could play with paper colors and textures, as well as combining watercolor, chalk, markers and airbrush. They could erase without leaving marks, manipulate values and hues, and change sizes. Interest in the program waned as students got their own computers, more sophisticated programs, scanners and PhotoShop.

At the time of our first experiments, we used the first digital camera to put figures into the painting program. The idea was to take photos of each actor and then paint costumes onto their bodies, allowing complete accuracy and realism of body shapes and sizes. One student designed a wedding dress for a friend using this method. But this technique has also lost favor now that Poser and scanners are available.

Computers still present many drawbacks for producing designs. One draws on a tablet but the image appears on a screen. The size of a design is limited by the printer. The designer's "spirit" doesn't flow through the equipment, as my student would wish. Moreover, the cost of buying and keeping up with the new hardware and software is daunting to many students—and professors.

I can see a time when all these problems will be eliminated. Already, the technology exists to overcome most of the objections, albeit for a price. Students may soon draw and paint directly on a screen of almost any convenient size. Printers will approach the size of plotters. Prices will continue to fall, making computers so ubiquitous that students will no longer even question the efficacy of using them. The transfer of "spirit" to paper may no longer be a consideration.

More is to come. Model making will be accomplished by either a computer-operated laser carver or a three-dimensional printer. Both are now available, but at prices that may equal the yearly production budget of a small school. But maybe a virtual walk through will make models obsolete. Likewise, computers will take costumes from the sketch to the cut cloth; computer controlled lights will be pre-programmed at the designer's studio. What is your desire? It's on its way.

The fly in the ointment is that each of these wonderful techniques requires learning a new language, a new code which is distanced from the substance of the end product, as we have known it. While we have been fond of referring to theatre as the last of the hand made enterprises, we have one foot over the threshold of a machine-made world. As is often said, each new technological advance distances us from our humanity. In theatre design, as with all else, a new language is able to express some things better while other messages suffer. Therefore, what suffers in our brave new world is the aesthetic of the hand-made, the unique. In other words, as we enter an age of computer design, we also embarque on a new aesthetic just as surely as aesthetics changed when models replaced sketches, when electric lights replaced gas, and gas replaced candles.

Humans tend to use new technology because they can, sometimes to the detriment of a desired result. Now that we mic musicals, singer/actors can no longer do without amplification. The direct personal contact between the audience and the cast of a musical has been interrupted by a wall of wires and dials, with both equipment and an operator interceding. The end product is a sound which may or may not be close to the actor's voice, or even produced by the actor at the time. As technology separates us from what is human, the availability of computer-controlled mechanics has permitted spectacular effects; does it matter that few have meaning. I know, audiences love these spectaculars about scenery, lighting, and costumes. It's just that for me, theatre has always been about the human condition, not hydraulics and limit switches.

My design students have a spectrum of opinions about the new technology in this era that straddles the formation of a new paradigm. Some students are reluctant to use computers; others find it impossible to do without them; a middle group is selective in how and when they turn to a computer. Any and all of these methods are acceptable to me if the end result works. Insisting on one or another process would be foolish when we don't know where we are going. Moreover, I have seen many a professional go from swearing they would never use a computer to depending on them. There are still some holdouts, but not many. And those professionals who do use computers, do so in different ways: drafting, scanning and manipulating pictures for models, producing painter's elevations. Some paint over printed images, some re-scale images. Even though I don't know of any, there may be professionals who use 3D modeling programs to render their sets. There certainly are academics who do. Adding to the confusion is the rapid availability of new programs. In the midst of this turmoil, pushing one or another method would be like shouting to a group of drowning students that they must only use the breaststroke.

Integrating computers into instructional programs is a challenge to teachers at all levels. In elementary schools, "keyboarding" may replace writing and calculators may make learning the multiplication tables unnecessary. In college, English essays can now be graded by computers as touted in a recent ad, "If you're smart, you've graded your last test" (Question Mark Co., 6).

Predictably, there is opposition to computers grading essays. A recent article starts, "It's time to put a stop to talk about new computer programs that can grade student's essays with less effort and more accuracy than any teacher could—and do so more cheaply and quickly, to boot. Such programs are neither necessary nor desirable" (Baron 1998, A56). Even computer experts find fault with how we are using computers and how they are using us. Donald Norman says the PC is neither personal nor used much for computing. "When I prowl the halls of my workplace, I often see people on their hands and knees beside their computers. No, not praying, but installing new things, rebooting, checking the cable connections, or just muttering under their breath.... Rather than being personal, friendly, and supportive, it [the computer] is massive, impersonal, abrupt and rude" (Norman 1998, B12).

Every new complicated technology—telephones, movies, airplanes—moves toward more and more reliability even as it increases in complexity. By being able to repair themselves, computers even contain the solution to being more reliable. And it is possible, though not often evident, to design programs which are simple, direct and friendly. My real concern is that computers are unlike other technologies which extend our abilities to accomplish tasks. Computers, as in the grading of essays, are becoming us, taking over tasks in ways which give us little control. So we watch with a kind of science fiction horror as our understanding of what it means to be human is eroded day by day. The titles of three new books, written by acknowledged scientists and reviewed seriously in the *New York Times*, tell the frightening story: "The Age of Spiritual Machines: When Computers Exceed Human Intelligence," "Robot: Mere Machine to Transcendent Mind," "When Things Start to Think" (McGinn 1999, 6).

What it means to be an artist is also in question. To quote a recent *New York Times* article:

The future of artwork is on the computer. You might not like what computers produce...but tomorrow's works are bound to be created digitally. On the plus side, children who learn to make art digitally can become old masters of the genre by the time they hit 10. (Leimbach 1998, D12)

Old masters indeed.

As I see it, the question is not if, but when. How soon will this paradigm shift be accomplished? How fast must teachers of design run just to keep up with the technology, the aesthetics, and, of course, the students? What part of the training from our old bag of tricks is still valid, and what part should be deracinated? Thinking about these questions, I sometimes feel as if I am being dragged by a speeding train. The train may or may not be going where I want to go; I can only predict the direction we are going by looking back and seeing what we have passed so far. Furthermore, being dragged is not my choice of locomotion.

My reactions to what I have seen in my own classes are mixed. Understandably, students also have mixed reactions depending on their skills. Those who can draw, paint, and make models are reluctant to abandon what they do well, while those who have problems with traditional methods of communicating, are becoming avid users of computers. Those designing sets are, generally, not using the paint/draw or modeling programs but are scanning images to manipulate. The results are sometimes wonderful. They can apply lighting effects, re-scale, scan in the most spectacular art work and photos, change colors and add or eliminate at will. The few students who have used the 3D modeling programs struggle with the complexities of the programs and take a long time to produce rather simple designs. Costume design students are also scanning images from historical research and then altering a few details, re-scaling and changing colors. Fewer seem to use the Poser program, possibly because it takes more time to move the figure than does scanning an image.

In evaluating student work, I try to find a consistent and logical philosophical platform on which to stand. If I wished, I could spend all my time learning and teaching the computer skills which would give students the very latest computer techniques. Instead, I believe that technical skill, while the easiest thing to teach, is not the most important thing that students need to learn or what I should be stressing. I want my students to see, because really seeing is knowing. I want my students to understand, because understanding a play and the psychology of its characters is the basis of true design. I want my students to be creative, because revealing worlds we have never imagined is the reason for the best theatrical design. I believe my students must tap into their personal visions to find styles that have unique voices. Do computers aid or hinder me in teaching these foundation requirements?

Computers are not yet the major reason why young people do not truly see the world. Hours spent peering into a TV screen came first. Computer use will only exacerbate the problem. My colleagues, including colleagues in disciplines other than theatre, complain about: our students' inability to see in three dimensions, their lack of understanding of the workings of the simplest objects which surround them, their difficulty sensing scale and proportion, and their frustration when asked to describe something by drawing it. Using a computer does not alleviate these problems—it adds to them by providing easy ends while ignoring the means to get there. One example might be a computer program which realistically shows how material drapes on a figure. As a learning tool it's a dud because the student has no more understanding of draping at the end of the process than at the beginning. To understand how fabrics drape, two old methods, together, work best: actually draping fabric, and draping fabric and drawing it. From seeing and knowing comes imaginative and innovative design. Applying what a computer program provides is slavery to what some programmer has chosen.

There was a reason for biology students to draw what they saw under a microscope or when dissecting a frog. There was a reason for young people taking the Grand Tour to make sketches of cathedrals. As my professor Josef Albers said, "If you really see it, you can draw it. . . . College students use their eyes all the time but they see nothing." His observations become truer as time passes. He would be dismissive of substituting contact with the real world for a menu of applied textures and shapes. As a way of knowing and seeing, he would have no problem choosing between reality and virtual reality.

Reviewing an art exhibit, Peter Schjeldahl wrote, "Painting is the medium of the need to see. It is the medium of the hand, which is the organic emblem of individuality and sincerity. When you paint, your hand distills matter from the rest of you—senses, brain, heart, guts, soul" (1998, 93). As an observation but not necessarily a criticism, he goes on to say that modern art was about process but not much about people. The same holds true for teaching computer design. It is a collage process, divorced from concerns of the heart and soul. It can help ten-year olds produce "masterpieces" but nothing that touches us deeply.

I often hear it said that computers are only a tool. As of now, this is not true. Tools are only useful when under our control. While I can imagine a time when we have passed through this transition to a new technology and can truly use computers as tools, we must presently struggle to master their complexities. As teachers of design, are we merely to teach how to control a machine or should we be teaching how to control the creation of a personal aesthetic statement? We must do both. The challenge is to find a suitable balance of our time, energy, and money.

The computer program I am using to write this corrects my spelling, which I need, and also suggests changes in style. If, over the years, I had not developed my own style, puny as it may be, I might be tempted to depend on the uniform and stiff usage of an anonymous programmer at Microsoft.

Isn't this analogous to sitting a director in front of a monitor screen showing a lit set, peopled by costumed figures who move through the space? I'm not sure that creative directors or actors would want their choices foreclosed any more than I want Microsoft to tell me how to write.

Contemplating my years as a teacher, I marvel at the acceleration of change. Neither with painting and drawing nor with model making did the techniques of visual presentation become obsolete the day after they were taught. Not so with computers. They are part of a rapid shift in the way we process information, not just in theatrical design, but in every segment of society. A provocative article in *Communication Arts* argues that we are entering a "visual age," when reading will become unnecessary. The falling literacy rate in our schools is a reaction to this phenomenon. The author, David Lance Goines, goes on to say that if we are honest with ourselves, we will see that most of the information we process from magazines, television and the internet comes from images rather than words, which makes illiteracy less of a problem than we think. But the article does not recommend abandoning reading, rather, it recommends a way of surviving in a swiftly changing environment. "When in the course of evolution it is time to bridge the technologies, or to make adaptations in an evolutionary sense, the adaptive strategy is always flexibility. The animals that can do both what has been and what is coming are most likely to survive" (Goines 1999, 16).

I am horrified by the idea of a post-literate society but agree that bridging technologies is a reasonable response to change. I believe that students should be computer literate but will become computer experts in ways and in programs of their own choosing. At the same time, I will continue to teach drawing and painting as the best means of training the eye and hand.

Perhaps my greatest concern is that in an age "When Things Start to Think," "When Computers Exceed Human Intelligence," the theatre will not stand in opposition to the de-humanization that the computer can represent. Will computers which exceed human intelligence have the capacity to feel love, friendship, jealousy, or pity? Will images be able to communicate complex concepts? Will the precision of words give way to the relativism of emotions? Will computers that think have personalities?

The computer work I have seen so far, even my own, is so slick, so perfect that it lacks personality. It has a machine made look. It is devoid of the individuality that allows us to recognize that we are communicating with another human. Teaching, for me, is nurturing individual talents. It has less to do with technique than with ideas, with seeing and with understanding. There are great designers who are not great draftsmen or painters. But there are no great designers without an "eye," who don't understand human character, or are without a strong personal vision. Teaching these intangibles has and will continue to be my priority and my greatest challenge.

Works Cited

Baron, Dennis. 1998. *The Chronicle of Higher Education* (November 20): A56.

Byatt, A. S. 1996. *Babel tower*. New York: Random House.

Goines, David Lance. 1999. Post-industrial post-literacy. *Communication Arts* (January/February): 16.

Liembach, Dulcie. 1998. *New York Times*, 12 Nov., D12.

McGinn, Colin. 1999. Hello Hal. *The New York Times Book Review*, 3 Jan., 6.

Norman, Donald A. 1998. *The invisible computer*. Cambridge: M.I.T. Press, quoted in *The Chronicle of Higher Education* (October 9): B12.

Pogrebin, Robin. 1998. Keeping *Titanic* dynamic. *New York Times*, 2 Oct., 5.

Question Mark Company. n.d. Advertisement. *T.H.E. Journal* (October): 6.

Rubin, Joel E. and Leland H. Watson. *Theatrical lighting practice*. New York: Theatre Arts Books, 1954.

Schjeldahl, Peter. 1998. Fairies welcome. *The New Yorker* (October 20): 93.

understanding and appreciation of content areas, many faculty still use "chalk and talk" in higher education. However, at the beginning of the new millennium, an increasing number of faculty use technology to manage classroom activities, assess student learning, or redesign learning activities beyond the traditional boundaries of the classroom. For some faculty, the jury is still out on the "new" technology and its reliability or usefulness. For others, they do not see any appreciable benefit to the use of IT as they meet with students face-to-face in studio situations or in regular classes. Students, on the other hand, seem to regard surfing the web as their constitutional right and cannot imagine a day without checking their e-mail for news from home or old high school friends.

Despite an apparent technology gap between students and faculty, both parties can benefit from the appropriate and considered use of IT in and out of the classroom. The positive impact of technology on learning in general and writing in particular has been well-documented (e.g., Milone 1996; Oblinger and Rush 1997; Somekh and Davis 1997; Sullivan and Porter 1997), but the impact of informational technologies on theatre pedagogy has not. We need only look at the ten-year index for *Theatre Topics* in 2001, our primary disciplinary outlet for articles on pedagogy, to note the paucity of work on technology and teaching. Indeed, with a few notable exceptions (e.g., Schrum 1999), theatre educators have been largely absent from studies on pedagogy and technology (e.g., Donlevy and Donlevy 1997; Nichols 1997; Kellner 1998), and few theater scholars participate in the national dialogue on the intersection of pedagogy and IT. Yet "technology" has been driving dramatic changes in theatre and performance since the introduction of electricity in the nineteenth century (Marranca 1996). Other forms of information technology, namely film and television, have influenced audiences, students, and artists for decades. Few, if any, of our graduates will go on to a career in live theatre as actors, but most will enter a world full of various forms of information technology in which they will need to be proficient.

Theatre departments are not usually perceived as technological leaders in academic communities, but this need not be the case. We use a great deal of technology in our theatre productions and, less so, in our teaching. Information technologies are a part of many design classes, especially at the graduate level, and most students and faculty use a word processing program to create papers, articles, and book chapters. IT has penetrated into the college experience so deeply that most of us find the daily contact with some sort of electronic device neither traumatic nor burdensome. We do not find similar penetration of IT into theatre classes. Some classes seem to use new information technologies more readily than others, but soon we are likely to face a world in which such use of IT, as was chalk, is pervasive and expected.

For some, the pressures to deliver instruction using new technologies have already wrought significant change. For example, a few but growing number of theatre departments like my own now offer regular, required classes in camera acting technique. Such classes not only satisfy a student's desire to be trained in camera acting but also can engage students and faculty in the pedagogical use of information technologies at a very sophisticated level. I will address such uses in more detail below, but my point is that technology, broadly construed, is arguably more important to the production and consumption of theatrical performances than ever before. I believe it is well past time, therefore, to focus attention on strategies that exploit technology in theatre pedagogy. Such a focus, however, may do more than give us new techniques to increase student learning or help build student appreciation. We may have to reassess what a theatre student is and what he or she studies.

Let me first, however, briefly situate IT within the literature of teaching and learning and summarize the major contributions to this dialogue by theatre educators. I will then examine how some instructors have used information technologies to solve specific pedagogical problems and to provide data that suggest the effects of those strategies. I conclude by assessing the potential impact of information technology within the discipline.

According to Kull and Halal (1999), a wave of unprecedented change, driven by recent advances in information technology, is causing a "technology revolution" whose effects are only beginning to be understood. Information technologies are catalysts of increasingly rapid change in how information in general, and education in particular, is delivered, understood, and consumed. The four informational technologies—computer hardware, computer software, communication systems, and information services—are changing the ways in which we share, create, and assess knowledge or content. Rapid advances in multimedia connectivity across all four IT categories allows individuals to accumulate, manipulate, and transmit increasingly complex content to ever-growing audiences, a factor that has both pedagogical and performative consequences.

Many scholars are trying to understand and assess the effects and possibilities of IT in pedagogy, and the opinions and conclusions concerning IT are neither uniform nor unequivocal. Some scholars (e.g., Oppenheimer 1997; Cuban 1986, 1993) believe that the hype far exceeds the promise. They point to past predictions, for example, that movies, radio, and computers would completely supplant teachers and textbooks. Others (e.g., Privateer 1999; Flowers et al. 2000; Girod and Cavanaugh 2001) contend that IT will fundamentally alter the face of teaching and learning in

American postsecondary education. They point to the dramatic increase in the accessibility to and adoption of IT by both faculty and students since the early 1990s. Despite many differences of opinion, most scholars agree that information technologies have at least altered the several important discourses—political, economic, and pedagogical—on the cost, means, and outcomes of postsecondary education.

Theatre scholars have also explored IT as such tools and capabilities intersect with theatre performance and training. The only substantial collection of such scholarship currently available is *Theatre in Cyberspace: Issues of Teaching, Acting, and Directing* (1999). Editor Stephen Schrum has assembled a collection of essays that surveys three conjunctions of theatre and IT: computers and theatre, computers and teaching, and computers and performance. The authors represent some of the earliest adopters of IT in theatre classrooms and performances. The first section, computers and theatre, suggests ways and reasons for theatrical educators and artists to actually use IT to make their administrative and artistic lives easier. The second, computers and teaching, offers three accounts of professors' use of various information technologies in their teaching. The third, computers and performance, explores performative applications of IT, namely the ATHE MOO and virtual reality. A MOO is a MUD (Multi-User Dimension) created with Object-Oriented programming. The result is a text-based environment in which users manipulate objects and their own "characters" in nearly infinite ways simply by typing at a keyboard. The authors explain and explore how the ATHE MOO was created and is used by performers, professors, and students. Several final articles examine how more complex technologies, most especially virtual reality, can be used with theatre, "the original three-dimensional interactive environment" (4). The book serves as an excellent introduction to the multiple uses of IT in theatre practice and training.

Both the four articles in *Theatre Topics* (e.g., Fliotsos 1995; McCoy 1995; Cummings 1998; Rustan 1998) and the three chapters on pedagogy in *Theatre in Cyberspace* are primarily "how-to" articles that introduce the use of technology in theatre education to fellow practitioners, many of whom are apparently reluctant technologists. Although I will also offer some practical suggestions and descriptions of the use of technology in theatre classes, I hope to model a scholarly approach to the use and assessment of technology in pedagogy that others in our discipline may build upon. Such an approach is important for several reasons. First, if we are to contribute to the national dialogue on technology and teaching, and perhaps to keep our place within the academy, we need to apply similar techniques to the scholarship of teaching as do many other disciplines that have well-established records of such scholarship, most notably the sciences (e.g., Mason and Verdel 2001). Second, the other disciplines will discover that we have much to contribute to this dialogue. As more distance learning is used and more courses are taught via IT (e.g., television, streaming media over the internet), questions about working in front of a camera, remote or present audiences, and balancing performative modes in different media with appropriate pedagogy will become important. Our acting teachers, for example, can uniquely contribute to that discussion. Finally, many faculty will find valuable outlets for such scholarship not only in *Theatre Topics*, but also journals such as *The Journal for Excellence in Teaching, The Teaching Professor*, and others. Our disciplinary voice should be heard at this level.

I first experimented with how specific pedagogical problems could be solved using technology in 1997, my first year at Ball State University (BSU). I began with placing my course syllabi, some handouts and lecture notes, and a brief Quicktime™ movie on a course Web site. The response from the students was overwhelmingly positive. I began to immediately track their attitudes and responses to my use of technology in pre- and post-tests and surveys that all students were required to take. In the fall of 1998, another faculty member at BSU searched our system servers for innovative users of Web sites and invited the 21 faculty he found to meet (Butler 2001a). At first, we simply demonstrated our use of IT to each other, but we progressed quickly to discussions about resources, tools, theoretical issues, and student reactions to our use of technology. After a few months, the group had shrunk to seven regular members and a few occasional attendees who were very interested in student learning and technology. Out of that group, I began working closely with Darrell Butler, Department of Psychological Sciences and University Computing Services, to develop a proctored, computer-based testing room (CBT) on campus for administering assessments (e.g., quizzes, tests, and surveys) to students.[1] After one pilot semester, the CBT was opened to the rest of the university community in the spring of 2000, and several faculty began collaboratively collecting data.

The CBT offered us several advantages. First, we were able to test students more frequently without sacrificing class time. Second, we could now experiment with various computer-based testing ideas. Third, we could harvest information from our students cheaply, quickly, and conveniently to assess their attitudes and success rates with our various experiments. Although some students grumbled at first, the data we collected over the past year and a half have yielded positive results.

I was particularly concerned with my students' learning experiences in the large lecture class, Introduction to Theatre.[2] Scholars such as Mason and

Verdel (2001) report that large classes are a cost-effective and efficient method for delivering instruction, one that is not likely to be replaced with a more effective method in the future. Most studies (e.g., Lindsay and Paton-Saltzberg 1987; Robertson and Ober 1997; Osborne et al. 2000) strongly suggest that the probability of student success is significantly lower in large classes than in smaller ones.

Most students take the introductory course in theatre to fulfill a requirement for a core curriculum or general studies program. Many such classes, therefore, are taught in large sections to particularly unmotivated students. Several smaller sections of the same class are offered at BSU, and the student success rate is higher in the smaller class, in concordance with the published literature. Given that the work was nearly identical in both classes, I wanted to study why students in the large classes were experiencing a lower level of learning. More importantly, given that a major goal for such a class, although often couched in the language of "life-long learning," is to encourage students to become future audience members, it seems foolish not to create as positive an experience as possible.

The surveys I have administered for the past three years suggest some patterns of behavior among my students. My results are unsurprising. First, many of my students have never been to a professional live theatre, and most have rarely attended live theatre of any kind. The language, history, and etiquette of live theatre are off-putting for many students. Many of them also assume, given the enormous number of hours most of them have spent watching film or television, that a theatre class is unlikely to teach them anything significant about performance. They think they understand actors and know what they like in a show and what they do not. Second, and perhaps related to the last point, my students report spending only about 8 hours per semester studying for my course, a figure that is fairly constant across freshman through seniors. Other studies at BSU have found that students report about 7 to 7.5 hours per class spent studying for exams or tests (e.g., Office of Academic Assessment 2000). Third, most students believed that the large class negatively affected their learning, making it even harder to stimulate student interest in theatre itself. Only 3 percent of my students agreed that they learned equally well in large or small classes, 47 percent reported better learning in small classes, 22 percent thought that they learned better in large classes, and 28 percent did not have an opinion. The problem I faced was how to encourage my students to spend more time studying, which would increase their learning, without my efforts appearing as an unreasonable burden on their time that they might come to resent. I still wanted my students to enjoy theatre, after all.

The literature suggests that one strategy to increase students' study time is to increase the number of scheduled exams (e.g., Turney 1931; Keys 1934; Pikunas and Mazzota 1965; Kika et al. 1992; Graham 1999). These studies show that students increased test scores between 7 percent and 12 percent when they were assessed more frequently. Students also improved on test scores when announced quizzes were used to prompt more productive study behavior. Graham (1999) shows a reliable 4 percent increase for such strategies, and Butler (2001b) suggests that lower success rate may be attributable to students' decision making, which may involve some kind of probability matching, that is, students try to guess when the next unannounced quiz will be given and study accordingly.

Butler and I believed that we would be able to use the computer-based testing lab to solve some of these problems. Out of class testing would not use up class time and would offer students considerable flexibility—they schedule when they wish to take exams or quizzes at their convenience. The CBT lab allowed us to administer a large number of tests without the additional costs of Scantron sheets or the staff necessary to feed the papers through a grading machine. Additionally, computer-based testing allowed us to use different types of test stimuli, such as recorded sound and still or moving images that are impossible to use with paper and pencil tests. Finally, the computer-based testing lab could give nearly instantaneous feedback to students and faculty, a feature that the students truly appreciated.

In order to harvest a rich data set, we assessed students in several different courses, including psychology, theatre, history, biology, and art. Several factors kept the variables constant throughout our data collection. The students were unaware of the pedagogical differences in the classes when they enrolled. An anonymous survey was created to assess students' attitudes about the testing environment and their learning. The same instructor had taught each course at the same time of day for the previous three years. The classes were similar in size (mean = 222) and had similar populations in regard to gender, high school rank, and SAT or ACT scores. All instructors were using the CBT but one. Among the professors using the CBT, some replaced their normal Scantron tests with electronic versions, some went from two or three exams to six or seven or more, and one even allowed students to take each test as many times as necessary to earn a satisfactory grade.

In my own class, I experimented with several different changes in my pedagogy based on the possibility of frequent testing. I use Cameron and Gillespie's *The Enjoyment of Theatre* (2000) as the primary text, and I had previously given three major exams and a writing assignment to assess student learning. I changed to eleven quizzes, three exams, a writing assignment, and a group project. The quizzes were designed to assess student learning on the textbook before I covered the topic in class. The students' performance on the quizzes suggested to me which concepts (or which of my own questions on the quiz) were confusing to them. I then adjusted my lectures and classroom learning activities to address those areas of weakness. One of my students called this method "just-in-time teaching," and I have come to adopt the term when I talk about what I am trying to accomplish.

The CBT lab had 24 450MHz Pentium II^{TM} computers, one of which was equipped with adaptations for students with disabilities. Each computer ran a severely restricted version of Windows NT^{TM} and browsers that were configured so that e-mail was limited to sending questions to the instructor. The multiple-choice tests were accessed on a web-based testing environment developed at BSU by Dan Fortriede and Vernon Draper, InQsit version 7.1. Faculty could create tests either by building a question pool in the InQsit system or by importing previously word-processed tests into the program. InQsit allows multiple test types and a user-friendly interface to manage question pools, record student scores, and analyze test items. Students access the system in the lab using their own e-mail account names and passwords and a proctor password that is shown only in the CBT lab. The password automatically changes every five minutes to minimize student access to materials outside of the proctored environment. <Complete documentation on InQsit is available on the World Wide Web at http://www.bsu.edu/inqsit/.>

Students using the CBT reserved a time to take assessments at their own convenience, usually over a two or three-day window, and were randomly assigned to computers within the room. A proctor with significant experience in University Computing Services monitored admission to the room, checking student IDs and reporting any suspicious activity directly to the instructor via e-mail. The proctor's verification screen also showed any special instructions given by the instructor for that assessment (e.g., the ability to use scratch paper) and gave the computer terminal assignment for each student. At the end of the semester, students who used the CBT lab were administered a survey in the lab, while the class that did not use the lab was given a paper version.

According to Butler (2001b), his class tested in the CBT facility scored higher on exams than did his previous students who were tested in-class. He conducted a between groups ANOVA and Sheffé tests and concluded that his students' test results for 1996, 1997, and 1998 were not significantly different from each other, but the 1999 results were significantly different. In my own class, similar results were obtained. As seen in figure 9.1, students did not significantly improve their scores on exams in the four semesters prior to

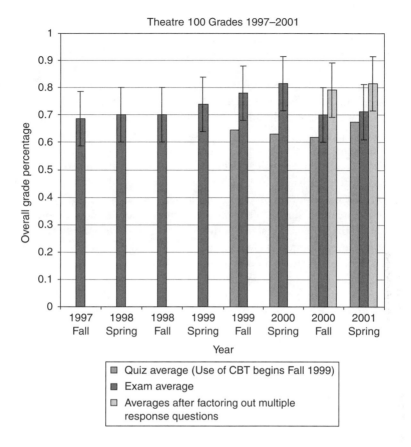

Figure 9.1 Student Grades for Introduction to Theatre from 1997 Through Spring 2001.

fall 1999, despite a variety of experiments in my teaching. The introduction of the quizzes and "just in time teaching," however, marked a significant increase in student performance on the same exams. In the fall of 2000, I added "multiple response" questions that asked students to identify one, some, or all of the possible choices as correct. These questions were significantly more difficult than traditional multiple choice or true and false questions, but when factored out of the results, students still showed remarkable improvement on exam scores over previous scores. More importantly, the exam scores showed significant improvement over their quiz scores, which suggested to me that more frequent testing was increasing their overall study time.

In general, most students improved their exam scores over the semester as they determined how to study for my tests, and the freshmen improved significantly more than the upper classmen. Figure 9.1 shows that in each fall semester, when at least half the class was entirely freshman, the scores on exams fell slightly. In 1998 BSU adopted a slightly more stringent admissions criteria, but our Office of Academic Assessment (2000) concluded that the effect of higher standards only predicts an overall academic improvement of between 3 percent to 4.5 percent. Because my data show an increase in scores on the exams well in excess of 4.5 percent, some of that improvement can be attributed to the pedagogical changes I instituted and some to the higher standards for admission. But, such a conclusion might be misleading as the older students admitted prior to the tougher standards apparently out perform the newer freshman. The reasons may have more to do with maturity, I suspect, than any other factor. Both groups, however, improved their scores over previous semesters suggesting that the "just in time teaching" method had a significant impact on their learning.

Students also reported positive attitudes about using the CBT facility. Only 4 percent of students reported preferring in-class testing at mid-semester. Furthermore, at the end of the semester, even after being forced to trudge across campus each time they were to take a test or quiz, only 10 percent reported preferring in-class testing. The students in the control class were less satisfied with the number of exams than those in the CBT lab and believed that they would have earned higher grades if there had been more exams. All students completed a 7-point preference scale asking them how much they liked the method of testing used. Students in the CBT preferred their method of testing (mean = 5.63 on 7 point scale) more than the control class preferred in-class testing (mean = 3.15 on 7 point scale). Students in the CBT environment also reported that they studied more often than in previous years. The mean for 106 respondents was 16 hours of study time for 11 quizzes and 3 exams, or a total of 14 assessments. Other classes in the study also reported increased study hours.

Although this study confounds using the CBT with more frequent testing, I believe that computer-based testing had less effect on student performance than the frequency of testing. Some students reported that they felt they had made fewer mistakes in the CBT, but no evidence suggests this was a factor. Because students could take an assessment over several days, they reported that they talked about the exams more frequently. Some of this communication was, no doubt, cheating, that is, students attempting to share questions and answers with each other. But, as one of our experimental colleagues pointed out, if they are talking about the material out side of class

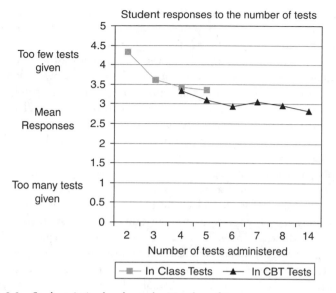

Figure 9.2 Student Attitudes about the Number of Assessments.

time, we have achieved something of a minor miracle. I attempted to minimize the impact of such cheating behaviors by using a large question pool, scrambling the order of those questions, and by offering a curve as incentive to students to keep the answers to themselves. I could not be completely sure, however, that each student faced an equally difficult test.

Finally, our data suggest that there may be such a thing as too many tests. Overall, student attitudes indicate that a moderate number of tests, probably five to eight assessments per semester or an exam or quiz every two to three weeks, are associated with better overall attitudes. As seen in figure 9.2, students rated how well the number of assessments correlated to their own learning. If students had fewer assessments, especially two exams, they indicated that more tests would have facilitated learning and better grades, and students associated fewer exams with higher anxiety levels and less feeling of control. Although fourteen assessments were rated better than a moderate number of exams in terms of anxiety, students indicated that fewer tests would have facilitated learning and better grades, and they rated fourteen assessments as significantly less convenient. In response to the data, my classes for fall 2001 employed six quizzes and three exams for a total of nine assessments.

Despite the addition of several test items that were much more difficult to answer correctly, students continued to rate the class and their experiences highly. Some students thought the class was too demanding for an introductory level course, and most agreed that the class was at least more challenging than they had expected. Notwithstanding the students' perception of the workload, their rating of my teaching remained high, and their perception of my organizational methods and skills actually increased slightly. I have come to view the CBT as an essential tool to help me facilitate student learning, one that allows me to make a difficult pedagogical situation, the large lecture class, a better one.

Although I had forced students into becoming more active outside of class time by giving them more assessments and had targeted my own teaching towards their areas of weak understanding, I had not encouraged them to become more actively engaged in the classroom. I wanted students to participate within the class and take an active part in the construction of their knowledge of and experiences in theatrical performances. I had gained three class days by having students complete exams outside of class, and I put those "free" days to use. I divide the entire class of 200 plus students into 40 groups balanced by gender (usually three women and two men or visa versa). Each group must create an original adaptation of a text or performance the class shares in common, one read or seen, submit that script to a peer group for evaluation and feedback, and then memorize and perform the skit before the entire class. What may seem an impossibly time consuming task was made tolerable by using various IT applications. A spreadsheet allows me to create, monitor, and record 40 group projects each semester without adding too much time to my administrative duties associated with the class. A Web-based grade book allows me to import my recorded grades to an interface wherein each student can see only their own grades. That same Web-based grade book allows me to record all the InQsit grades, calculate the final percentages, and submit the final grades to the registrar with a few mouse clicks.

Additionally, the course Web site facilitates student learning and communication in a variety of other ways. First, the Web site forms a scaffold for student learning that guides several of their assignments. Lev Vygotsky (1997) was among the first to document the effects of "scaffolding," namely using other students who have greater resources than the individual to improve learning, and the Web site is structured to mimic that process. Detailed instructions, interactive guides to assessment of materials, and previous examples of student work are all made available to students to guide their efforts. Interested readers may visit the site at http://www.bsu.edu/classes/o'hara/theat100/ and view many of those materials.

Second, the Web site facilitates communication among students and with me in ways that a large class often prevents. For example, one of the tools within the site is a complete class list with e-mail address links. In the case of their group projects, students click boxes of the students in their group, write one e-mail message, and can easily send it to the entire group. These students meet virtually using e-mail to share ideas, drafts of scripts, or questions. E-mail is also used to send scripts to their peer evaluators. In fact, other than the paper forms they use in class to evaluate the performances and the notes they take, the entire class is "paperless." All written work is submitted as attachments to e-mail. Students must still rehearse for the required in-class performance in a face-to-face environment, but they report that the electronic communication tools ease many of the problems that students associate with group project work. Using forms available on the Web site, the entire class assesses the performances, which are performed in clusters of eight groups on five days spread out through the semester. The results of the student assessments are made public in a faux Tony Awards ceremony, and the winners of the awards have their pictures posted to the Web site. Students report that an unusual sense of community, one that they never expected in a large lecture class, is created by the group projects, and that the pictures help make the large class seem more personal.

Technology also serves as a catalyst for pedagogical change, or at least a change in student behavior, in my classes for theatre majors. I use the InQsit system to insure that assigned readings, such as plays, have been read before class begins. These quizzes do not take up class time and sufficiently motivate students to keep up with the reading to insure richer and livelier discussions in our regular face-to-face meetings. Another advantage to using the CBT lab for my script analysis and history classes is two-fold: first, all essay tests are typed and thus easily readable, and second, only a student ID number identifies the essays. I grade all the essays, therefore, without really knowing whose work I am reading. When all the grading is finished, I match ID numbers to student names and enter their grades in the Web-based grade book. Both my students and I feel that this method yields results that tend to be fair and more reflective of their work. Keeping all written work electronic allows me to quickly copy and paste text in Web sites that check for plagiarism (e.g., http://plagiarism.org/, http://parallel.park.uga.edu/~ego/plagiarism.html). In this way, I have found several students who made use of the growing number of essay factories that populate the Web.

Studio classes can also benefit from IT, and several other instructors at Ball State University use various electronic resources to not only increase student learning and skills acquisition, but also to change the way they are teaching.

Dr. Rodger Smith, for example, in his Acting for Camera classes uses IT to coordinate three different colleges and departments into an integrated learning experience. The English Department's Scriptwriting class, the Telecommunication Department's Directing for Camera class, and the Theatre Department's Acting for Camera class all meet at the same time in the fall semester. Students meet both face-to-face and virtually to generate original scripts which are then rehearsed and filmed for credit in all three classes. All three groups continue to work together through the spring semester, though the writers are now acting in advisory positions. As acting students prepare for their parts in these short films, they also make their own films using each other as cameramen, technicians, and editors. Taking advantage of the ease and power of iMovie™ and Apple Computer's powerful Quicktime™ format, acting students have become makers of performance pieces from beginning to end. They generate or find scripts, rehearse roles, film scenes, review rushes, retake scenes, edit footage, add sound and effects, and show finished performance pieces.

Our students' learning goes beyond new skills and IT tools; they also deepen their understanding of the craft of acting in ways they cannot in traditional acting classes. Students watch, evaluate, and assess their own acting. They can critique their recorded work while the professor coaches the student's assessment of their own work. The benefit of using electronic media to increase public speaking effectiveness is widely used, but not so in acting classes. Most acting classes rely upon the analysis by other class members and the instructor. Students who record their work can examine it with the same eyes as their audience, allowing them to target specific moments in which they could improve their tactics or actions.[3]

Based in part on the success of his Acting for Camera program, Rodger Smith was awarded a significant grant for the fall 2001 to teach a class in BSU's Virginia B. Ball Center for Creative Inquiry. The class is composed of students from Telecommunications, Business, English, Public Relations, Journalism, and Theatre; it will be their only class. The students will generate, create, and launch a Web Entertainment Site that will culminate in the hosting of a festival of Internet specific performance pieces modeled on Sundance, Cannes, and other such festivals. We will be documenting their experiences in hopes of furthering our understanding of how IT can be used to facilitate learning.

In addition to pedagogical uses, IT can be a means to increase the resources performers use to assess and network their work. Notable actors and directors can assess and provide feedback remotely, asynchronously or synchronously, allowing young actors to interact with more experienced artists in ways most universities could not otherwise afford. Rich alumni bases can be developed and strengthened through IT. Ball State University has developed an alumni Web site that allows us to contact and share news with our recent and not so recent alumni. Our program has already reaped some benefits through an increased number of young alumni visiting for pedagogical purposes, such as professional readiness workshops, and so on. We have found that our most recent alumni point with pride to our Web presence.

As I hope this essay has demonstrated, IT not only can make many administrative tasks associated with pedagogy easier, it can also serve as a catalyst for pedagogical change and development. Theatre programs can become academic leaders in technology, exploiting the latest developments in streaming media, digital recording, and image manipulation. The power and presence of IT within our lives should give us pause for thought, which can be developed into more meaningful student learning if we are willing to reach beyond our traditional boundaries and seek partnerships with our colleagues and IT professionals. As theatre scholars and teachers we have too often been guilty of training our students to use only the quill pen when they also need to know how to sharpen their pencils.

Notes

1. This essay would not have been possible without the development of the proctored, computer-based testing room. This testing room was the result of a collaborative effort among myself, Darrell Butler, faculty member in the Department of Psychological Sciences at Ball State University; Yasemin Tunc and Dan Fortriede, staff at Ball State University Computing Services; and a number of other BSU employees. The data presented here were collated and interpreted by Darrell Butler and me.
2. The class is populated each fall with 100 freshmen who are linked in a first year learning program across campus and over 100 non-freshmen who register normally. We believe that the mix of freshmen and upper classmen provides positive role models for the younger students. In the spring, the class has over 200 students at various levels.
3. Interested readers should look to Rustan (1998) who points to ways in which most departments can easily and cheaply begin to develop a media acting program.

Works Cited

Bolter, Jay. 2000. *Writing space: Computers, hypertext, and the remediation of print*, 2nd ed. Mahwah, NJ: Lawrence Erlbaum.

Butler, Darrell. 2001a. Faculty interested in teaching, learning, and technology. The Technology Source (July/August). July 1, 2001 <http://horizon.unc.edu/TS/default.asp?show=article&id=904>.

———. 2001b. Proctored, Computer-based testing outside of large classrooms: The impact on student learning, attitudes, and cheating. Article under review.

Cameron, Kenneth and Patti Gillespie. 2000. *The enjoyment of theatre*, 5th ed. Boston: Allyn and Bacon.

Cuban, Larry. 1993. *How teachers taught: Constancy and change in American classrooms, 1890–1990*, 2nd ed. New York: Teachers College Press.

———. 1986. *Teachers and machines: The classroom use of technology since 1920*. New York: Teachers College Press.

Cummings, Scott. 1998. Interactive Shakespeare. *Theatre Topics* 8, no. 1: 93–112.

Daiute, Colette. 1985. *Writing and computers*. Reading, MA: Addison-Wesley.

diSessa, Andrea. 2000. *Changing minds: Computers, learning, and literacy*. Cambridge, MA: MIT Press.

Donlevy, James and Tia Donlevy. 1997. Teachers, technology, and training. Perspectives on education and school reform: Implications for the emerging role of the teacher. *International Journal of Instructional Media* 24, no. 2: 91–98.

Fliotsos, Anne. 1995. Listservs for laymen: Accessing theatre information through the Internet. *Theatre Topics* 5, no. 2: 81–87.

Flowers, Lamont, Ernest Pascarella, and Christopher Pierson. 2000. Information technology use and cognitive outcomes in first year of college. *The Journal of Higher Education* 71, no. 6: 637–667.

Girod, Mark and Shane Cavanaugh. 2001. Technology as an agent of change in teaching practice. *T.H.E. Journal: Technological Horizons in Education* 28, no. 9: 40–47.

Graham, R. 1999. Unannounced quizzes raise test scores selectively for mid-range students. *Teaching of Psychology* 26: 271–273.

Kellner, Douglas. 1998. Multiple literacies and critical pedagogy in a multicultural society. *Educational Theory* 48, no. 1: 103–122.

Keys, W. 1934. The influence of learning retention of weekly as opposed to monthly tests. *Journal of Educational Psychology* 25: 511–520.

Kika, F. M., T. F. McLaughlin, and J. Dixon. 1992. Effects of frequent testing of secondary algebra students. *Journal of Educational Research* 85: 159–162.

Kull, Michael and William Halal. 1999. The technology revolution: The George Washington University forecast of emerging technologies. *On the Horizon: the Strategic Planning Resource for Education Professionals* 7, no. 1: 1–9.

Lindsay, R. and R. Paton-Saltzberg. 1987. Resources changes and academic performance at an English polytechnic. *Journal of Educational Research* 85: 159–162.

Littleton, Karen and Paul Light. 1999. (ed.), *Learning with computers: Analysing productive interaction*. London: Routledge.

Mason, Diana and Ellen Verdel. 2001. Gateway to success for at-risk students in a large-group introductory chemistry class. *Journal of Chemical Education* 78, no. 2: 252–255.

Marranca, Bonnie. 1996. *Ecologies of theater: Essays at the century turning.* Baltimore: Johns Hopkins University Press.

McCoy, Ken. 1995. A brief bibliography of Internet theatre resources beyond email: Excerpts from Ken McCoy's "Guide to Internet resources in theatre and performance studies." *Theatre Topics* 5, no. 1: 89–94.

Milone, Michael. 1996. *Beyond bells and whistles: How to use technology to improve student learning.* Arlington, VA: American Association of School Administrators.

Nichols, Randall. 1997. A critical approach to teaching educational technology. *Proceedings of Selected Research and Development Presentations at the 1997 National Convention of the Association for Educational Communications and Technology.* Albuquerque, NM, February 14–18.

Oblinger, Diana and Sean Rush. 1997. (eds), *The learning revolution: the challenge of information technology in the academy.* Bolton, MA: Anker.

Office of Academic Assessment. 2000. *Making achievement possible and freshman year experience survey.* Muncie, IN: Ball State University.

Oppenheimer, Todd. 1997. The computer delusion. *Atlantic Monthly* 280, no. 1: 45–62.

Osborne, R. E., W. F. Browne, S. J. Shapiro, and W. F. Wagor. 2000. Transforming Introductory Psychology: Trading ownership for student success. *To Improve the Academy* 18: 128–146.

Pikunas, J. and E. Mazzota. 1965. The effects of weekly testing in the teaching of science. *Science Education* 49: 373–376.

Privateer, Paul Michael. 1999. Academic technology and the future of higher education. *The Journal of Higher Education* 70, no. 1: 60–79.

Robertson, T. and D. Ober. 1997. General studies assessment data—average grade earned and average section size. *BSU Campus Report.*

Russell, Michael. 2000. *It's time to upgrade: Tests and administration procedures for the new millennium.* White paper for US Department of Education: Secretary's Conference on Educational Technology. September 22, 2000 <http://www.ed.gov/Technology/techconf/2000/russell_paper.html>.

Rustan, John. 1998. Media acting: An affordable reality with portable equipment. *Theatre Topics* 8, no. 2: 205–218.

Schrum, Stephen. 1999. (ed.), *Theatre in cyberspace: Issues of teaching, acting, and directing.* New York: Peter Lang.

Sullivan, Patricia and James E. Porter. 1997. *Opening spaces: Writing technologies and critical research practices.* Greenwich, CT: Ablex.

Somekh, Bridget and Niki Davis. 1997. (eds), *Using information technology effectively in teaching and learning.* New York: Routledge.

Turney, A. H. 1931. The effect of frequent short objective tests upon the achievement of college students in Educational Psychology. *School and Society* 33: 760–762.

Vygotsky, Lev. 1997. *Educational Psychology.* Boca Raton, FL: St. Lucie Press.

CHAPTER 10

Deconstructing the Dominant: Educational Theatre in Historically Black Colleges and Universities as Critical Pedagogy Sites

Gail S. Medford

T hroughout history, educators have argued the importance of theatre within educational institutions. Historically, reasons given for including theatre in education were: (1) to teach language and literature, (2) to bind society and culture, (3) to teach Christian virtue, (4) to teach oratory and delivery, (5) to teach self-confidence, and (6) to teach memory (Phillip A. Coggins 1956 and Patti P. Gillespie 1990, 33).[1] During the twentieth century, two additional reasons have been emphasized: to train theatre professionals within academe and to establish a relationship between the college campus and the surrounding community. Towards the end of the century, Clar Doyle, in his groundbreaking text *Raising Curtains on Education* (Doyle 1993), introduced another reason for the existence of the discipline in academe: drama/theatre as a site for critical pedagogy in education. In the text's Forward, Henry Giroux, one of critical pedagogy's foremost advocates and spokesmen, applauded Doyle for his insightful work by noting that he

...demonstrates a keen sense of the importance of drama as a pedagogical practice that links theory and practice, on the one hand, and politics of representation and the body in the other. Drawing upon a vast array of work in critical pedagogy and critical theory, Doyle uses drama as a form of cultural production to enable students to utilize their bodies and minds in the service of being able to link language and experience, desire and affirmation, and knowledge and social responsibility. (Giroux in Doyle 1993, Forward)

Although the arguments for including theatre in the Historically Black Colleges and Universities (HBCUs) paralleled those cited by Coggins and Gillespie, and are just as sound, Doyle's theory of critical pedagogy in educational theatre offers even greater justification for theatre in the HBCU world of academe. As relative to the historical missions of these institutions, theatre as an academic discipline had and has the added purpose of cultivating and perpetuating African American drama and theatre in America. S. Randolph Edmonds, who gained the title "dean" of educational theatre in African American schools, stated during his time that the "Negro college theatre, more so than any other organization, provide[d] fertile soil for the development and growth of the Negro Theatre [and its students]" (Edmonds 1934, 232). Further, many African American artists and aestheticians from the cultural renaissance of the 1920s and the black theatre movement of the 1960s called upon institutions of higher learning to cultivate "Negro" or African American theatre, respectively. Playwright and scholar Paul Carter Harrison captured well the thoughts regarding theatre in these African American institutions when he said, "Ideally, the [Black American artist and scholar] should have the opportunity to investigate the viability of his [or her] ethnic impulses in [a Black American] non-commercial environment such as the Black university" (Harrison 1974, 5). These exhortations, together with Doyle's treatise, offer educational theatre scholars another dimension of study that could empower students and give them opportunities to explore their complex connections with daily life.

A historical study of educational theatre in seven HBCUs suggests that Edmonds' and Harrison's calls for the development of an African American voice in theatre helped to lay the fertile ground for the use of critical pedagogy within HBCU drama/theatre programs (Medford 1994). Further, the study revealed that these institutions historically developed under the thumb and within the context of the dominant Eurocentric culture and ideologies of America. From the beginning, when most African American institutions of higher learning began during the Reconstruction period, to the 1920s when most became accredited and engaged in a black cultural renaissance (the decade of the "New Negro"), these HBCUs found themselves too often financially dependent on white philanthropists and their ideological approvals. Even the politically, socially, and culturally challenging 1960s, with its nonviolent Civil Rights drive and militant Black Power movement, did not find these institutions satisfactorily separated financially or ideologically from the Eurocentric hegemony. However, as James Anderson so adequately states, these HBCUs continue to

> ... steer between two equally critical courses ... On the one hand, dependence on the benevolence of industrial philanthropists ... On the other hand, their [HBCU] mission to represent the struggles and aspirations of black people and to articulate the very source of the masses' discomfort and oppression. (Anderson 1988, 270)

The institutions selected for the historical study of HBCUs (Howard, Hampton, Dillard, Prairie View, University of Arkansas at Pine Bluff, Morgan State, and South Carolina State) represent a cross section of private and state-supported schools located in metropolitan areas, small cities, or rural sites. This examination of educational theatre from 1867 to 1990 focuses on the development of departmental organization, curriculum progression, and the selections of plays for mainstage seasons. *Department organization* refers to the location of the theatre program within the administrative structure of the college or university. *Curriculum* is defined as those courses offered by the department that are included and described in the college catalogues. *Selections for mainstage* refer to works offered as part of a theatre season for a paid public viewing. Two types of theatrical activities are excluded: (1) activities planned and supervised by non-theatre faculty but involving students of the theatre department, and (2) activities planned and supervised by theatre faculty, but occurring outside the department. The study of play selections, then, is limited to those offered by the theatre programs as a part of their mainstage seasons.

Based on this study of educational theatre in HBCUs, this essay aggregately explores Doyles' assertion of drama/theatre as a site for critical pedagogy by considering: (1) how the drama and theatre curriculum developed to include African American voices, and (2) the use of critical pedagogy (knowingly or unknowingly) in deconstructing "canonical" plays selected for mainstage theatre productions. Finally, on a personal note, I will offer specific experiences and sites where I engaged in critical pedagogy as a practitioner and scholar in academic theatre. But before we delve into the considerations of this essay, it is important to offer some workable definition of the rather complex theory of "critical pedagogy."

Critical Pedagogy

Throughout literature on critical pedagogy, recurring concepts and terms such as "transformation," "empowerment," "voice," "liberation," "critical consciousness," "conscientization," "generative language," "power," "praxis," "dialectic," and "humanization" attempt to define its framework and complexities. Joan Wink, in her *Critical Pedagogy: Notes from the Real World* (Wink 2000), suggests that the true definition of this term lies in its praxis. To offer "stated" definitions may tempt the reader to "memorize any one of them as if it were the *one true* definition" (Wink 2000, 28). Nonetheless, through a generative exercise, she proposes a working characterization of critical pedagogy as

> ...a prism that reflects the complexities of the interactions between teaching and learning.... enabl[ing] us to see more widely and more deeply.... [with] a tendency to focus on shades of social, cultural, political, and even economic conditions...under the broad view of history. Critical pedagogy forces educators to look again at the fundamental issues of power and their relationship to the greater societal forces that affect schools. (Wink 2000, 30)

Quoting critical pedagogist and theorist Peter McLaren, Wink further points out that "critical pedagogy asks how and why knowledge gets constructed the way it does, and how and why some constructions of reality are legitimated and celebrated by the dominant culture while others clearly are not" (McLaren 1994, 169; Wink 2000, 36).

In a 1997 interview with Carlos Torres, Giroux submitted that "Critical pedagogy...addresses how to construct ideological and institutional conditions in which the lived experience of empowerment for the vast majority of students becomes the defining feature of schooling" (Torres 1998, 127).

After studying the writings and work of Paulo Freire, patriarch of this pedagogy, who introduced and named it in the 1970s, Laurie Williams summed up the following foundations for critical pedagogy that may be found in Freire's most salient work, *Pedagogy of the Oppressed* (1970):

- Man's ontological vocation is to be a subject who acts upon and transforms his world, and in so doing moves toward ever new possibilities of fuller and richer life individually and collectively.
- Every human being, no matter how "ignorant" or submerged in the culture of silence he or she may be, is capable of looking critically at the world in a dialogical encounter with others.

• Provided with proper tools for this encounter, the individual can grad-
ually perceive personal and social reality as well as the contradictions in
it, become conscious of his or her own perception of that reality, and
deal critically with it. (Williams 1999)

Drawing upon these elucidations, a workable "definition" of critical
pedagogy for this essay may be as follows:

A mode of interwoven teaching and learning where instructor and
student unite to recognize voices silenced by a cultural hegemony and
where together teacher and student engage in praxis that brings them into
a cohesive critical consciousness, which eventually breaks the silence, lib-
erates the voices, empowers the once muted, and transforms educational
theatre to a critical site beyond the realm of theatrical performances and
an art for the elite.

Critical Pedagogy in the Curriculum Development

In the seven HBCUs studied, educational theatre developed along very
similar paths to those in historically Euro-American colleges. As in Euro-
American schools, theatrical activities and drama groups came before curricular theatre. Educational theatre then moved from drama as literature in
English departments, to drama as a tool for oratorical exercises in Speech
departments, to drama as a text in performance in theatre programs.

All institutions, except Dillard, introduced students to academic drama
and theatre through Greek, Latin, French, or Shakespearean readings that
were included in courses offered by language departments. Students further
experienced these plays through recitations required in early speech training
and through public speaking events encouraged by various literary societies.
The earliest studies of plays began at Howard University in 1868–1869 and
Hampton Institute in 1888–1889. During these periods, students read
works by Moliere, Racine, Aeschylus, Euripides, and Plautus, both in original languages and in translation.

The seven schools at some time required students to examine
Shakespearean works in courses such as "English Drama," making
Shakespeare the dominant playwright in studies of English literature. Again,
Howard University offered the first of these courses in 1907–1908, and the
following year included a course called "Shakespeare," thus leading these
schools in developing specific courses in Shakespearean studies (e.g.,
"Tragedies of Shakespeare" and "Elizabethan Drama and Shakespeare"). In a

radical move, the two city institutions and South Carolina State deleted all Shakespearean studies from their drama curricula during the 1950s; the metropolitan schools did likewise during the early 1970s.

Many of the institutions deleted specific courses in Shakespeare, but continued to offer various types of studies in European drama. In the 1950s, the schools began offering drama survey courses as well as specific studies of modern and American plays. Between the late 1960s and the mid-1970s, six of these HBCUs included, for the first time, a course in African American drama. Prairie View was the only institution in this study that failed to have offered this course by 1990.

Although students in these HBCUs began to study drama as early as the late 1800s, their acquaintance with theatre production courses did not begin until the 1920s. Again, Howard University pioneered this curriculum with "Technique of the Drama" in 1920–1921, followed by Hampton in 1926–1927 with "Advanced Play Reading and Production." With the exception of University of Arkansas at Pine Bluff (UAPB), the remaining institutions began their theatre curricula in the 1930s. The initial theatre studies focused on basic elements of play production: acting, directing, stagecraft, costuming. However, only the metropolitan schools included playwriting in their first comprehensive courses in theatre.

Soon after introducing these comprehensive courses in theatre production, all seven institutions began developing individualized courses. The metropolitan schools first offered courses in acting, directing, history, and criticism in the late 1930s and 1940s; both city schools started in the 1950s; the remaining two rural HBCUs began in the late 1950s to late 1960s. Courses in technical theatre, such as "Lighting" and "Scene Design" entered the curricula at various times between the 1930s and 1970s.

During the 1970s and 1980s, all institutions in this study expanded the theatre curricula to include several advanced courses in acting, playwriting, and various areas in technical theatre. Most notably, the schools began offering "Introduction to the Theatre" in the 1960s and 1970s.

From this overview, we see that educational theatre grew out of studies in English and along with courses in speech. Generally, the curricula progressed in two directions: one in drama, the other in speech and theatre. Although English departments kept courses such as "Shakespeare," the drama areas or departments often included that course and various other studies of plays (i.e., "Modern Drama," "American Drama," and "Black Drama"). The second direction took these plays from the texts to the stage, as drama areas developed their theatre production and performance tracks. In most cases speech took its own direction apart from theatre. These institutions began with one or two comprehensive studies in theatre production (i.e., "Technique of the Drama"), then moved to numerous specific courses in production and performance ("Stagecraft," "Lighting," "Acting," "Directing"); theatre history, theory, criticism, and pedagogy were interspersed evenly throughout. Interestingly, these institutions, unlike their white counterparts, also offered at some time unique studies in areas such as "Ritual Theatre," "Religious Drama," "Community Dramatics," and "The Art of the Little Theatre."

Between 1920, when Howard offered the first theatre production course, and 1990, the development of the educational theatre curriculum suggested that these HBCUs focused more attention on theatrical production and performance than on other academic aspects of theatre. Metropolitan schools appeared to be the most innovative of the HBCUs in their educational theatre curricula. They were the first to offer playwriting and led in producing original works for the mainstage. Their progressiveness probably occurred because these schools housed larger student populations and employed noted figures such as Alain Locke, who was a leading personality in the Harlem Renaissance; Edmonds, who was a theatre scholar and playwright; and Owen Dodson, a prominent scholar, poet, and playwright. Conversely, rural and small town institutions were the slowest to develop. They were the last to offer a major in theatre. Budgetary factors, as well as a smaller student population with more local interests, may have caused these schools to lag behind.

Given the historical and cultural context of HBCUs, the progression of educational theatre could not help but produce various courses grown out of a critical pedagogy. Throughout the years of development, the "playwriting" curriculum was instrumental in addressing the need for African American voices in a Eurocentrically dominated theatre, as noted by the number of original scripts selected for mainstage. Such a curriculum must have certainly engaged students and professors together in some levels of "conscientization" (breaking through established myths and stereotypes to heightened awareness of self apart from the hegemony). Additionally, other special courses such as the "Ritual Theatre," "Religious Drama," and "Community Dramatics" could offer environments beyond the academic that would be rich and ripe for critically examining black culture's dialogical encounter with other minorities and the dominant culture.

Critical Pedagogy in the Selections of Plays for the Mainstage

The investigation of play selections in this study expanded on methods used in comparable research (Sister Mary Peter Doyle 1935; Alexander Marshall 1980; Jean Marie Fishman 1992). Unlike these studies, this examination covered a longer span of time, reviewed all mainstage selections, and gathered data from primary sources such as production lists, playbills, programs, newspapers, portfolios, and annual reports from university archives. Secondary sources include department histories and interviews.

The categories for the selections in this study were those John Dietrich proposed in 1948: standard, original and miscellaneous. He referred to the categories as "broad classes":

> A play was defined as *standard* when by virtue of a passage of time or the dignity of the style or idea, it had survived or gave promise of surviving as a contribution to world drama... An *original* play was any script which was given its premiere performance by the schools... *miscellaneous* included all plays which could not be contained in the major classifications. (Dietrich 1948, 186)

Various other secondary sources served as guides in examining the play selections and playwrights.[2] For this study, the definition of *original* was extended to include all works written for little theatre and for educational theatre by those in theatre programs at colleges and universities.

Between 1908 and 1990 the seven institutions performed a total of 1,203 works representing 1,072 playwrights on their mainstages. The greatest number of selections came from Howard, a private metropolitan school; University of Arkansas at Pine Bluff, a city school, produced the smallest number. Although miscellaneous works comprised the majority in six of the seven repertoires, most of these educational theatre seasons also offered a sizable number of standard and original plays, as seen in table 10.1.

Table 10.1 Overall Number of Selections by Institutions

Institutions	Classics	Standard	Musicals	Originals	Misc..	Specials
Howard	18	56	13	46	91	16
Morgan	11	44	7	27	78	6
Dillard	13	50	10	34	66	0
Hampton	22	32	11	9	18	11
UAPB	7	23	9	18	39	7
Prairie View	11	39	4	10	52	12
S.C. State	8	34	19	5	80	13
TOTAL	90 (8%)	278 (24%)	73 (6%)	149 (13%)	491 (43%)	65 (6%)

Viewing educational theatre's development through play selections suggested that these institutions tried to adhere to standards and practices of their historically Euro-American counterparts as well as to cultivate African American theatre. A broad analysis displayed a concentration of classics and European dramas before 1920 and a significant number of popular plays, Broadway shows, standard works, and musicals between 1920 and 1990. The early concentration of classics and European dramas occurred perhaps because of the strong influence from English. The move toward more con-temporaneous works may have been influenced by theatre's move away from English toward an alignment with speech or toward its own autonomy.

Evidence also indicated that the number of selections usually increased as educational theatre grew apart from English and speech. Such increases may be explained by several factors. For example, the fact that these institutions carved out little niches for educational theatre, either as areas within English or speech or as independent departments, indicated more student interest that may have encouraged faculty to direct more or varied plays. Another influence may have come from the expansion of theatre in Euro-American institutions that may have encouraged HBCUs to give more attention to college theatricals on their (HBCUs) campuses.

The analysis also demonstrated that these HBCUs addressed the challenge to meet specific cultural needs of their students. Thus, we saw a marked number of original works appear in the 1920s and 1930s and a significant increase of selections written by African Americans in the 1960s and 1970s. Additionally, unlike their historically Euro-American counter-parts, these HBCUs produced a notable amount of special programs high-lighting African American history and culture. Although these institutions offered the students opportunities to explore African American culture in theatre, black culture as a whole entity in the art received far less attention. That is, the institutions generally overlooked many playwrights and theatrical experiences across the African Diaspora.

Some differences in repertory appeared because of institutional support and location. Rural and small town institutions, which were state supported, produced the largest number of special programs and the smallest number of original works. Reasons for these trends may lie in budgetary constraints, a small student population, and a lack of courses in playwriting. In contrast, private and metropolitan schools led in producing classics, musicals, and standard works. Because these institutions comprised larger and more diverse student populations and often received larger budgets, this trend was expected. A larger pool of students creates more diverse interests and needs as well as offers a larger selection of talent. Larger budgets possibly translate into the ability to produce more works of greater variety and those, such as musicals, that require a large and expensive physical production.

Works by white male writers comprised most of the play selections at all schools in this study. Selections written by white rather than black playwrights were roughly double, while selections written by males overwhelmingly surpassed those by female authors. This trend was probably attributable to two factors: more white male authors have been published and produced than either black or female authors overall, and these HBCUs selected similar works to those selected by their historically Euro-American counterparts.

Perhaps unsurprisingly, rural and small town HBCUs tended to be more provincial and more conservative, less willing to challenge established standards of the majority's culture. Metropolitan and private schools selected the largest number of works by African American writers. These institutions were located in areas largely populated by African Americans and often found encouragement from African American community theatres existing in the same areas.

During the 1920s, unlike the previous years, the HBCUs unquestionably responded to contemporaneous trends in African American culture through curricular and extra-curricular activities in theatre and drama. Because African American intelligentsia represented a significant proportion of the New Negro movement, particularly in the Harlem Renaissance, African-American higher education, and, thus, drama or educational theatre, could likely have been affected. Howard University was particularly affected by the movement as Alain Locke and Montgomery Gregory, significant figures in the Harlem Renaissance, served as prominent professors at that institution and worked to establish a national African American theatre from that school. Thus, of the seven institutions examined in this study, Howard formed a symbiotic relationship with the movement and the Harlem Renaissance.

The seven schools in this study demonstrated three trends surely tied to the events of this and the previous decade. First, most of these HBCUs formed drama or theatre groups during this period, perhaps in response to the Harlem Renaissance, to DuBois' call for true African American theatre and drama, and to expanding theatricals in Euro-American institutions. Second, in addition to forming areas in drama, two institutions began offering theatre production courses that comprised various facets of stagecraft, directing and acting; students at metropolitan schools also received instruction in playwriting. This curricular change evidenced an answer to the call for both African American native and folk drama written by African Americans. Third, three institutions displayed the talents of students and faculty by selecting significant number of original plays for the mainstage, again demonstrating a desire to participate in developing a race or folk drama by African Americans about African Americans.

Interestingly, however, these schools did not display the talents of many African American writers from the Harlem Renaissance or the Krigwa literary contest.[3] Many of these writers, especially females, were completely overlooked. In view of the marked number of original pieces, we may then conclude that these institutions simply chose to focus on developing new talents and plays rather than producing the works of those already receiving attention.

These institutions responded in a similar manner to the cultural events and trends of the 1960s and 1970s. Educational theatre answered the call of the Black Theatre movement in three principal ways: by offering first-time courses in African American drama, by selecting a significant number of works by African American playwrights for mainstage, and by producing a noticeable number of original plays and special programs concerning African American life and history.

However, a closer look at educational theatre's response to the movement revealed that it offered a somewhat conservative answer. For example, evidence revealed that the contents of the "Black Drama" courses primarily focused on African American playwrights (usually modern and contemporaneous), omitting writers from Africa and the African Diaspora. Similarly, mainstage selections included a nominal number of works by African writers. Of the few writers represented, Fugard received the most attention. Further, the mainstage selections favored non-militant theatre and contemporaneous musicals; thus works representing protest theatre (such as those by Jones/Baraka) were presented infrequently. Such a conservative response may have reflected the views of conservative administrators and faculty as well as an adherence to some standards set by predominantly Euro-American groups such as the American Theatre Association.

Critical analyses of mainstage play selections, particularly for HBCUs, provide insight into the culture of the educational theatre program, the department, and possibly the institution. These selections carry implications that may go beyond the scope of box office receipts, as productions not only give the theatre student a practical training ground, but also serve as a form of publicity for the department. Theatre seasons, whether selected by students, faculty, administrators, or any combination of the three, reveal the cultural voices that dominate the program. For example, seasons that rarely, if ever, offer selections by Hispanic writers would imply that particular culture is silent or nonexistent in that theatre program, department, or institution.

Further, an examination of the selections within the cultural contexts of American higher education and of the dominant culture could give rise to discussion and praxis of empowerment and a "liberatory" education in theatre and drama. The selection of plays by drama departments of HBCUs may well serve as a cultural enrichment and education for its surrounding communities, both inside and outside the university. The works performed may reveal trends, which may in turn give theatre departments of African American institutions further insight into what they have offered their audiences individually and collectively. Such insight may serve to encourage cultural transformation, if needed.

Critical Pedagogy Up Close and Personal

Doyle offers dramatic texts and theatre as tools of critical inquiry that allows for powerful reflection and examination of various political, social, cultural and ideological constructs. He asserts that although the student and teacher must acknowledge and respect the playwright as originator of the cultural work, they must also recognize that the play is out of the author's historical and cultural context. Therefore, "one of the first moves toward a critical drama pedagogy is to give ownership of the dramatic play back to the students (1993)," but with the understanding that while doing so is liberating and empowering, that ownership does free the work from social, political, and ideological influences. Giroux points out,

> ...for Doyle, drama becomes a site where critical pedagogy comes alive [as it] offers opportunities to employ the critical categories of voice, difference, and community in ways that integrate the dialectical relationship between affective and rational investments, individual experiences, and the collective stories that mark out our sense of place, culture, and community.... drama becomes the dwelling place in which identities can affirm their differences, students can speak from the diverse locations of their own histories, and strive to engage their desires within rather than outside of the movement of the body, creative expression, and the language of theory. (Giroux in Doyle 1993, Forward)

Throughout my years as a theatre practitioner and scholar, either as a student, professor, and colleague, I personally have engaged in some aspects of critical pedagogy, although often unwittingly. Whether working with non-African-American scripted plays or developing "specialty productions," critical pedagogy has offered an added dimension to the entire theatrical process. I offer three of those pedagogical experiences in the following descriptions.

Euripides' *Medea*

Of the plays most produced by the seven HBCUs examined in this essay, Euripides' *Medea* was on the top of the list. My role in this 1980 production was to play the lead character. The director was a professor who saw this work strictly as a "universal" piece that transcended any racial or ethnic concerns: Medea's plight was just like that of any wife scorned by her husband, the father of her children; Jason did what men sometimes do or fancy to do; the nurse was like any other confidant and the chorus of women was an uncompromising part of Greek theatre that functioned as a signpost and guide to the story.

To the director's dismay, the performers were not as ready to accept his rather simple character placements as he would have liked. After the cast's third reading of the script, the director/professor was drawn into a critical discussion and deconstruction of the classic Greek play. The first set of questions put to him included the following: "Why must we study and perform these plays at an HBCU?" "Of what value will knowledge of this genre of theatre/drama have to us?" "Why do you see this play as 'universal?'" "What is a universal drama anyway?" "What makes this play a theatre/drama standard that should be studied by everyone?" His careful and interactive responses led to further discussions surrounding classical Greek culture versus that of African Americans in 1980 and the place that knowledge of theatre/drama had in a liberal arts education.

Another query led him and the performers to examine together the relationship of Jason and Medea in light of the historically stereotypical views of relationships between African American men and women. Most interestingly, the cast queried and sought an answer to the concern that this play, when performed by a black cast, would become yet another stereotyped epitome of the dysfunctional black family: the husband-father is absent and off to make another family, the wife-mother is left to find a way to make it alone, and the children are eventually destroyed. Medea also could personify "a vengeful black woman" who "messes with voo-doo" and does not care about her children.

Although the cast understood the function of the nurse and chorus to the play itself, they queried how these entities might be rearranged to reflect more of a "community concern" for Medea and her children than was proposed by Euripides. This particular analysis helped the cast understand the tenets of narration and storytelling, as related to Greek theatre.

Conversely, the discussion raised the professor's/director's awareness of the cast's need to have this group function a bit more intimately with the main character and her children. Thus, some of the chorus' physical blocking and stage movement intimated a relationship of "neighborliness" or "community" with Medea and her boys. One piece of directorial blocking and stage movement between the chorus and Jason elicited an audience comment that warned, "Those women are going to get you, Jason. Those are Medea's girls."

Tennessee Williams' *A Streetcar Named Desire*

A popular playwright with these seven HBCUs was Tennessee Williams. In addition to several of his other works, most of the institutions produced *A Streetcar Named Desire*, his Pulitzer Prize winning play, which is quite interesting, as Williams was a white Southern playwright whose themes often reflected tragic and frustrating aspects of his own personal life. A 1991 reading of this play by a mixed cast of African American, white, and Hispanic students led to a very thought-provoking discussion of the supporting characters in this piece. As the white professor/director sought to explain the relationships between the main characters in this play, a student asked about Williams' insertion of the other characters that sometimes are nameless. This question led to a discussion of the dominant culture in America and its relationship with other cultures. "In what ways does Williams seem to reflect views of white America?" "Does the namelessness of the 'Negro Woman' and the 'Mexican Woman' indicate a white view of minorities as window-dressings for American culture?" "Could Blanche have become romantically involved with Pablo Gonzales rather than with Mitch, if Pablo had been as attentive to her?" " How might the story be played if all the main characters were Mexican?" "How might Stanley and Stella change their circumstances?" "What choices could the men have made in this play that may have changed the outcome for Blanche?" "What choices could Stella have made to change the outcome for her sister?" "Does Williams offer hope and desire for any of these main characters?"

Ntozake Shange's *for colored girls who have considered suicide/when the rainbow is enuf*

Feminist theatre did not find great acceptance in the educational theatre programs of these institutions. Although students and professors may have been interested in adding such plays to the mainstage repertoire, many administrators were not so inclined. In 1999, at a HBCU, three students, an academic administrator, a colleague and I engaged in an interesting discussion regarding the exclusion of feminist plays from the mainstage theatre seasons. Although the students and I stressed that by this exclusion, the department had done and was doing a disservice to the theatre students and the university community, the administrator and my colleague were not swayed. The administrator took great pains to explain that one theatrical piece turned him off completely from any such theatre. That piece was Shange's very notable choreopoem, *for colored who have considered suicide/when the rainbow is enuf.* For him, if this work was an example of feminist theatre, he would have none of it. The piece and its performance left him feeling emasculated and angry. He felt he had been attacked, with no defense for himself or his fellow "brothers."

Shange's piece is a collection or "system" of poems that speaks of the joys and sorrows, the discoveries and reflections, and the hopes and wishes of some African American women. Although there are parts of the choreopoem that do not speak well of black men, there are other parts that are very illuminating to and of African American men and women. This work offers something of a panoramic view of the dialectic dance between woman and herself within the context of male relationships. During the 1970s and 1980s, this unique work raised the consciousness of some women (and some men), while delivering the voices of others from a much too long silence.

One of the students engaged in this discussion recalled those illuminating parts and offered his insights as a young man. With his testimony, I proceeded to encourage the administrator and the professor to give permission to perform Shange's work in a small laboratory setting as a classroom activity, if the cast and director would engage in a critical pedagogy that would bring to the audience the stilled male voice that the administrator felt was needed to "balance" the piece.

The initial cast of all women met for several reads of the work to gain an understanding of the scope and shape of the choreopoem. As a female ensemble, they explored the various poems within their own individual contexts and then as African American. They engaged in queries and discussions surrounding the topic of being female, of being female and black, of being at varying ages and stages of their lives, and of experiences that brought women of the choreopoem to the point where the audience meets them in each piece. It was then that four males were brought in to "join" the ensemble.

During this phase of rehearsals, the men engaged in similar queries and discussions that centered on the male roles in lives of these "colored girls" of the choreopoem. Their critical discussions took them to explorations of males as lovers, friends, supporters, cheaters, abusers, rapists, and even killers. One very poignant discussion centered on the piece called "a nite wid beau willie brown," which told the story of a war veteran and his failed relationship with Crystal, his girlfriend and the mother of his two children. The poem portrays him as a ne'er-do-well who physically abuses Crystal, as he tries to convince her to become his wife. In the end he drops their two children out of a window because she cannot speak the words to say she would marry him. The males sought to answer questions such as "What choices did Beau have that could have improved his life?" "What social, political, and cultural milieus may have affected Beau's and Crystal's plight?" "What might have been the scenario if the roles were reversed?"

Finally, the two groups formed one ensemble and choreographed the entire chorepoem out of their discussions. Voices of the males were added, not so much as responses to Shange's words, but as contexts to the rhythms of the poems. The male vocalizations and movements did not offer justifications or excuses, but gave a three-dimensional work of art that truly gave the women of the choreopoem

> a layin on of hands,
> the holiness of [themselves] released (Shange 1977, 50)

The administrator and my colleague came to view this classroom exercise as part of the "audience." They both declared a greater sense of the chorepoem and a more sympathetic view of the women in it.

Conclusion

As educators, whether K-12 or higher education faculty, we are called to challenge, expand and cultivate minds of those who lead society into a greater and better tomorrow. Critical pedagogy is one way to do that, with an even better promise—to deliver the oppressed, the silenced, the powerless into humanization and heightened awareness of mind, body, and spirit. As Clar Doyle evidences, educational theatre is a great site for this, as the discipline, the art itself, with its entrenched modes of reflection, allows for creative exploration, limitless queries, and empowerment.

The HBCUs in this study (and other such institutions) historically have faced challenges of cultivating and perpetuating African American ideologies and considerations within a structure of a direct or indirect Eurocentric hegemony. This complex association and ongoing dialectic begs for critical pedagogy to be employed as a method of keeping African American and other "minority" voices alive and heard above the hegemonic din.

As noted in this essay, within the higher education structure of these HBCUs, educational theatre provided a fertile place for its students and professors to share in the exercise and power of legitimizing and raising their voices. Courses such as "Playwriting" and "Ritual Theatre" encouraged the development of original works to be performed on the mainstages, along with the Eurocentric standards or "canons" of drama. Performance courses in acting and directing offer many opportunities for African American students to explore a liberatory praxis and thus, transform themselves beyond the Eurocentric prescribed theories and methods. These courses further present openings to discussions on the "given challenge" of non-traditional casting of black students in plays written by, for, and about white people. Additionally, these HBCUs cannot escape the argument that the selection of plays for their stages carry many implications and, to some degree, responsibilities that go beyond box office receipts and displaying cultural knowledge of the "great dramas of the world." These institutions inherently remain charged with cultivating consciousness.

Doyle says it best as he declares the following:

At its best, a critical drama pedagogy can make breaks with dominant expectations and alienate the familiar. Drama must become... a tool toward a consciousness of what might be.... [and] aid in bringing about needed changes, that through critical consciousness, could result in freer human development. (Doyle 1993, 89)

Notes

1. These reasons for academic theatre are fully discussed throughout Phillip A. Coggins, *The Uses of Drama* (New York: George Braziller, 1956) and addressed in Patti P. Gillespie, "Theatre Education and Hirsh's Contextualism: How Do We Get There and Do We Want to Go," *Journal of Aesthetic Education* 24 no. 1 (Spring, 1990): 32–37.

2. The "AETA Production Lists," a yearly study until 1976 and based on Dietrich's work, helped with the categorizations. These production lists surveys were published in the *Educational Theatre Journal* almost regularly in March, April or May between 1948 and 1976 by the following authors: John Detrich 1948–1949; Theodore Hatlen 1950–1953, 1957–1958; Edwin Schoell 1954–1955; Theodore Shank 1959–1961; Alan Stambusky 1965–1966; Leighton Ballew and Gerald Kahan 1968–1971; Leighton Ballew 1972–1976. Milton Smith's *Guide to Play Selection* (1933) and the second edition of that guide by the National Council of Teachers of English (1958) provided references for discerning which works were "standard."

CHAPTER 11

"Imaginative Collaboration": Pedagogical Issues in African-American Theatre History

Joni L. Jones

> *Vernacular performance ... is as much a struggle for possibilities of*
> *meaning as 'about' any particular thematic ideographic content.*
> Kimberly W. Benston
> *Performing Blackness: Enactments of*
> *African-American Modernism*

The first day of class holds such promise. On that first day, mistakes have not yet been made, there are no painful moments trying to unravel the events that led to a class' emotional melt down, no reworking the syllabus after I have once again allowed class discussion to get us further and further behind, no failed attempts at discussions of racism in the United States. Maybe this time I will really get it right. After 23 years of teaching, maybe this will be the time when my classroom practices finally yield my grandest visions of beauty and social change. Maybe my process will unfold in an elegant and insightful series of provocative discussions, deeply meaningful exercises, and clearly relevant assignments. On that first day, the students look at me with what seems to be similarly grandiose expectations. Maybe this will be the class that pulls all of their learning together. Maybe this will be the place where they discover their position in the world. Just maybe this will be the class that respects them while pushing them to grow. None of the students are reading the newspaper, or studying for another class, or masking their frustration, boredom or absolute disagreement with what is happening in the course with the feigned attention they have mastered over the years of sitting in classrooms. None of this is happening. Not yet. It's just the first day, and the possibilities lay before us.

But as the semester evolves, this class too is likely to succumb to the series of hits and misses that have characterized my teaching of African American Theatre History in the past. Throughout the semester, the students and I tackle representation and appropriation, the complications of historical documentation, and U.S. aesthetics and iconography mired in racism, sexism, homophobia, and classism. Sometimes class discussion becomes bogged down in an artificial and debilitating political correctness; other times we skim the surface of both history and performance in this survey course; and on rare occasions the participatory structures in the course are intimately linked with the palpable transformation of the students and of me.

At its best, the structure of this course should reflect the nature of the theatrical art and artists covered throughout the semester. My pedagogical approach rests on the premise that the content of the course should shape the learning strategies employed in the course. Such an approach might be an "emergent pedagogy," following the lead of anthropologist Stephen Tyler who identifies an "emergent ethnography" that grows from the specifics of the fieldwork experience. An emergent pedagogy for African American Theatre History echoes the sentiments of the quotation that begins this essay. I envision the classroom itself as a "vernacular performance" that is as much about the transformative potential of participatory/embodied learning as it is about specific theatrical historical content. When the classroom exists as a vernacular performance, the course builds on Yoruba theatre scholar Oyin Ogunba's notion of "imaginative collaboration," (1978) a multi-layered term that describes the relationship between Yoruba audiences and Yoruba performers. This relationship is characterized by mutual participation and the formation of the appropriate atmosphere that will enable the performance to move toward transformation. Participation and theatrical environment are two key features of many of the works we study in African American Theatre History. But as soon as students come to understand the ways in which the course will rigorously examine race, I am in danger of having spoiled the very atmosphere that is necessary for their participation and for our mutual growth. The atmosphere is the roux into which the participation is stirred while transformation is the intended result. This is a spiraling relationship of interdependency. The atmosphere permeates participation and transformation; participation and transformation strengthen the atmosphere.

This atmosphere, in both the classroom and the performances examined in the class, has a kinship with *ase*, a Yoruba concept meaning life force, power, and authority. It is the ability to make things happen, and the energy that pervades all things. In Yoruba cosmology, this power is "the ability to change, manipulate, and transcend the physical realm" (Olomo 2002, 54). *Ase* is the special property of Esu, the Yoruba deity of indeterminancy. Yoruba theologian John Mason explains that "Esu is not just the guardian of vital life force but is synonymous with it" (1992, 54). *Ase* is the force that unifies all persons and things into symbiotic relationships. When the *ase* of one is depleted, others may offer theirs to replenish it; in this way we have a deep and abiding responsibility to one another and to the planet. The classroom should practice what the aesthetics of the course preach. Students can best understand the important sense of atmosphere that is revealed in the plays and practices of the course by experiencing the dynamics of imaginative collaboration in the classroom.

Ase as atmosphere shares power with the Dogon concept of *nommo*, or word force. *Ase* gives power to words through *nommo; nommo* is the life energy in the word just as *ase* is "the motive force inherent in the Word, the living pulsation of [scripture] ... " (Wenger 1990, 198). Indeed, during Yoruba prayer, the word *ase* is intoned in order to acknowledge the power of the prayer. In this way *ase* is used to signify "so be it"; it is used to mark the action in words. The union of *ase* and words is crystallized in Esu, the bearer of *ase*. Esu is the communicative impulse "that activates all physical-metaphysical, intellectual communicative affinities and reaches" (Wenger 1990, 77). Henry Louis Gates, Jr. noted Esu's ability to activate and animate through words when he likened Esu to the messenger Hermes or Mercury in Gates' analysis of African American literary traditions (5–10). Words, life force, and action are inextricably bound.

Given this principle in the dramatic texts of the course, the classroom must likewise underscore the relationship between the words in our discussions, our shared life force, and the actions we engage in as a class. Relating the aesthetic philosophy directly to the structure of the class seriously raises the stakes of our interactions, and I believe also raises the potential for profound, even if unspoken, personal revelations about identity, politics, aesthetics, and the confluence of these elements.

While participation is important in the class as a West African-based performance feature and as precursor to the intellectual and psychic under-standings of the course, the participation in class cannot be solely based on identification. I cannot assume that the students have a vested interest in the subject matter, no matter what their racial identification. In the predomi-nantly European-American institution where I teach, most of my students are not African American. And, of course, the African American students might not identify with the aesthetics presented in the course. The participation has to move toward Edward Said's notion of the beauty and worldliness of the literature. He writes "One of the great pleasures for those who read and study literature is the discovery of longstanding norms in which all cultures known to me concur: such things as style and performance, the existence of good as well as lesser writers, and the exercise of preference" (1993, 313). Said encourages readers to experience the overall quality of the work, not only the politics of the content. While I may want the students to see the ways in which race factors into the dramas we read, I cannot rely on this being their only form of participation with the work. I must be certain to offer them strategies for critiquing the structure of the plays, the development of the characters, and the theatrical and narrative conventions of the period in which the play was written. In this way, they may participate due to pleasure rather than identification. Just when my harangue on race in the classroom becomes especially strident, I can remember that my pedagogical mentors, for the most part, have been white men who loved literature and encouraged me to do so as well—Dr. Philip Decker of MacMurray College and Dr. Wallace Bacon of Northwestern University, both of whom died in 2000. I, too, want the students to love the literature as they love the possibility of a life less encumbered by race, gender, sexual practice, and class.

I mention my mentors here not for sentimental reasons, but because it demonstrates the complexity of "teaching race." I had so few African American teachers from kindergarten through doctoral work, that I really learned to teach from white people, specifically white men. Though I begin African American Theatre History with a discussion of West African-based performance practices, I have to acknowledge the ways in which those practices have been shaped by an array of cultural influences. And if my teaching strategies are to mirror the performance practices discussed in the class, my teaching, too, has borrowed from black sermon traditions as well as British-inspired pedagogical strategies of lectures, tests, and grades.

In "teaching race" I inevitably confront the debate around essentialism. A course that is called African American *anything* must examine what exactly makes that thing being studied African American. And to name it African American requires distinguishing African American from all other things. Gayatri Spivak calls for a "strategic essentialism" in order to gather forces around social issues and to generate solidarity among those who self identify in specific categories. Students seem to understand this need and accept how it functions particularly as they review Willis Richardson's and Zora Neale Hurston's outlines for "Negro Theatre" that emphasize "the Negroes gift for language," yet students also see how this "gift" connects to stereotypes and an essentializing predisposition. In class, I find myself wanting to demonstrate the uniqueness of African American theatre by listing the features that have occurred most often in my field work, in my work with professional theatre, and in my traditional research—simultaneity, seriation, participation, improvisation, monologue/storytelling supported by an active chorus, enlivening the *ase*—while realizing that this list is reductive. Gena Caponi recognizes this problem and cites Mintz and Price, M'biti, Raboteau and Hord and Lee to support her own use of an "African-derived cultural aesthetic." In spite of this intellectual corroboration, the questions of stereotyping and essentializing a diverse group of artists, and claiming a commonality of cultural features is difficult to defend without the awkward caveats of "not *all* African American artists," "not *only* African American artists," and "not this particular artist *all* the time." There are simply tensions between artists who are immersed in identity politics to help create a necessary social schism (such as Ntozake Shange, Imiri Baraka, Alice Childress) *and* Nineteenth Century African American playwrights who modeled their work after the dramatic conventions of the day rather than the West African-based performance structures the class has been studying. It may be that the best way to address essentialism is to explore the powerful potential of simultaneity— one of the very aesthetic choices central to the class. Ira Aldridge's adaptation of "The Black Doctor" uses the structure of Nineteenth Century melodrama *and* its content points to the specifics of a "blackness" that the lead character is only beginning to understand.

Said also suggests that another antidote to essentialist rhetoric is situating the literature in its context. By placing the literature alongside other works of its day and within the world at large in which it was generated, the literature expands outward to embrace the world rather than isolating itself away from the rest of life. Toward that end, the course packet includes chronologies of events relevant to the plays and periods we examine. The chronologies list important African American theatrical dates along with events in U.S. Theatre, U.S. History, and world history. When I review that list, I am reminded of how much whiteness remains the ground on which the course resets. I have scant information about Latina/o Theatre, Asian American theatre, Jewish theatre, or Native American theatre.

Essentialism also rears its head in establishing voices of authority and authenticity in the classroom. At times, African American students speak forcefully about some aspects of their own experiences to help buttress a particular argument. Finally, they have a place where their lives are presented as truth rather than whining paranoia. Some of them feel the course gives them an opportunity to see themselves as subjects and agents in their own histories. However, sharing their racialized experiences can silence all questions and critiques as the African American students are given the positions of authority. bell hooks addresses this problem when she writes, "If experience is already invoked in the classroom as a way of knowing that coexists in a nonhierarchical way with other ways of knowing, then it lessens the possibility that it can be used to silence"(1994, 84). Creating nonhierarchical ways of knowing requires that I share "facts" as well as my experiences; it means giving all students an opportunity to come to know the world through the literature, through their daily lives, and through whatever else they have to bring with them to their learning.

It seems that as we do what I feel is the necessary discussion in the class, we have less and less time to examine the "beauty of the literature" as Said suggests. And there is always the problem with dramatic texts of *discussing* them and not *experiencing* them in performance. Even in a classroom full of "non-actors" there is great benefit to having them spontaneously perform scenes from the plays we read. Here they can confront issues of casting, blocking, pace, and rhythm that remind them that in theatre, bodies are always on the line. Ideally this will underscore the embodied politics that I present to the class through an examination of race. On the fourth class period, I asked students to flesh out the opening scene from Duro Ladipo's "Oba Koso," the story of a Yoruba king's deification. One student was called on to direct the scene, and I asked for volunteers to perform. The class felt there should be three students representing the king's court. Given our recent discussions about the fusion of music, dance and spoken word in West African performance traditions, they decided this non-acting king's court should dance! I gave them a simple clapping rhythm, but as the scene progressed the clap evolved into a full body movement. The townspeople who had come to the king to argue against the ongoing war, were told to mime carrying weapons. After the scene, one student commented on the irony of them carrying weapons and asking for a cessation of the war. The king and his wife improvised dialogue as they fed each other imaginary fruit. These 15 minutes were well spent. The students had to take the words off the page and imagine them living in space. It is my hope that doing this early in the course will give them ways to read the plays throughout the semester.

Ogunba's notion of participation not only generates a fertile atmosphere, but it also includes the actual participation in the work itself. This is a hallmark of much African American performance and can be found in the impulse toward call and response and toward improvisation, yet in this history course, much time is spent with me lecturing and the students (hopefully) listening. I incorporate group work into the course so they can feel firsthand the theatrical requirements of collaborating and negotiating. The semester culminates in this group project. Ideally they work on this assignment for several weeks before presenting it to the class. The groups are asked to choose a play, performance company, or historical event, and shape a 15-minute presentation around their choice. Every group member must participate in the class presentation, but I can never know how thorough the participation was outside of class. Inevitably, a few group members do more work than others and some, I am often told, do no work at all. While it is time-consuming and "unfair," this assignment is the only one which approximates the close, trying, rewarding relationship of a theatrical company. Through this assignment the students might better understand the rise and fall of the American Negro Theatre that had to split its meager resources between uptown theatre classes and small productions, and a downtown hit; they might come to see how the potentially strong Zora Neale Hurston–Langston Hughes collaboration ended with the artists no longer speaking to each other; they might feel the excitement of creating something new with their peers.

Participation is also integrated into the course by requiring that the students attend an African American church service. This assignment is connected to the union that many scholars see between African American theatre and the African American church—especially, Baptist, A.M.E., and Pentecostal churches. Some of these churches are rampantly homophobic, frequently sexist and often speak of their brand of Christianity as the one true way. Fortunately, all of this narrowness can produce healthy classroom conversation. For instance, what is the role of Christianity in the history of African Americans? How does Christianity relate to the West African spiritual practices covered in the course? What is the relationship between spirituality and theatre? How do sexist and homophobic perspectives "serve" African American communities? What are the ethics of engaging in a religious activity merely to fulfill an assignment? Going to church as an assignment even allows us to ask whether this promotes the worst form of ethnography, in which the ethnographer does not even have an interest in the "subject" but has a purely utilitarian relationship with the culture? The questions help situate theatre alongside the ethics of everyday living rather than in elitist isolation. The questions also reveal what is at stake with theatrical representation.

I also require the students to attend an African American performance event—a play would be ideal, but a concert, poetry reading or other live events would also meet the aims of the course. Fulfilling this assignment can be difficult in Austin, where the major theatres do a "black show" once every two or three years, and the one black company in town produces sporadically.

Participation as a pedagogical strategy requires that the students see a relationship between the theatrical theories and productions of the course to the large and small dramas of their everyday lives. I have found Victor Turner's exploration of the mutual influences of stage and social dramas to be very useful in this regard. As if the State of Texas had not already given us a wealth of social dramas to confront, on September 11, 2001, as I walked toward class thirty minutes after the World Trade Center was destroyed and thousands of lives were lost, I wondered what I could possibly say about stage drama that would not trivialize this particular real life drama. Just one class period prior to the attack, the class had discussed Turner's theory, and that discussion served as a tool for talking about the terrifying events of that morning. After watching the horror together on television and trying to honor the specifics of that event, we then tentatively moved toward relating this to Turner's work. How will this social drama effect stage drama? What stage dramas support this social drama? My teaching assistant asked the class, "What do you think the terrorists look like." This risky question opened up issues of stereotypes, media-generated understandings, and the nature of civil liberties. Who are the major players? How do we avoid reducing the victims to mere extras in this drama? And finally, I ended this class day by asking the students to list the possible forms of redress, again returning to Turner's concepts. The responses ranged from trial and truth councils to assassinations and war. The class had to vote on which form of redress they would choose if they were a part of a delegation appointed by George W. Bush to decide what the United States should do in response to the attack. They tried to avoid the task—could they pick two or three answers rather than just one? Could they think about it and vote during the next class period? Since they would never be appointed to such a delegation, why do the exercise? I was disturbed to see that the most number of responses called for assassination and war. We now know that the students were prophetic.

Because race is such a focus of the course, the class operates with a level of tension that I must constantly monitor. It is difficult to balance vigorous discussion with protecting the feelings of each student. Sometimes I fear they are left feeling exposed and confused—perhaps in need of greater counsel than I can provide. And I too need such counsel after many classes. This work is really about all of us teaching each other, in the way Paolo Freire says classrooms work best. When I allow myself to be honest in the classroom, I share the authority with my students—and often need to seek solace after a particularly difficult discussion.

I remember one such discussion after reading a series of lynching plays. The plays are short and this allowed us to look closely at them in their entirety. I noted how one of the characters simply said "let us pray" after her grandson had been taken away without cause by the police. I questioned this as an effective strategy against the impending lynching. Immediately, students—African American Christian students jumped into the discussion— "Why can't you see prayer as an effective strategy?" "Do you know the power of prayer?"—and suddenly my own spirituality and my limited reading of the play were exposed to the class. The period was over, students unceremoniously filled their backpacks, sucked their teeth, and left the room. A hurricane had just swept through and I was left dazed.

Chandra Mohanty reminds us that when we engage in pedagogical practices that challenge the social and political structure, and when we expose our own blind spots, prejudices, and biases, we are not likely to receive strong teacher evaluations. This simply adds insult to injury. All that work, all that risk, and to end the semester with evaluations that scream, "Dr. Jones is a racist," "Dr. Jones doesn't allow any opinion that differs from her own," "This course should go back to African American Studies where it belongs." Even if these were written in the heat of finishing a semester with papers to write, exams to take, and projects to complete, they still sting.

I would like to create a classroom experience that practices the freedom that Henry Giroux describes—a place where the students and I journey along a sometimes frightening road, but where we always find our way to strength and safety and a new world order. Of course Giroux is wiser than to make such predictions, but it is still early in the semester—just the fifth class session—and I am still hopeful that maybe this time I will get it right.

Works Cited

Benston, Kimberly. 2000. *Performing Blackness: Enactments of African-American modernism*. New York: Routledge.

Caponi, Gena Dagel. 1999. *Signifyin(g), sanctifyin', & slam dunking: A reader in African American expressive culture*. Amherst: University of Massachusetts Press.

Freire, Paulo. 1996. *Pedagogy of the oppressed*. New York: Continuum Publishing Company.

Gates, Jr., Henry Louis. 1988. *The signifying monkey*. New York: Oxford University Press.

hooks, bell. 1994. *Teaching to transgress: Education as the practice of freedom*. New York: Routledge.

Hurston, Zora Neale. 1970. Characteristics of negro expression. In Nancy Cunard (ed.), *Negro: An Anthology*, New York: F. Ungar.

Ladipo, Duro. Oba Koso. 1984. In *The Yoruba Popular Traveling Theatre of Nigeria*. 'Biodun Jeyifo. Nigeria: Nigeria Magazine.

Mohanty, Chandra Talpade. 1994. On race and voice: Challenges for liberal education in the 1990s. In Henry A. Giroux and Peter McLaren (eds.), *Between borders: Pedagogy and the politics of cultural studies*. New York: Routledge.

Mason, John. 1992. *Orin Orisa: Songs for selected heads*. New York: Yoruba Theological Archministry.

Ogunba, Oyin. 1978. Traditional African festival drama. In Oyin Ogunba and Abiola Irele (eds.), *Theatre in Africa*. Nigeria: Ibadan University Press.

Olomo, Aina. 2002. *The core of fire: A path to Yoruba spiritual activism*. Brooklyn, NY: Athelia Henrietta Press.

Richardson, Willis. 1919. The hope of a Negro drama. In *Crisis* 19: 338–339.

Said, Edward. 1993. The politics of knowledge. In Cameron McCarthy and Warren Crichlow (eds.), *Race, identity and representation in education*. New York: Routledge.

Turner, Victor. 1990. Are there universals of performance in myth, ritual, and drama? In Richard Schechner and Willa Appel (eds.), *Means of performance: Intercultural studies of theatre and ritual*. New York: Cambridge University Press.

Tyler, Stephen. 1986. Post-modern ethnography: From document of the occult to occult document. In James Clifford and George E. Marcus (eds.), *Writing culture: The poetics and politics of ethnography*. Berkeley: University of California Press.

Wenger, Susanne. 1990. *The sacred groves of Oshobo*. Austria: Augustine Merzeder.

CHAPTER 12

Balancing Acts: Teaching Theatre in British Higher Education Today

Rob Brannen

Balancing Acts:

Theory	Practice
Academic	Vocational
Research	Teaching
Product	Process
Transmission of information	Experiential learning
Cognitive skills	Subject skills
The Epistemological	The Ontological
Classical	Contemporary

The "balancing" list appears to be endless for those engaged with teaching theatre at a higher education (HE) level; I am sure we could all create our own list of tensions, considerations, pushes, and pulls. Here I want to share a number of the current concerns in terms of a "balanced approach" from my experience of working as a theatre lecturer at a British university today. These concerns have been shaped over the past few years by a series of four developmental events, or national educational undertakings, within the British HE system.

Firstly, the late 1990s saw a comprehensive Subject Review (Drama, Dance, and Cinematics) undertaken by The Quality Assurance Agency (QAA) for HE, during which each HE Institution was subject to a review of its provision in the field. The QAA produced a Subject Overview Report detailing the strengths and shortcomings of the national provision as a whole. Secondly, in 2002 the QAA produced a Subject Benchmarking Statement (Dance, Drama, and Performance), which aimed to "describe the nature and characteristics" of the subject and also to present the standards expected at the level of bachelors degree with honors. In other words we now have a benchmark for Theatre "graduateness" (the qualities of being a Theatre graduate). Thirdly, at about the same time, a learning and teaching subject centre for Performing Arts was established at Lancaster University, as part of a national initiative for creating a Learning and Teaching Subject Network. In recent years our Subject Centre, The Performing Arts Learning and Teaching Innovation Network (PALATINE), has helped to identify key concerns in teaching theatre and facilitating projects, workshops, discussion, and the dissemination of information in this area. Finally, I have been personally involved with one of the subject specific learning and teaching projects aided by PALATINE, a project entitled The Performance Reflective Practice Project (ReP).

Through a discussion of these four key developments affecting my own teaching practice, the aim is to indicate the current nature of teaching theatre in British Higher Education and the current debates which are moving us forward. The work of the QAA allows for a general overview. The work of PALATINE begins a broad debate about learning and teaching, and ReP provides one example regarding the exploration of a specific concern.

We have now reached a point where the majority of British universities offer Theatre courses; either as Single honors subject or Joint/Combined honors, usually with one other subject. The QAA reports indicated a very diverse offering of distinct fields within the broad subject title, and importantly, that the spectrum of the provision ranges right across the academic/vocational, classical/contemporary range. This range has been broadened in recent years due to the degree of specialization and different educational approaches now found at post-16 level education, prior to university entry. Although many still arrive at the British university with three Advanced Level qualifications, an equal number now arrive at my own university through a vocational route: the National Diploma. Those with vocational training will have studied Theatre or Performing Arts alone, with no other subject, from the age of sixteen. Even those who have taken the traditional route can now do so having theoretically specialized in Performing Arts two years prior to coming to university, for example by taking Performing Arts, Theatre and Dance at Advanced Level. Within both of these major routes to Theatre at university level we have no way of discerning the "balance" of their education prior to joining us. In other words, those delivering post-16 courses have a degree of flexibility in their delivery whereby, for example, one vocational course might place emphasis upon a theoretical underpinning to practice evidenced through the written essay and another course might require almost no formal writing at all. In the same way, those offering courses in the HE sector may choose where to place the emphasis starting from the point of admissions. Vocational courses will choose to place evidence of performance skill above formal qualifications and allow entry with the bare minimum permitted to progress into higher education. On the other hand, university departments may require an entry points score as high as any other subject area requirement in the country. Alongside drama schools and conservatoires, some of the new universities specifically offer actor training, while some of the older universities deliver Theatre Studies courses with their roots firmly in the department of literature.

However, perhaps the majority of us, whilst acknowledging the extremes of the spectrum which exist, will take the middle ground. For example, my own university selects students through audition, interview *and* conditional entry points. A point of balance comes from considering the candidate's potential to understand through critical analysis *and* the potential to "do." Indeed, for the other end of the degree course, the QAA panel choose their words carefully to balance the selected criteria for a graduate. Under "Knowledge, understanding and abilities" we find: "to be able to demonstrate comprehension, *and* creative and intelligent engagement with . . ." [italics mine] prior to criteria concerning text-based approaches, collaborative group work, and considerations of the individual performer. Under "Subject Skills" we find that the graduate should "be able to engage creatively *and* critically with . . ." [italics mine] prior to criteria relating to production work, text-based approaches, performance skills and independent research into performance (QAA 2002). What is clear from the work of the QAA is that somehow through *combining* these considerations we manage to produce theatre graduates who go on to make their professions within a very wide range of vocations. These graduate destinations for the most part fall into the broad areas of performance, the arts, the media, marketing, administration, teaching, and community work.

This brings us to the question most often asked by prospective theatre students prior to point of entry. Upon Open Days and Audition Days I am almost guaranteed to be confronted with the enquiry: "What is the balance of theory and practice?" The PALATINE overview replies: "Most courses stress the interdependence of theory and practice, and the majority aim to offer students opportunities to engage with practice in an academic context" (PALATINE 2001). But if I gave that reply to a prospective candidate, I am sure they would regard me quizzically, and it would raise a number of questions in my own mind too. It would appear that most of us do it, juggle with it, balance it, but what exactly do we mean by "theory and practice"? It was with some curiosity that I came across a recent university Drama Studies course proposal which boasted ". . . a unique balance of theory and practice." Given the QAA benchmarking criteria above and the question on every seventeen-year-olds' lips as they search for the right course, it would appear to be an odd claim indeed.

In her paper "the curiosity of writing (or *who cares about performance mastery?*) [sic.]," Susan Melrose informs us:

> It might seem from commonsensical uses of the expression "theory and practice"—used as though we all already actually understand what these nouns stand for, if not the reasons for the one's preceding the other—that "theory" either is writing, or is necessarily mediated by it. Certainly enough expert academic writers (some of whom actually do know better) use the noun "theory" as though what it stood for was writerly and written, to cause this misunderstanding to be replicated throughout the land, in the university as well as other sites. (Melrose 2003, Abstract)

Melrose writes this within the context of a discussion regarding the role of written research outcomes "as external measure against which other practices are compared" (ibid.), which leads us, toppling somewhat, to our next related "balance." PALATINE's base-line survey of the national provision tells us:

> Staff research and professional experience, together with considerable input from visiting practitioners are significant strengths and help to ensure that curriculum content and delivery are current and relevant. The input of and reliance on relatively large numbers of part-time staff—often professional practitioners of national or international renown around a small permanent "core" team is a particular characteristic of the entire subject area. (PALATINE 2001)

Theory and practice? Research activity and professional experience? Lecturers and practitioners? Professional practitioners balance their work with their university input or, often, undertakings for formal qualifications. But, also, many lecturers within the field are currently balancing two jobs, or have done so in their past: their professional performance practice and their educational vocation. Within my immediate staff team, lecturers have experienced work as professional performers, directors, choreographers, playwrights, and artistic directors of building-based practice whilst in university employment. This "particular characteristic" is possibly unique within the university sector and raises questions regarding the knowledge-based (researchers), the experiential (practitioners) and the educative (teachers), alongside the intersection and interface between those positions.

It is no wonder that the nature of post-graduate work in the subject area has seen a significant shift in recent years. Traditionally, post-graduate provision may be seen to focus upon the depth of academic research evidenced through written tomes. In other words the best post-graduate courses produce great academics or researchers. These post-graduate activities lead to the extension, or pushing back the boundaries, of knowledge or how we look at/write about practice. Within the university context there is an obvious tension between the challenging of existing subject frameworks and a vocational training for performance or the cultural industries (and indeed market-led university admissions policies), as the outcomes of such activities are perceived to be leading to a reaffirmation of, rather than challenge to, the status quo. Training for West End musicals has, quite rightly, been resisted. Producing Andrew Lloyd-Webber fodder remains firmly off the curriculum, and the prime considerations for post-graduate study would still appear to be about challenging dominant structures, a depth of enquiry, discovery and the evolution (rather than stasis) of the subject, not employability. What *has* generally been viewed as a significant development is the emerging role of *performance* as research, alongside its contested nature. A forum has been provided for this continuing and fairly pre-occupying present debate through the Practice as Research in Performance project (PARIP), one of a number of nationally funded learning and teaching projects.

> A growing number of Performing Arts departments in Higher Education are now offering higher degrees which place practice at the heart of their research programmes. [I would note, not *training* programmes.] This represents a major theoretical and methodological shift in the performance disciplines—traditional approaches to the study of these arts are complemented and extended by research pursued by the practice of them. (PARIP 2003)

There can be no doubt that the identified "participatory nature" of the subject was key to an overall positive report from the QAA and a direct practical engagement with the subject led to a high level of enthusiasm by students and staff being highlighted as "a striking characteristic." Generally the teaching of the subject was viewed in a glowing light, with praise for the QAA assessors observed over seven hundred teaching sessions across all institutions delivering the subject. Ninety percent of the teaching was reported to be "good" or "very good" and, "... the best sessions were judged to be adventurous and inspirational" (QAA 1998). But if there is a pervading sense of an enthused ongoing interrogation of practice at the heart of delivering the subject, what were the concerns raised by the QAA review in terms of getting the balance right, and what was the response of the academic community?

For one example, the report states: "... in most institutions, the assessment of practice presents difficulties. This is particularly true of group work..." (ibid.). Funding for national learning and teaching projects has enabled a response to such concerns. In direct response to the above, The Assessing Group Practice project was founded as a collaborative undertaking involving a number of institutions across the sector. This project, "... aims to ensure that assessment of collaborative activity within the performing arts can be demonstrated as fair, robust and practicable across the sector" (Assessing Group Practice 2002). Through website and workshop dissemination their work provides case studies and assessment process and practice models in order to inform delivery. In a similar way, PALATINE has been instrumental in bringing the subject community together to explore learning and teaching issues constructively and supportively. Aside from supporting such projects as PARIP and Assessing Group Practice, PALATINE has initiated and facilitated events and workshops throughout Britain exploring such issues as Teaching Theatre History Today, Enhancing Graduate Employability and Assessing Improvisation.

My own learning and teaching research activity over the past few years has similarly been supported by our subject network and is a response to a further QAA concern. It is a point which directly relates to the "balancing" difficulties referred to earlier. The QAA report states:

In 60 per cent of cases an appropriate balance is achieved between practical production or performance and cultural, historical, theoretical and critical approaches. However, 40 per cent fail to provide for adequate developments of students' powers of analysis and critical reflective practice. (QAA 1998)

PALATINE's baseline survey reiterates the point as follows: "In a number of cases... there is an emphasis upon breadth at the expense of depth and... achievement in written and theoretical work generally does not match the level of achievement of their practical work" (PALATINE 2001).

But we can see how very easy it is for those designing and delivering a balanced curriculum to be faced with huge dilemmas. An English graduate's entire study, for example, might be focused upon critical analysis and the demonstration of their ability through the traditionally accepted written assessment forms. An expectation would not be for them to engage creatively with their subject by producing a short story, let alone a whole novel. What adds significantly to our dilemmas of delivery is the fact that "doing" is central to performance and primacy is given to the presence of the body in performance as the site in which meaning is ascribed, both verbally and nonverbally, within the creation of performance process. At a national level, and within our own institutions, this leads us into debates concerning the primacy given to certain kinds of knowledge and the communication of that knowledge. There are pressures from all sides. "But the students *must* keep on top of Derida in terms of cultural theory *whilst* mastering the Feldenkrais technique, otherwise they simply won't have *any* currency in terms of contemporary practice." "How can we possibly justify a graduate award in Theatre when they have not experienced all ten of Grotowski's principles of the creative act *or* deconstructed *Titus Andronicus* to any demonstrable level of 'deep' learning." I am teaching theatre students at a *British* university and we rarely mention Shakespeare, for goodness sake. How *can* I sleep at night?

Yes, the acquisition and transmission of certain kinds of knowledge is debateable within our subject area, and the time that we give and the level of depth possible is open to question. However, the view and purpose of analysis and critical reflective practice is, it would appear, less open to debate. If there is a problem with critical reflective analysis on practice, then both as a subject-specific and transferable life-skill it should be of great concern to those teaching theatre. The great theatre practitioners show the way and provide examples of ongoing reflective practice: Stanislavski, Brecht, Littlewood, Strasberg and Adler, Brook, Grotowski, Barba, Boal, Mamet, and in the United Kingdom the oft quoted Tim Etchells, director of the performance company, Forced Entertainment. Such models of practice tell us that in terms of a serious engagement with our subject, the continual reflection upon experience—readjusting practice, testing, and further critical reflection—would appear to be crucial.

The Performance Reflective Practice Project (ReP) was proposed by my university (De Montfort) as a direct response to the QAA concern that a significant proportion of the HE provision were delivering courses where their students were found wanting in this area. The formal recognition and teaching of reflective practice appeared to be a significant issue. My particular role in the project focused upon compositional creativity and learning processes within the light of recent discussion in HE surrounding experiential learning and the concept of reflective practice. For this investigation I worked in collaboration with my colleague Helen Bailey, Dance Lecturer, seeing the issue to have resonances across the two traditional disciplines into a wider consideration of performance process and practice. Of particular interest was that our investigation into recent educational theory has, to a certain degree, legitimized our own practice, and highlighted the contribution that educative tools aligned to our subject area can make to generic learning and teaching debates. The project allowed us the opportunity for a dialog within our own institution, between the performing arts teachers, and an expanded dialog with staff and students from six HE Institutions in the United Kingdom nationally. At times this dialog was furthered or enhanced through experiential engagement in studio-based exploration. What emerged was a value given to the personal ongoing experience, a shared vocabulary which deals with the subjective, the personal, and the emotional. Consequently, what also emerged was a challenge to the dominance of theory and product and a repositioned emphasis upon process and practice. However, this rebalanced position was not arrived at through the sacrifice of critical analysis skills, but through questioning regarding the frameworks of their use.

We began to look at underpinning educational theory to our own instinctive practice. Here we discovered that there often exists a tension between those promoting experiential learning and the academic context within which they are working. Again the notion of "doing" appeared to be problematic and provided a challenge to the accepted learning and teaching practice within our universities. For example, the last major report concerning HE practice within the United Kingdom, The Dearing Report (1997), indicated that 98 percent of all students view the lecture as the prime teaching method during their learning experience at this level. It would appear from the report's findings that the vast majority of their taught experience is concerned with the transmission of information. On a basic level, we found ourselves aligned to those educationalists who have extreme difficulty with the all too often held concept of the mature academic transmitting information into the empty heads of students. Here the British educationalists Anne Brockbank and Ian McGill summarize the traditional position, central to our often troublesome existence within the university: "The reference to experience has been dismissed by many as it deals with the body, appetites, the senses, the material world, while thinking proceeds from the (perceived) higher faculty of reason and spirit" (Brockbank and McGill 1999, 23).

However, the framework for the practice of our critical abilities within theatre begins to be shaped by a reading of recent theorists who require a more holistic approach to learning. British educationalist Ronald Barnett (1997) calls for a "critical being" rather than simply the activity of "critical thinking," placing an emphasis upon the emotional and active aspects of learning and not simply the cognitive and the knowledge-based. As the eminent American psychologist Carl Rogers tells us:

> Self-initiated learning which involves the whole persona of the learner—feelings as well as intellect—is the most lasting and pervasive.—This is not learning that takes place "from the neck-up." It is a gut-level type of learning.—An important element in these situations is that the learner knows it is his [/her] own learning and can thus hold onto it or relinquish it in the face of a more profound learning, without having to turn to some authority for corroboration of his [/her] judgement. (Rogers 1969, 36)

Key to this principle, and to a certain degree the possible focusing of our curriculum, is the conceptual framework provided by the idea of a reflective practitioner. By making my own pedagogical practices explicit to the learner they can be allowed to take responsibility for their learning and their performance practice. We can be freed to some extent from the overcrowded curriculum where so many demands of theory and practice are placed upon us through an explicit conceptual framework for the learners'/practitioners' role within clearly identified examples of practice. In other words, within my role as teacher I might reconsider the balance between the transmission of content and the facilitation of reflective practice within models of learning: how to approach performance skills, how to approach theoretical models, and so on.

The American educational theorists Patricia King and Karen Kitchener suggest that we do not reflect on straight-forward, or "well-structured" problems, however, reflection is central to solving "ill-structured" problems. They state, "Ill-structured problems result when either the acts open to the decision maker, states of nature, possible outcomes, or the utility of the outcome is unknown or not known with a high degree of certainty" (King and Kitchener 1994, 11). In other words, at a basic level, we do not reflect upon the answer to $2 + 2$, nor upon the route which we take to work everyday. However, Jennifer Moon tells us that we *do* engage in reflection when our thought-processes are applied to, "relatively complex or unstructured ideas for which there is no obvious solution" (1999, 23). Through our own reflective dialog, Helen Bailey and I (2002) considered that not only does creative performance practice require the solving of ill-structured problems, but the *creation* of ill-structured problems for both performers and audience. It is consequently fundamental to our role as performing arts teachers to understand the nature of learning through reflection and to facilitate an enabling environment in which the students' own reflection can be most creatively productive and educationally beneficial.

At the same time, there needs to be an awareness and wariness of an approach to teaching which belongs solely to the mature, all-knowing academic category at the expense of being engaged *ourselves* with an ongoing reflective process. We might employ the same principle to those who see themselves as falling within the mature actor or mature director category, and, having mastered their subject, transmits their knowledge through the "master" class. If the learner's or performer's role is *only* to receive that which is transmitted by the "master" then how are they to take responsibility for their learning, or development as a practitioner?

Choosing to examine the role of reflection within compositional/devising work Helen and I questioned how we might facilitate studio-based learning, which allowed students to move towards self-sufficiency both as learners and artists. We began to apply to our own teaching, concepts developed by the educationalists David Kolb (1984), Donald A. Schön (1983, 1987) and further developed by John Cowan (1998), regarding the cycle: "reflection-for-action" (reflection prior to an experience), "reflection-in-action" (actions influenced by the reflective process), "reflection-on-action" (reflection following experience) and so on. We communicated the outcomes of this questioning through a reflective practice workshop both for students and staff from our subject area as discipline specific, and for a cross section of university lecturers from other disciplines as a generic learning and teaching exercise. The aims of the workshop were to legitimize and provide frameworks or parameters for the following: the role of peer dialog, the sharing of process and group discussion, reflective writing and the conscious recognition and role of the subjective experience. During the workshop the participants *experienced* the outcomes of research from the position of the *learner*, this non-traditional form of communicating/discussing research outcomes being all important to the debates already outlined (in other words not the transmission of an academic paper). Susan Melrose states, "Our writing will always be *about* performance" (2003, Part 1). She fears that as a university discipline we may move towards what she calls "spectator-studies," " . . . practiced . . . at a safe and readily-resourced distance from expert performing arts practices and practitioners" (ibid.). Within the context of ReP research, a further consideration is that we might also fear an externalized learning process which "happens over there" and then is "done to me," rather than *my* doing, *my* experience, *my* response, *my* learning.

Of course, all these points of "balance" are interconnected, presently arising from an over-riding tension produced by the fact that we engage with a subject where "the experiential is a key principle of study" (QAA 2002), yet we attempt to deliver the subject within academic contexts slow to recognize or legitimize this very educational principle. On the other hand, the majority of those teaching theatre, and those drawing up the standards for delivery of the subject, are also resisting the tidal shift toward the market-led employability slogan, in which our role is only to produce the practitioner without the "critically reflective."

In his article "Tomorrow's Theatre—and How to Get There from Today's," John Russell Brown warns of theatre as a deeply conservative, endangered art form which must make very basic changes before it can "hold up a mirror to our lives and once more draw crowded audiences" (2002, 339). In stark relief to the apparent condition of the art form itself, he draws our attention to theatre's boom and expansion in the education sector. Here we find the younger generation, more in touch with their times, and here he tells us ". . . is a crucible for change . . . that is not confined by commercial considerations and not easily intimidated by tradition or other people's successes" (ibid., 342). Likewise, Vera Gottlieb, in her article "Theatre Today—the new realities," pleads for a theatre of relevance ". . . to be a means of empowerment, rather than merely 'populist,' engaging with the questions which both arise from society *and* require debate" (2003, 9). There would appear to be a huge responsibility on our shoulders in our attempt to get the balance right: both the critical skills to question and the practical skills to communicate the debate through performance. It is not necessarily the teachers of theatre who must question the form for their students, but who must teach how to question and act upon that questioning, so that the form might be changed by and for a new generation of practitioners and audience members.

The QAA Subject benchmarking report summarizes the national British provision of teaching our subject in HE in the following way:

> The practice and conceptual bases of performing arts . . . do not embrace a stable body of knowledge and skills [for my purposes here "a *balanced* body of knowledge and skills"] but are characterised by changing social, political and artistic values and practices; it is the dynamic nature of these cultural practices and their frequently contested nature that sustains the vitality of the subject areas. Reciprocally, the activities of students and

staff in HEIs [Higher Education Institutions] impact and change those practices." (1998)

John Russell Brown concludes his article: "In a classroom, with its own kind of energy and freedom, someone may be finding the means by which tomorrow's theatre will thrive and win back its public" (2002, 342).

Off-balance is a suitable starting point and one to be embraced; just before we move, just before we fall, just before we run.

Works Cited

Bailey, Helen and Rob Brannen. 2002. Creative dialogues: Connecting the learning process and the creative process through reflection. <www.lancs.ac.uk/palatine/ s-v-presentations/brannenpaper.htm> Paper presented at the Shared Visions Conference, Brighton, UK.

Barnett, Ronald. 1997. *Higher education: A critical business*. Buckingham: Open University Press and The Society for Research into Higher Education.

Brockbank, Anne and Ian McGill. 1999. *Facilitating reflective learning in higher education*. Buckingham: Open University Press and The Society for Research into Higher Education.

Brown, John Russell. 2002. Tomorrow's theatre and how to get there from today's. *New Theatre Quarterly* 13: 334–342.

Cowan, John. 1998. *On becoming an innovative university teacher: Reflection in action*. Buckingham: Open University Press.

Dearing, Ron. 1997. *Report of the National Committee of Inquiry into Higher Education*. <www.leeds.ac.uk/educol/ncihe>.

Foundation for the Development of Teaching and Learning (FDTL) projects: Assessing Group Practice. <www.assessing-groupwork.ulst.ac.uk>. Practice as Research in Performance. <www.bris.ac.uk/parip>. Performance Reflective Practice Project. <www.hum.dmu.ac.uk/Research/PA/ReP/>.

Gottlieb, Vera. 2003. Theatre today. *The Contemporary Theatre Review* 13, no. 2: 5–14.

King, Patricia M. and Karen S. Kitchener. 1994. *Developing reflective judgement: Understanding and promoting intellectual growth and critical thinking in adolescents and adults*. San Francisco: Jossey Bass.

Kolb, David A. 1984. *Experiential learning*. Englewood Cliffs, NJ: Prentice Hall.

Melrose, Susan. 2003. the curiosity of writing (or *who cares about performance mastery?*) [sic.]. <www.sfmelrose.u-net.com> of writing. Paper presented at the Practice as Research in Performance Conference, Bristol, UK.

Moon, Jennifer. 1999. *Learning journals: A handbook for academics, students and professionals*. London: Kogan Page.

Performing Arts Learning and Teaching Innovation Network. 2001. Performing Arts Base-line Survey 2000–2001. <www.lancs.ac.uk/palatine>.

Quality Assurance Agency for Higher Education. 2002. Subject benchmark statement: Dance, drama and performance. <www.qaa.ac.uk>.

———. 1998. Subject overview report: quality assessment of drama, dance and cinematics. <www.qaa.ac.uk>.

Rogers, Carl. 1969. *Freedom to learn*. Columbus, OH: Charles E Merrill.

Schön, Donald A. 1987. *Educating the reflective practitioner*. San Francisco: Jossey Bass.

———. 1983. *The reflective practitioner: How professionals think in action*. New York: Basic Books.

CHAPTER 13

Preparing Future Teachers of Theatre: Pedagogical Issues and Current Practice

Michele A. Pagen

The premise to this study began as a personal one, indeed. As a doctoral student in the early 1990s, I found myself standing in front of a classroom of students for the first time. I thought that this notion was exciting, yet odd, for I had never had a formal education class in my entire academic career. Nonetheless, there I was in front of a roomful of students faced with the task of teaching them a specific area of theatre, which compelled me to give some profound thought to the transmission of knowledge. I was fortunate in that the graduate program in our department required that first year doctoral students enroll in a course entitled "Theatre Pedagogy." At least I would have exposure to numerous teaching theories and practices through the required readings in the course. However, I wanted to teach at a college or university upon graduation and did not feel that one course in pedagogy would provide me with enough knowledge to teach others. Doctoral programs traditionally provide the student with academic knowledge, yet the majority of graduates, many of whom have little or no prior teaching experience or teacher education background, will be employed in higher education.

I was faced with a dilemma: Is knowledge of a subject matter enough to teach that subject matter? Essentially, my concern was that I would not be able to effectively communicate the knowledge I had acquired to students. This led me to investigate other graduate theatre programs in an effort to discover whether doctoral students in other departments and at other universities were required to participate in a teacher-training program different from the one offered at my university.

During the 1992–1993 academic year, I began a preliminary search on pedagogy requirements in theatre doctoral programs across the country, but found little information. Therefore, I broadened my search to include doctoral programs in general, not limited to the theatre discipline. It was here that I found a great deal of information debating the quality of teaching in higher education. Many scholars indicated a need to improve teaching assistant training in graduate programs that would, as a result, improve college and university teaching. I began to wonder where theatre fit into this discussion. Therefore, this essay is divided into four areas of investigation. The first three areas describe the results of my initial study. The fourth area examines the current state of theatre doctoral programs. Therefore, the essay begins with a brief description of the issues confronting those in academe at the time of my initial investigation. Next, pedagogical practices concerning teaching assistant training are presented, addressing graduate programs in general and theatre doctoral programs specifically. Additionally, priorities with which theatre graduate programs must concern themselves when preparing future teachers are defined. Finally, an investigation of current doctoral theatre programs is conducted in order to ascertain whether these programs have adopted or implemented suggested priorities of the new professoriate.

Pedagogical Issues in the Early 1990s

In investigating the preparation of graduate students (future university professors), I found that the earliest discussions referred often to Ernest Boyer's 1990 study *Scholarship Reconsidered: Priorities of the Professoriate* sponsored by the Carnegie Foundation for the Advancement of Teaching. In this report, Boyer indicates that "teaching," "research" and "service" may no longer accurately describe the professoriate. Instead, Boyer introduces four terms as replacements to the outdated three. His idea is that we, in higher education, need to develop a more "creative" view of the professoriate. His professor is a scholar, who comprises "discovery," "integration," "application" and "teaching" (Boyer 1990, 15–25). Although teaching remains a component of Boyer's scholar, it is given a new definition, one that incorporates the first three.

"Discovery," according to Boyer, "comes closest to what is meant when academics speak of 'research' (Boyer 1990, 17). Despite criticism against "publish or perish," original, independent research discoveries conducted by professors help to keep the academic discipline fresh and alive. However, discovery should not be conducted in isolation, but rather in connection with the remaining components.

Boyer's "integration" signifies that one should apply the "discovery" in order to search for connections between existing research or research in a discipline other than one's own (Boyer 1990, 19). This area reveals an opportunity for interpretation of one's own work according to the "grand scheme of things."

"Application" would appear to indicate an active task. This term signifies a specific approach to discovery, in effect, putting the theory to practice (Boyer 1990, 22). "Application" could seek to answer questions relating to the advancement of the discovery itself or the institution or society. An earth shattering discovery is not necessary; all academic research seeks to answer a question of some type, whether sought for the good of the researcher, the discipline, or mankind.

The final component of Boyer's scholar is "teaching." In Boyer's terminology, teaching is the successful communication of the discovered knowledge to individual students (Boyer 1990, 23). Discovery and teaching are and should be connected according to Boyer. The two should not be unrelated tasks, completed because that is what is required.

Boyer's 1990 discussion concerning the new professoriate occurred during a time when both society and those in academe were searching for ways in which to improve the reputation of higher learning. His report indicated a need for those in higher education to re-prioritize the research, teaching, and service elements of a professor in order to address the rise in the public concern about the quality of education received by the students. Those enrolled in colleges and universities were concerned with the amount of time their professors devoted to teaching. Boyer concluded that because of this, there is more attention being paid to the education of the undergraduate student (Boyer 1990).

In 1997, The Carnegie Foundation for the Advancement of Teaching sponsored a follow-up report to Boyer's 1990 study. *Scholarship Assessed: Evaluation of the Professoriate* serves as a sequel to the initial study. Its authors attempted to examine colleges and universities across the country in an effort to ascertain how faculty and administrators were incorporating this new definition of the professoriate. What was found was that the scholarship of discovery was in transition. Efforts were being made to break free of traditional research procedures and move toward the more inclusive process of discovery. As a result of this, faculty and administrators were struggling to develop a clear method of assessment for this new type of scholarship.

Simply, "the effort to broaden the meaning of scholarship simply cannot succeed until the academy has clear standards for evaluating this wider range of scholarly work" (Glassick et al. 1997, 5). Those in academe had recognized public outcry for improved teaching in higher education and were, indeed, making strides to change.

Boyer's initial report on the priorities of the professoriate also stemmed from society's search for "accountability" in higher education, and its demands that those in academe justify their profession and the activities which define it and occupy this time. Robert B. Wagner, in his 1989 book, *Accountability in Education: A Philosophical Inquiry* addressed this concern by indicating that the criticism surrounding education deals primarily with "educational purpose, procedures and reform [and] questions of accessibility and whether the results of education justify related expenditures" (2). Wagner indicated that it is the professor who faces the greatest criticism where accountability is concerned because society "assume[s] that teachers are responsible for student performance and ultimately for what students learn or fail to learn as a result of their classroom experience" (Wagner 1989, 2). And now, with the rapid increase of technology, information is being shared at an alarming rate. Lifelong learning programs are exploding, as there is an increase in the number of non-traditional students matriculating through the university. Those in academe are faced with a larger number of students, from all facets of society. Faculty are being asked to incorporate the use of technology as an instrument of both teaching and learning. Because of this, there has been a gradual shift in the purpose of a college degree. "Policy makers, legislators, and the media increasingly view higher education not as an investment in the collective public good but as a private benefit to individuals" (Glassick et al. 1997, 6). As educational purpose is being questioned, society is calling for a justification of the old research, teaching and service components of the professoriate. There is a necessity for higher education to "relate the work of the faculty more directly to the realities of contemporary life" (Glassick et al. 1997, 6).

In her discourse, which was published in March of 1992, Carol Cartwright implies that higher education has failed to concern itself with the changing needs of society. In effect we have "lost the public's trust" (Cartwright 1992, 14). It is her opinion that much of the criticism that befalls the academy resides within society. Part of that reason is because "[h]igher education has evolved from something available to and desired by the very few, to something practically required—indeed, demanded—by the majority" (Cartwright 1992, 15). Because higher education exists for the public, then it is with the public that higher education must hold itself accountable. This is something that must be done if higher education wishes to continue to exist. Cartwright argues:

[. . .] we are not talking about "business as usual" for higher education. We are talking about possible and very fundamental changes in *who* we serve, *why* we serve, *how* we serve, and *how* we are accountable to those who pay the bills. (Cartwright 1992, 16).

If the public is demanding that greater attention be placed upon teaching, then those within the academy must redefine the priorities faced by the professoriate in an attempt to update the duties of the professor and focus them more directly to meet the needs of the student. Boyer's definition incorporates all elements of a university professor equally in order to create a more balanced scholar; one who partakes in the scholarship of teaching as well as the scholarship of research. Teaching, however, has not traditionally been considered a scholarly activity. Researchers indicate, however, that those in academe must change this outdated method of thinking as they attempt to improve the quality of university teaching.

The acceptance of teaching as a respected scholarly activity will occur only if we maintain active, ongoing communication with others about teaching. Because teaching has not been considered on the same level as the scholarship of research, appropriate awards and recognition have been lacking. According to Boyer, "[A]t most four-year institutions, the requirements of tenure and promotion continue to focus heavily on research and on articles published in journals, especially those that are refereed. Good teaching is expected, but it is often inadequately assessed" (Boyer 1990, 28). Only recently have institutions of higher learning begun to recognize and reward effective teachers on their campuses with some degree of regularity. Most faculty are reluctant to discuss teaching in terms of an academic discipline possibly because they feel that their own academic preparation was lacking in this area. This reluctance is dissipating, however, due in large part to "increasing concerns about excellence in post secondary teaching currently being noted by legislators, college administrators, faculty, parents and students" (Ronkowski 1993, 86).

Preparing Doctoral Teaching Assistants in General

Traditionally, graduate programs provide the student with a strong background in a specific academic discipline; however, based upon the discussion of the reforms occurring in the area of college teaching, knowledge of the subject area is no longer sufficient. Thomas Angelo and Patricia Cross specify in their article, "Classroom Teaching for Teaching Assistants," that

> to maintain and imoprove the quality of higher education, we must prepare [...] future faculty members to teach more effectively and to value teaching as a profession that requires a mastery of skills, as well as a knowledge of subject matter. (Angelo 1989, 99)

This would mean that university professors would have to have a greater understanding of pedagogy and how to apply it to their content area. This notion would indicate that programs and departments devoted to preparing future faculty should incorporate pedagogy into their curricula. In many instances, they contend, graduate students are given the impression that teaching is something that is tacked on, an obligation that comes—perhaps "naturally"—after research and publication. However, in order for new faculty to be prepared to recognize teaching as a scholarly activity, should pedagogical methods and theories be included in the graduate program?

The responsibility of the graduate program to devote more time to the pedagogical preparation of its students is manifest in two areas. First, the graduate program, as a member of higher education, has a responsibility to the undergraduate student to remain abreast of the changing qualities, in both physical traits and learning styles, and to inform potential faculty members of these changes. "The on-the-job activities of new faculty members call for knowledge and skills not inherent to the standard Ph.D. program. In all fields, at all institutions, the greatest need is for scholars to teach undergraduates" (Richlin 1993, 1). Second, graduate programs have an obligation to the graduate student to assure that he or she is prepared with the knowledge and skills necessary for employment, a topic that has been primarily ignored in most graduate study.

As graduate programs strive to meet the responsibility of better preparing its graduates for teaching careers, a discussion of changing the graduate program inevitably arises. This discussion falls into three distinct categories. On one end of the continuum are those who reject the notion of incorporating change into the Ph.D. program. Typically in support of the traditional research oriented degree, advocates, including Jaroslav Pelikan author of *Scholarship and Its Survival: Questions on the Idea of Graduate Education*, contend that for the integrity of the doctoral degree to remain intact, change should occur through the acceptance of degrees devoted to producing college and university teachers, such as the DA or D.Ed. degrees (Pelikan 1983). By developing the separate degrees, the focus of the Ph.D. can then remain on producing the research scholar.

In contrast, are those who support the inclusion of pedagogical procedures into the existing curriculum of the Ph.D. program. These departments and programs are more accommodating and open to the change that Richlin and others conclude will be necessary for the successful preparation of future faculty.

A third group supports the addition of a pedagogical training program, but feel that a university-wide program would suffice. Programs such as these would inform the graduate student of various teaching and learning methods without regard to the curricular content. Faculty from numerous departments would participate in the education of the doctoral teaching assistant (DTA) through a faculty development unit.

As academic theatre is a member of higher education, it is vital that theatre concerns itself with the issues facing academe in general. Burnet Hobgood, editor of *Master Teachers of the Theatre*, identifies the lack of information in publication addressing theatre pedagogy in terms of higher education. He laments:

One looks in vain for general statements attesting to the qualities or attitudes needed in one who is or who would become an especially effective instructor of students interested in theatre. (Hobgood 1988, 6)

There do exist, however, statements attesting to the qualities or attitudes necessary for anyone seeking to become a college or university professor. Theatre must work to adapt the general methods to suit its own discipline.

Preparing Doctoral Teaching Assistants in Theatre

My initial survey was conducted in 1993. The survey document itself was ten pages long and consisted of a variety of types of questions, from short answer to multiple choice to rating scales. The instrument was developed in order to gather data regarding theatre doctoral teaching assistants, their courses and supervision. Graduate programs surveyed were identified in the 1992 edition of the *Directory of Doctoral Programs in Theatre Studies in the U.S.A. and Canada*. The information learned through this process revealed the amount and type of pedagogy offered to students in doctoral theatre programs. The complete 1993 survey and the empirical data are relatively extensive (Pagen 1994). Much of the information revealed in the survey, while certainly informative, does not directly apply to the issues addressed in this essay. Only responses specifically addressing the amount and type, or lack thereof, of pedagogical training existing in the graduate program is given below. Additionally, an investigation into existing graduate theatre programs has been conducted in order to determine what, if any, changes have been made to the training of theatre doctoral teaching assistants from the time of the initial survey of 1993 through the turn of the century. For the purposes of this essay, the information learned from the initial data collection is explained below and then compared with the information gathered recently.

An effort in the 1993 document was made, in part, to determine how theatre doctoral programs prepare their graduates for the professoriate of the future as conceived by Ernest Boyer and others. From the results of the survey it is possible to describe DTA training in theatre doctoral programs and suggest areas for change. When my initial research began, there were 38 doctoral programs in theatre in existence, all of which were invited to participate in the study. Twenty-seven programs replied to the invitation. Six schools indicated that they would be unable to participate in the survey process for reasons which included they no longer had a doctoral program, their doctoral students did not teach, or that they did not have the time to participate. This left 21 of the original 38 (or 61 percent) of the schools responding to the survey. The responses to the survey interpreted in light of the issues and practices identified earlier in the study, some interesting information is revealed concerning the level of pedagogy training within doctoral theatre programs and the preparation of the professoriate of the future.

According to the information revealed in the survey, doctoral students are given teaching assignments based on their academic standing and their potential as effective teachers. Prior teaching experience is not required in order to be given a teaching assistantship, which could leave many DTAs to experience the "learn by doing" method of teaching, which education researchers indicate will no longer be sufficient for a professor of the future.

The course supervisor—a faculty member within the department—generally provides any pedagogical training that is available to the DTA within the department. The pedagogical background of the supervisor is limited, possibly learned through trial and error. Course supervisors responding to the survey stated that they do not have enough time to devote to their position. This could indicate that the supervisor might not recognize the importance of pedagogical training or the difference between training for a particular course and training for the theatre discipline. This could also indicate that the department may not provide release time to the faculty member serving as course supervisor.

The facultys' attitudes toward pedagogical training might have determined the number of surveys returned incomplete. Several DTA supervisors returned the survey blank, stating that they had little time or inclination to complete the questionnaire. Perhaps the importance of pedagogical training for doctoral theatre students was not a departmental priority. This might indicate that teaching is not considered an important area for investigation.

Similarly, faculty attitudes revealed in the "Impression" section of the survey would indicate a reluctance to consider teaching an activity equal to research. For example, in response to the statement, "Faculty members are more often rewarded for research and publication than for effective teaching," one DTA supervisor responded, "As they should be." Many respondents indicated that there existed no need to investigate pedagogy courses or teaching methods.

It is curious to note that the same number of respondents who favored investigating philosophies of higher education, university-wide teacher training and instructional procedures also indicate that additional research into this area is not necessary. Possibly things will begin to change in terms of research into theatre pedagogy when more faculty become convinced of its necessity.

The attitudes held by course supervisors toward their positions could be in direct relation to the departmental treatment of DTA training and supervision. Theatre doctoral programs do provide at least minimal pedagogical orientation and consistent mentoring for doctoral teaching assistants. All respondents indicated that either a departmental or university-wide orientation program was available to doctoral students. The training, as well as the teaching assignment, still appear "tacked on" and are generally not included in the formal curriculum of the graduate program. Both are in addition to the required course work necessary for the completion of the degree. However, three of the programs represented offered a formal pedagogy course for their doctoral students. Based on the information revealed in the data, DTAs teach courses for the purposes of departmental exigencies and teaching experience. In only four of the responding institutions do DTAs receive credit for teaching an undergraduate course. While teaching experience could be considered a valid reason, the training offered to the student is limited to the theatre course for which the DTA is responsible. The majority of the doctoral programs surveyed did not offer a formal course in pedagogy for their graduate students despite the fact that all respondents consider a doctoral degree as preparation for a career with an institution of higher learning. This supports the notion that college and university teaching is one profession that allows its members to practice on their clients with little formal training. The necessity to include the education of the college teacher into the curriculum is apparent in order to stress the necessity for quality undergraduate teaching.

When considering the future of higher education, theatre educators must begin to discuss, formally, teaching in higher education. Theatre is a unique discipline, offering both "academic" and "practical" courses, which could require different pedagogical techniques. The lack of published information concerning pedagogy and theatre in higher education might indicate that this topic has not yet become a priority for academic theatre, but, to remain in tune with society and higher education, steps must be taken in this direction. As it exists, pedagogical preparation either exists in isolation of the academic discipline or with the limited background of the DTA supervisor. There appears to be a lack of cross discipline discussions of teaching in terms of sharing discoveries and teaching methods.

The single, fundamental change that must occur within theatre doctoral programs is the re-evaluation of the philosophy of the Ph.D. degree. The traditional duties of the professoriate must be redefined in order to address more specifically, the scholarship of teaching. Because it is in graduate school where the majority of college and university professors are prepared, graduate programs must begin to incorporate the new definition into their programs. Once theatre doctoral programs include, more formally, the art and science of teaching theatre within their programs, other areas of change will inevitably occur. As teaching becomes recognized as a scholarly activity, recognition of effective teaching among faculty and DTAs will follow. Course supervisors may be rewarded with release time in order to devote more time to the training of the teaching assistant. Subsequently, teaching assistants might recognize the importance of teaching and develop a much-needed respect for this neglected task. In addition, teaching may become less of an individual experience. Both DTAs and faculty may become more willing to share their experiences with each other and members of other disciplines in order to improve their own teaching.

Doctoral theatre programs have numerous options available when incorporating teacher training within the curriculum. Whether a pedagogy program exists university-wide or within the department, faculty should consider the many choices their institution has to offer.

As it exists, almost all of the doctoral theatre students enrolled in the colleges or universities represented in this study participate in a university-wide orientation program. The goals of these programs are not limited to pedagogical preparation, but most DTAs are exposed to teaching methods and techniques during the orientation period. In addition to orientation programs, doctoral teaching assistants could be encouraged to visit their university's teaching enhancement center, if available. In addition, courses in the education discipline could be included in the student's degree program.

Possible courses could include an educational theory and philosophy courses as well as curriculum design. By taking these courses, doctoral students would be provided with pedagogical knowledge, which they could then apply to their discipline.

To strengthen a doctoral student's pedagogical knowledge within the discipline, the department could require the DTA to observe or assist a "master" DTA in teaching the theatre course before he or she is given a section of his or her own. Another option to consider is to enable the student to assist a faculty member in teaching an upper level course. In addition, all DTAs could be required to attend a weekly meeting at which DTAs could discuss problems or challenges they face when teaching their particular course. By doing this particular option, all DTAs are exposed to at least an idea of the teaching techniques and challenges of numerous theatre courses, as opposed to those they face in only the course they teach. If an objective of the doctoral theatre program is to develop teachers for higher education, then pedagogy must be formally included in the student's curriculum.

The Current State of Theatre DTA Training

The above results of the 1993 study do not paint a very comforting picture. Happily, according to information gained in the third edition of the *Directory of Doctoral Programs in Theatre Studies, Performance Studies, and Dance: U.S.A. and Canada 1999*, this outlook has changed. As of 1999, there were 36 graduate theatre programs in existence. Of these, six programs now include some formal experience in pedagogy, be it a specific course within the curriculum or a yearlong program required of its students (Davis et al. 1998). While this *is* an increase of 100 percent, it is still only roughly 17 percent of the existing programs, which require even this limited exposure to pedagogy. This evidence does reveal an attempt, however minor, by those in higher education to improve teacher-training programs; however, is one course or a yearlong program devoted to teaching a specific theatre course enough to address pedagogical issues faced by future theatre faculty? Departments may find it necessary to develop a sequence of required pedagogy courses. All programs must include such courses if we are to truly redefine the professoriate for the future.

As I was conducting my investigation into the preparation of theatre doctoral teaching assistants for careers in academe, a program organized by the Council of Graduate Schools and the Association of American Colleges and Universities was being developed. This national program, still at work today, is funded by The Pew Charitable Trusts. The "Preparing Future Faculty"

(PFF) program began "as part of a nationwide initiative to encourage research universities to enhance the preparation of graduate students for future careers in the professoriate" (Castner 2001). My initial research into the pedagogical preparation of theatre graduate students occurred prior to the implementation of this program; therefore, the PFF program was not included in my early findings. However, a brief overview of the program reveals a strong, organized effort to address societal concerns as to the purpose of college and university faculty.

According to the description of the Preparing Future Faculty Program found on the organization's website, the PFF program

> addresses the full scope of faculty roles and responsibilities that include teaching, research, and service [by giving] doctoral students opportunities to observe and experience faculty responsibilities at a variety of academic institutions with varying missions, diverse student bodies, and different expectations for faculty. (Preparing 2001)

Obviously this program directly addresses the concerns held by both the public and by educational researchers during the early to mid-1990s. Those doctoral students selected to participate in the program emerge better prepared for a career in academe.

While the PFF program definitely moves in the right direction in terms of better preparing doctoral students for careers in higher education, there is no documented information demonstrating an increase into the amount of formal pedagogical training included in the program. Participants are given *more* opportunities to teach and at numerous types of institutions; however, this only supports the "learn by doing" method of education. Any additional focus on teaching in doctoral programs is certainly beneficial and the PFF program requires that participating students "have multiple mentors and receive reflective feedback not only for their research activities but also for their teaching" (Preparing 2001). The results of this reflective feedback require the mentor and student to discuss what it is that they do on a practical as well as philosophical level.

This program definitely demonstrates positive movement toward preparing stronger, more pedagogically aware students than those graduating before the implementation of this program. Upon examination of the research universities selected to participate in the program since its inception, 15 of the participating schools had doctoral theatre programs as of 1999. The PFF program has moved through four phases since its development; however and only recently have the Council of Graduate Schools and the Association of

American Colleges and Universities expanded the PFF program to include the Humanities and Social Sciences. This expansion occurred in phase four of the program, which began in 1999 and will be completed in 2002. Six of the selected 15 institutions participating in PFF 4 had doctoral theatre programs in 1999. The opportunity for doctoral theatre students to participate in this program exists, but it is unknown how many DTAs in the six universities with doctoral theatre programs are currently participating. No indication was given that the doctoral theatre programs at any of the six institutions participating in phase four were directly involved in the PFF program. It would be interesting to investigate the PFF program since its inception through 2002 to see how many theatre graduate students participated in the program and to what extent. The doctoral theatre programs participating in the program could be surveyed in order to determine the impact this program had on the specific department's required pedagogical training. The Preparing Future Faculty program has made definite strides in the preparation of future faculty of many disciplines; the amount of participation of doctoral theatre programs appears to be limited at this point.

Perhaps the best pedagogy program is one that includes several of the suggested options. The ideal pedagogy program is subject to the needs of the department, therefore no blanket prescription can be made. It is only through a thorough investigation of the needs, objectives and resources available that an ideal pedagogy program can be tailored for an individual department.

Conclusion

The amount of pedagogical information in existence relating to theatre programs specifically has not seen much growth in eight years. Perhaps theatre educators overall have not yet adopted the notion of the changing face of the professoriate. DTA training programs exist; however, a clear philosophy behind the purpose of the orientation programs appear to be lacking or, if stated, are extremely vague and limited to departmental exigencies. It would appear that theatre doctoral assistants teach courses out of departmental necessity and to provide general experience in this area. For most of those programs surveyed, teaching is not formally related to a student's course of study, although more graduate programs are making strides in this direction. The number of graduate theatre programs that include some formal study of pedagogy doubled between 1993 and 1999. Doctoral theatre students participating in any phase of the PFF program is, at this point, unknown, but the opportunity now exists. Perhaps, as theatre educators continue to become more aware of the changes that researchers contend are still occurring in higher education, the philosophy behind pedagogy in theatre Ph.D. programs will change as well, from an activity only tangential within the research oriented doctoral degree, to one that is a vital part of graduate education.

Works Cited

Angelo, Thomas and K. Patricia Cross. 1989. Classroom research for teaching assistants in the 1990s. In Jody D. Nyquist et al. (ed.), *Teaching assistant training in the 1990s*. San Francisco: Jossey-Bass, 99–108.

Boyer, Ernest. 1990. *Scholarship reconsidered: Priorities of the professoriate.* Lawrenceville, NJ: Princeton.

Cartwright, Carol A. June 1992. Reclaiming the public trust. *AAHE bulletin.*

Castner, Amy. Brief overview of the PFF Program. Preparing Future Faculty. 5 June 2001. <http://www.preparing-faculty.org/PFFWeb.Contents.htm#. about> (28 July 2001).

Davis, Peter and Thomas Postlewait. 1998. (eds.), *Directory of doctoral programs in theatre studies, performance studies and dance: U.S.A. and Canada 1999.* Philadelphia: American Society of Theatre Research.

Glassick, Charles E., Mary Taylor Huber and Gene I. Maeroff. 1997. *Scholarship assessed: Evaluation of the professoriate.* San Francisco: Jossey-Bass.

Hobgood, Burnet M. 1988. *Master teachers of theatre.* Carbondale: Southern Illinois.

Pagen, Michele A. 1994. *Preparing future teachers within theatre doctoral programs: Pedagogical issues, current practice and priorities for change.* Unpublished dissertation. Bowling Green State University.

Pelikan, Jaroslav. 1983. *Scholarship and its survival: Questions on the idea of graduate education.* Princeton: Carnegie Foundation for the Advancement of Teaching.

Preparing future faculty. Howard University Graduate School. July 25, 2001. <http://www.founders.howard.edu/gsas/PFF/main.html> July 28, 2001.

Richlin, Laurie. 1993. (ed.), *Preparing faculty for the new conceptions of scholarship.* San Francisco: Jossey-Bass.

Ronkowski, Shirley A. 1993. Scholarly teaching: Developmental stages of pedagogical scholarship. In Laurie Richlin (ed.), *Preparing faculty for the new conceptions of scholarship.* San Francisco: Jossey-Bass, 79–90.

Wagner, Robert B. 1989. *Accountability in education: A philosophical Inquiry.* New York: Routledge.

Index